W9-DED-087

TOWARDS SUSTAINABLE DEVELOPMENT

Towards Sustainable Development

On the Goals of Development – and the Conditions of Sustainability

Edited by

William M. Lafferty
Programme for Research and Documentation for a Sustainable Society (ProSus)
Research Council of Norway
Oslo

and

Oluf Langhelle
Programme for Research and Documentation for a Sustainable Society (ProSus)
Research Council of Norway
Oslo

First published in Great Britain 1999 by
MACMILLAN PRESS LTD
Houndmills, Basingstoke, Hampshire RG21 6XS and London
Companies and representatives throughout the world

A catalogue record for this book is available from the British Library.

ISBN 0–333–71521–7

 First published in the United States of America 1999 by
ST. MARTIN'S PRESS, INC.,
Scholarly and Reference Division,
175 Fifth Avenue, New York, N.Y. 10010

ISBN 0–312–21669–6

Library of Congress Cataloging-in-Publication Data
Towards sustainable development : on the goals of development – and the
conditions of sustainability / edited by William M. Lafferty and
Oluf Langhelle.
p.   cm.
Includes bibliographical references and index.
ISBN 0–312–21669–6 (cloth)
1. Sustainable development.   2. Economic development–
–Environmental aspects.   I. Lafferty, William, 1939–   .
II. Langhelle, Oluf.
HD75.6.T695   1998
363.7—DC21   98–19806
                                                          CIP

This book is printed on paper suitable for recycling and made from fully managed and
sustained forest sources.

10   9   8   7   6   5   4   3   2
08   07   06   05   04   03   02   01   00

Printed and bound in Great Britain by
Antony Rowe Ltd, Chippenham, Wiltshire

Contents

Preface

'The concept that became a problem': that is how Norway's leading newspaper, *Aftenposten*, summed up the idea of 'sustainable development' two years after the Rio Earth Summit. The purpose of the present book is to direct systematic attention to this 'problem'. Though the concept of sustainable development has deep roots in conservationist thinking, it was not before the publication of *Our Common Future* by the World Commission on Environment and Development in 1987 that the term became an internationally recognised symbol. Though numerous critics have since predicted a quick and definitive end to the idea, they have been proved decisively wrong. With the possible exception of 'democracy', there currently exists no more widely endorsed symbol for positive socio-economic and political change than 'sustainable development'. It is, quite simply, everywhere – at least in the industrialised and 'developing' world. From the smallest local NGO, through all types of intermediate organisations and nation-states, to the United Nations, World Bank and European Union – it is what we all (at least on paper) are striving for.

Yet there remain considerable differences of opinion as to just what the concept signifies, particularly in practical terms. For some, it represents but the most successful in a long line of deceptive neo-imperialist values and goals; while, for others, it contains just the right balance of radical and conservative ideas to *really* achieve world-wide and lasting progress. The goal of the present collection is to focus the major points of controversy in the debate, at the same time that we try to move the 'discourse' in a more consensual and effective direction. Our conviction is that 'sustainable development' is an 'essentially contestable concept' which neither can nor should be 'resolved' through debate alone. It is the very 'robustness' and 'staying power' of the idea *as* a controversial idea, which renders it so interesting as a basis for planning and implementation. Our aim is to try to move the discussion from polemics to pragmatics without claiming that the one or the other is 'wrong-headed'. We feel that time has proven the notion to be an ideological 'stayer', and that it is time to bring the original conceptual logic of the idea back into focus and to place it in its current global-political context. The book explores what Benjamin Constant referred to as the 'intermediary principles' between ideal and reality (Sartori, 1987), an area of discourse beyond purist semantics but short of technical operationalisation. Given the very widespread acknowledgement of the goal, how can we lay a better foundation, with clearer comprehension and more consensual priorities, for moving forward towards more effective realisation?

The basic structure of the book follows the logic of the concept as put forth in *Our Common Future* (1987). 'Sustainability' is viewed as a qualifying condition for 'development'. It is the latter which is in focus, and it is the need for the former which provides guidelines for the latter. Our contributors first look at the goals of development, and then at the conditions for sustainability. The individual topics of discussion are viewed as key interrelated elements from the world-view first presented by the World Commission, and later followed up within the United Nations Conference on Environment and Development (UNCED). We use the term 'the UNCED programme', and aim, through the different contributions, to explicate the underlying strengths and weaknesses of the position. If we are successful in establishing semantic 'boundaries' for this particular discourse, they will demarcate an exchange devoted more generally to 'social engineering', more particularly to the planning and implementation of the Rio accords.

The idea for the book was originally conceived as an integral part of the Project for an Alternative Future (PAF) in Norway. PAF was started in the early 1980s by a very small and very loose coalition of environmental activists and environmentally concerned centre-left politicians. Its original (very ambitious) goal was to develop a comprehensive alternative scenario for social, economic and political development in the Nordic countries. After producing a number of stimulating but relatively unconnected books and reports (accompanied by considerable internal dissension), the project was transferred to the Norwegian Research Council for Science and the Humanities (NAVF) in 1990. In 1992, with the fusion and reorganisation of research councils in Norway, the project was transferred to a new Division of Environment and Development within the new Research Council of Norway (NFR). At the end of its allocated five-year period in 1995, PAF was reorganised as a new Programme for Research and Documentation for a Sustainable Society – ProSus.

The present work on sustainable development and its companion volume on a 'sustainable economy' (Hansen, Jespersen and Rasmussen, 1999), can be seen as major attempts to realise *some* of the original goals of the Project for an Alternative Future. They are both conceived with the understanding that sustainable development and the UNCED programme represent *viable* alternative futures: futures where the combination of a global political process and globally sanctioned texts for change (the Rio accords) provide both comprehensive democratic arenas and feasible action plans. Both works reflect, we believe, the aspirations of the original founders of PAF – and of their parliamentary allies who supported them through nearly 15 years of 'alternative research' – even though both the language and level of optimism are clearly dampened.

On a more immediate level, the idea for the present volume grew directly from a previous work under PAF with the title 'Don't Just Say – Do It' (Stenseth and Hertzberg, 1992). As co-editor of this work (which provides more than 40 contributions on the idea of sustainable development from a broad spectrum of Norwegian academics, politicians and activists), Nils Chr. Stenseth provided much of the inspiration for a more focused follow-up volume. He is thus the first to warrant our thanks. In addition to providing an intellectual point of departure for our efforts, he has served as Chair of the Governing Boards of both PAF and ProSus, and has played a vital role in providing the conditions whereby this type of research could be carried out.

We would also like to thank (without naming names) the many individuals, both staff and associated academics, who have had administrative responsibility for PAF/ProSus within the previous NAVF and current Research Council of Norway. Had it not been for their belief in, and enthusiasm for, sustainable-development research, the present collection would not have materialised. The Division for Environment and Development was directly responsible for organising a 'national hearing on sustainable development' in 1995, providing an excellent forum for several of the authors represented in the present collection and leading to a series of 'consensus conferences' on sub-topics of the problematic.

In this connection, it is also necessary to extend a special thanks to several of the authors of the original work in Norwegian who, due solely to constraints of space, have not been included in the English version. Fortunately, all of these authors have works already available in English. Thanks for the co-operation and understanding of Raino Malnes, Eivind Hovden, Aanund Hylland, John Hille and Nina Witoszek.

We are also very grateful to our colleagues at ProSus, where all have contributed on an ongoing basis to the views here presented in the introductory and concluding chapters. Special thanks to the successive heads of information and publications at ProSus, Runar Malkenes and Pål Mugaas, as well as to Jon Wetlesen, Per Ariansen, Hanne Svarstad, Ørnulf Seippel, Ingeborg Rasmussen, Pål Føyn Jespersen, Stein Hansen and Tor Brostigen for comments and suggestions. Finally, the normal acknowledgement of what has become an increasingly abnormal debt: the gratitude we owe our families for putting up with our ridiculous work schedules. Possibly development – hardly sustainable.

WILLIAM M. LAFFERTY
OLUF LANGHELLE

List of Abbreviations

CFC	Chlorofluorocarbon
COP	Conference of the parties
CSD	Commission for Sustainable Development
ECE	UN Economic Commission for Europe
ECOSOC	United Nations Economic and Social Council
FAO	UN's Food and Agriculture Organisation
GATT	General Agreement on Tarriffs and Trade
GDP	Gross Domestic Product
GEF	Global Environmental Facility
GNP	Gross National Product
GREEN	OECD economic (equilibrium) model
HDI	Human Development Index
HWE	Human Welfare Ecology
IIASA	International Institute of Applied Systems Analysis
IMF	International Monetary Fund
IPCC	Intergovernmental Panel on Climate Change
IUCN	International Union for the Conservation of Nature
IWC	International Whaling Commission
MR	Mortality Rate
NAFTA	North American Free Trade Association
NASA	National Aeronautics and Space Administration (USA)
NAVF	The Norwegian Research Council for Science and the Humanities
NFR	The Research Council of Norway
NGO	Non-governmental organisation
NOK	Norwegian crowns (monetary unit)
NPP	Net Primary Production
OCF	*Our Common Future* (the Brundtland Report)
OECD	Organisation for Economic Co-operation and Development
PAF	Project for an Alternative Future
POL	'People in Ordinary Life'
POP	'People in the Original Position'
ProSus	Programme for Research and Documentation for a Sustainable Society
SAMMEN	Norwegian research programme for energy and society
SEEM	European energy-sector model
UNCED	United Nations Conference on Environment and Development
UNDP	United Nations Development Programme
UNEP	United Nations Environment Programme

UNESCO	United Nations Educational, Scientific and Cultural Organization
UNICE	Union of Industrial and Employers' Confederations of Europe
UNICEF	United Nations Children's Fund
UNIDO	United Nations Industrial Development Organisation
WCED	World Commission on Environment and Development
WCS	World Conservation Strategy
WHO	World Health Organisation
WMO	World Meteorological Organisation
WTO	World Trade Organisation
WWF	World Wildlife Fund

Notes on the Contributors

Per Ariansen is a Lecturer in the Department of Philosophy, University of Oslo. His most recent work focuses on issues related to environment and philosophy. In addition to numerous articles in this area, he is the author of *Miljøfilosofi* ('Environmental Philosophy', 1992).

Geir B. Asheim is Professor of Economics at the University of Oslo. Part of his research has been directed at natural resources and environmental economics, linked in particular to the themes of equity between generations and sustainable development.

Andreas Føllesdal is a Research Associate at the ARENA Center (Advanced Research on the Europeanisation of the Nation-State), University of Oslo. He has an MA from the University of Oslo in 1982, and a PhD from Harvard University in 1991. He has also studied at Harvard Law School, the Harvard Negotiation Project, and the Harvard Program on Ethics and the Professions. He writes and teaches political philosophy, with a special interest in international justice, ethics in the public and private sector, negotiation justice and the welfare state.

Stein Hansen is an economist and international consultant in the areas of developmental and environmental economics, resource use and transportation. He is a partner in Nordic Consulting Group A/S and a Senior Research Associate at both the Fridtjof Nansens Institute in Oslo and the ProSus Centre. Among his recent publications are *Er vi rede til nullvekst?* ('Are We Ready for Zero Growth?', 1993); *Miljø og fattigdomskrise i sør* ('Environment and the Crisis of Poverty in the South', 1993); and *Towards a Sustainable Economy* (with P.F. Jespersen and I. Rasmussen, 1998).

Wenche Håland is Professor in Clinical Psychology and Head of the Polyclinic for Youths and Adults at the University of Bergen. She was previously a Board Member of the Project for an Alternative Future and currently on the Board of ProSus. She has served in numerous capacities for the Research Council of Norway, and is at present a member of the Norwegian Ethical Committee for Sociology and Humaniora. She has written several books and articles on psychotherapy, developmental psychology, management and social problems.

William M. Lafferty is Professor of Political Science at the University of Oslo and Director of ProSus. Among his major publications are *Participation and*

Democracy in Norway (1981); *Demokrati og demokratisering* (1984, with Bernt Hagtvet); *The International Handbook of Participation in Organisations* (1994, with Eliezer Rosenstein); and *Democracy and the Environment* (1996, with James Meadowcroft).

Oluf Langhelle is a Research Associate at ProSus and a doctoral student at the Department of Political Science, University of Oslo. His major field of interest is normative political theory with a special emphasis on issues of social justice, democracy and sustainable development. He has recently published articles in both English and Norwegian and is co-editor of *Rio+5* (1997), an evaluation of Norway's follow-up to the Rio Earth Summit.

Ingunn Moser is a Research Associate at the Centre for Technology and Human Values, University of Oslo, and at the Centre for Technology and Sociology, University of Copenhagen. Her major field of interest is the relationship between social theory and technological development. She is co-editor (with Vandana Shiva) of an anthology, *Biopolitics: A Feminist and Ecological Reader on Biotechnology* (1995), and is presently involved in a project on information technology for the physically disabled.

Jon Birger Skjærseth is a Research Fellow for the Research Council of Norway at the Fridtjof Nansen Institute in Oslo, as well as a researcher at the International Institute for Applied Systems Analysis (IIASA), Laxenburg, Austria. He works mainly on studies of international environmental protection cooperation, particularly related to the efficiency and national implementation of international environmental agreements.

Nils Chr. Stenseth is Professor of Zoology at the University of Oslo, Chairman of the Governing Board of ProSus, and Chairman of the Norwegian Research Committee on 'Man And the Biosphere'. Among his most recent publications are co-edited volumes on resource management in the Barents Region (1991); the debate on sustainable development in Norway (1992); the minky whale (1993); and nature, society and foreign aid in Africa (1995).

Jon Wetlesen is Professor of Philosophy at the University of Oslo. His works include a doctoral dissertation on Spinoza (*The Sage and the Way: Spinoza's Ethics of Freedom*); an introductory textbook on 'practical argumentation' (1976); and an analysis of Buddhist philosophy (1982). His current interests focus largely on human rights, global ethics and sustainable development.

1 Sustainable Development as Concept and Norm

William M. Lafferty and Oluf Langhelle

The words 'sustainable' and 'sustainability' seem to have lost any semblance of meaning recently through overuse. We need to recapture the concepts, provide them with real meaning, and begin a process of dialogue to make the concept reality. There is no running away from it.

Stephen Viederman, 1994

1.1 AN ESSENTIALLY CONTESTED CONCEPT

The idea of sustainable development has survived nearly a decade of rhetorical excess and academic criticism. From the Brundtland Report *Our Common Future* to *Agenda 21*, it has remained the central goal and guiding norm of environment-and-development politics. Though an 'essentially contested concept', it retains a widespread moral appeal. This is possibly due to the concept's dual ethical foundation. By giving expression to both 'realist' (natural-law) and 'consensualist' (democratic) norms, it can claim support with respect to a broad spectrum of moral imperatives. The potential of the idea as a mobilising force for domestic political change lies in a combination of scientifically based moral urgency and a near-unanimous global acclamation. In addition, the politics of the UNCED process provide new and effective arenas for an emerging global civil society at a time of declining influence for national interest groups.

Just as every country and ideology after World War II wished to profile itself as 'democratic', we find the same trend today with respect to 'sustainable development'. The underlying idea of sustainability is, of course, much older than the 1987 report from the World Commission on Environment and Development. It is, however, only since the publication of *Our Common Future* (WCED, 1987) that sustainability, coupled to the notion of 'development', has become a rhetorical talisman for our common present. Pity the politician, the party programme, the long-term plan or the international agreement which does not pay respect to the idea. The prospect of a 'nonsustainable society' is on a par with that of a nondemocratic society. It's simply not on.

Yet there is a tremendous diversity of definitions and interpretations.[1] Competing understandings of 'sustainable development' are surely as numerous as

1

competing understandings of 'democracy'. The idea has evolved into an 'essentially contested concept' (Gallie, 1962; Connolly, 1983); an idea characterised by different types of 'openness of meaning' (Kaplan, 1964) over which we pursue endless semantic debates. For many, this points towards a relatively simple solution: avoidance. Unclear concepts lead to unclear communication, and unclear communication is the source of both nonsense and trouble. Any idea which attempts to attach relatively simple normative connotations to the complex notion of 'development', as applied to widely diverse global settings and populations, deserves to be scrapped.

There is, of course, much to be said for this position, particularly from a scientific and analytic point of view. The matter can, however, be viewed in another light. As conceived here, the most significant potential of the concept lies in neither science nor academic analysis but in politics. The promulgation of the idea by politicians and bureaucrats is in inverse proportion to its rejection by critical social scientists. The more the politicians use it, the less the intellectuals like it. There is surely an interesting problematic here for political psychologists, but this is less important in the present context than the problem of implementation. Denying the usefulness of 'sustainable development' as an analytic concept, or the attractiveness of it as a normative concept, does nothing to impinge on either its popularity or import as a political concept.

The world has use for political scientists only insofar as political scientists can help us to make a better world. If a concept like sustainable development is being used to manipulate political values and emotions, then we must be prepared to demonstrate this in a systematic and effective way. But we must also allow for the very real possibility that the term can be used in good faith, and that some of us, at any rate, have a responsibility to assist in the conversion of values and goals into specific results which conform with the normative aspirations.

This is a very different – more constructive and pragmatic – approach from that usually taken to the concept by academics. There can be little doubt that the majority of books and articles on sustainable development run from the sceptical to the outright critical. Nevertheless, the Brundtland Report has had enormous influence. It has set the standard and become the point of reference for every debate on sustainable development.

The Brundtland Report can be regarded as an attempt to reconcile two themes which have long been in an antagonistic relationship with each other, namely environment and development (Adams, 1990; Shanmugaratnam, 1992; Pearce and Warford, 1993). While the concept of sustainability – with its origin in ecology – has a reasonably clear meaning, the concept of development is a semantic, political and, not least, moral minefield (Adams, 1990). The concept of development has widely different meanings, and a generally accepted definition of the concept does not exist (Svarstad, 1991). On the one hand, development is taken to mean social change over time, and involves changes that are regarded as both positive and negative. In other contexts, it is taken to mean only positive changes with regard to certain value-based criteria. In the latter case, development is associated with a desired realisation of values, principles or actual conditions.

The Brundtland Report links sustainability to development in the context of the latter connotation.[2] Hence the definition of sustainable development sets a normative frame for the concept's meaning. It indicates the direction for development and within which scope or limits this development must take place in order to be sustainable. Raino Malnes (1990) calls these elements 'the goal of development' and 'the proviso of sustainability'. Of the two components in sustainable development, developmental goals have logical priority over the requirements for sustainability. Sustainability is, in other words, a conditional restriction on human development (Malnes, 1990:5).

There have been several attempts to expand on the definitions in the Brundtland Report. As Olav Stokke (1991) points out, the definitions in the report call for further expansion and refinement. What is alarming, however, is that these attempts at making the definition more precise and operational have partly shifted the normative scope stipulated in the Brundtland Report. As used in *Our Common Future*, sustainable development is linked to both the relationship between generations and to that within our own generation, on a national and global basis. There has been a strong tendency, however, to apply the concept only to the relationship between generations. This apparently marginal change in perspective has a number of normative implications which alter the meaning of the concept. In the extreme case this can mean that the North–South dimension – the relationship between rich and poor – becomes more or less defined out of the concept. In our opinion, this is clearly a turn in the wrong direction with respect to the intentions in the Brundtland Report.

In spite of the diversity in people's understanding and use, and of the term being in danger of becoming a new hackneyed phrase, there is much to indicate that Timothy O'Riordan is right when he asserts: 'Like it or not, sustainable development is here to stay' (1993:37). Sustainable development emphasises normative dimensions that no ideology or politics can ignore or fail to address, and one would be hard put to find a set of values that has attained a comparable level of political recognition.

In this introduction, we shall sketch some of the major contradictions in understanding the concept of sustainable development, and try to present an understanding and usage which is constructive with respect to the numerous programmes employing the idea as an overriding goal. We structure the discussion in five steps:

1. The origin and development of the concept.
2. An interpretation of the concept as used in the Brundtland Report.
3. An overview of alternative definitions and their implications compared with the Brundtland Report.

4. An explication of contradictions arising in connection with operationalisation.
5. Some preliminary conclusions on the overall usefulness of the idea.

1.2   ORIGIN AND EVOLUTION OF THE IDEA

The word 'sustainable' comes from the Latin *sustenere*, which means 'to uphold' (Dixon and Fallon, 1989; Redclift, 1993). In modern times, the term has its origins in German forestry in the eighteenth and nineteenth centuries. The basis for the use of the term by the Germans was a relatively long-term perspective for forest management (Stenseth, 1992a; Jacobs, 1995). According to Donald Worster (1993), 'sustainable development' first appeared in *World Conservation Strategy* (WCS), in 1980; then in the book *Building a Sustainable Society*, by Lester R. Brown of Worldwatch Institute (1981); then in *Gaia: An Atlas of Planet Management*, edited by Norman Myers (1984); and subsequently in *Our Common Future*.

There has, however, been a gradual development in both the usage and meaning of the term. John A. Dixon and Louise A. Fallon (1989) identify three distinct types of usage that reflect this development:

1. Sustainability is used as a *purely physical concept for a single resource*. The idea here is quite simple: applied to the forest as a renewable resource, the exploitation of the forest is sustainable if one does not take out more trees than are replenished in growth. In this way, the resource is exploited without depleting the physical stock.
2. Sustainability is used as a *physical concept for a group of resources or an ecosystem*. The idea here is the same, but it is immediately more problematic to determine the effects of the exploitation due to the complexity and the interaction between the different parts of the ecosystem. The exploitation of virgin forest, for example, would influence and change the constitution of animal and plant species. Even though a logging operation can be sustainable when the forest is regarded as an individual resource, it is not necessarily so for the original ecosystem. From this perspective, there would be major consequences depending on whether we regard the forest as an individual resource or as a single ecosystem. And already here the question arises as to what it is that is actually maintained. Is it the original ecosystem? Or is it the resource or resources one chooses to exploit?

   Such a method of utilisation may be applied to renewable resources (circular-flow resources), but is more difficult to apply to non-renewable resources (stock resources). Each utilisation of non-renewable resources will either reduce the stock or will lead to these being depleted in time. For example a sustainable utilisation of oil in the sense of being 'maintainable'

is, in this context, meaningless. The continuous utilisation of a non-renewable resource is clearly not maintainable over time.
3. In the final type of usage, the concept encompasses a broader social context. Sustainability is here used as *a social-physical-economic concept related to the level of social and individual welfare that is to be maintained and developed*.

The definition of sustainable development in the Brundtland Report clearly comes under this third category.

1.3 THE DEFINITION OF SUSTAINABLE DEVELOPMENT ACCORDING TO THE BRUNDTLAND COMMISSION

The Brundtland Report is an explicit attempt to form the basis for a global ethic in which the understanding of sustainable development is fundamental: 'human survival and well-being could depend on success in elevating sustainable development to a global ethic' (WCED, 1987:308). According to the report, it will be difficult to reverse the negative trend without such a new orientation in attitudes and values.

The Brundtland Commission defines sustainable development as 'development that meets the needs of the present without compromising the ability of future generations to meet their own needs'. According to the report, this contains within it two key concepts:

- The concept of 'needs', in particular the essential needs of the world's poor, to which overriding priority should be given; and
- The idea of limitations imposed by the state of technology and social organisation on the environment's ability to meet present and future needs' (WCED, 1987:43).

There are several aspects to this definition which are worth noting. Firstly, the basis of the definition is not the environment, but humans and human needs. '*Our Common Future* starts with people' (Adams 1990:59). The commission deliberately chose this emphasis, and rejected the suggestion that they should concentrate on discussing environmental problems only. In the foreword, Gro Harlem Brundtland provides the following reason for such a standpoint:

This would have been a grave mistake. The environment does not exist as a sphere separate from human actions, ambitions, and needs, and attempts to defend it in isolation from human concerns have given the very word 'environment' a connotation of naivety in some political circles (WCED, 1987:xi).

As J.G. Soussan (1992) has argued, this standpoint in the Brundtland Report can be seen in light of the criticisms that were raised against the 1980 World Conservation Strategy (WCS) Report. The WCS Report was the first to make use of the concept of sustainable development. WCS was prepared by the International Union for the Conservation of Nature (IUCN), and published in 1980 with support from the World Wildlife Fund and the United Nations Environment Programme (UNEP). The report was criticised for having an 'anti-poor' profile. Poverty in general, and the conduct of poor people in particular were identified as the main causes of environmental damage, without considering poverty itself as an integral part of the same existing pattern of development (Soussan, 1992:24).[3]

In the WCS Report, development and nature conservation were seen as two sides of the same issue. Three ecological goals here formed the basis for sustainable development: (1) maintenance of essential ecological processes and life-support systems; (2) preservation of genetic diversity; and (3) ensuring the sustainable utilisation of species and ecosystems.

The message was that ecological principles and the environment in general, should set the limits for human actions and activities. As W.M. Adams (1990) notes, this was also a deterministic message: Nature itself will set these limits no matter what humans do.

The Brundtland Report is not characterised by the same degree of determinism. According to the second key concept, nature's carrying capacity is highly influenced by technology and social organisation: 'The accumulation of knowledge and the development of technology can enhance the carrying capacity of the resource base' (WCED, 1987:45). According to Adams (1990), this 'involves a subtle but extremely important transformation of the ecologically-based concept of sustainable development, by leading beyond concepts of physical sustainability to the socio-economic context of development' (Adams, 1990:59). In this context, the carrying capacity of nature is not static, although the report does stress that ultimate limits exist. At a minimum, however, sustainable development requires that the natural systems which support life on Earth, atmosphere, water, soil, and other living beings, are not endangered (WCED, 1987:45).

In the Brundtland Report, this minimum requirement is characterised as 'physical sustainability' (WCED, 1987:43). A development path that fulfils the minimum requirement is maintainable, and may 'theoretically be pursued even in a rigid social and political setting' (WCED, 1987:43). Several authors have in fact argued that the concept of sustainable development should be understood exclusively as physical sustainability (see Beckerman, 1994, and Wetlesen in Chapter 2). In this sense, sustainable development becomes a purely technical concept that says something about whether development is sustainable over time or not. Whether this should be followed or not is a broader normative question that sustainable development so defined, cannot address.

The Brundtland Report dismisses such a viewpoint, however. According to the report, even physical sustainability 'cannot be secured unless development policies pay attention to such considerations as changes in access to resources and in the distribution of costs and benefits' (WCED, 1987:43). Whether a certain development is physically sustainable will depend on both of these considerations, that is, changes in access to resources and in the distribution of costs and benefits form part of the process in determining the level of physical sustainability. For example, under a situation where resources are scarce, a distribution in which a small minority of the world's population controls most of the resources will be possible to maintain over a longer period of time than one where scarce resources are distributed equally among the world's population. Consequently, the question of what is *physically* sustainable cannot be answered without taking into consideration the question of distribution and *what* one wishes to maintain and develop.

Hence even the narrowest concepts of physical sustainability – the minimum requirement for a sustainable development – includes considerations of 'social equity' (WCED, 1987:43). These questions must be considered in relation to each other if one is to follow the general admonitions of the Brundtland Report. Inherent in the goal of development, therefore, is social equity: that is, meeting the needs of the present without compromising the ability of future generations to meet their needs. It is partly this which should be maintained and developed. Furthermore, the Brundtland Report claims that social equity between generations 'must logically be extended to equity within each generation' (WCED, 1987:43). Hence social equity as an inherent developmental goal in sustainable development has two different dimensions, a time dimension and a space dimension. This is represented in Figure 1.1.

Figure 1.1   The temporal and spatial dimensions of sustainable development

Space Dimension

		National	Global
		National	Global
	Within the same generation	National equity within the same generation	Global equity within the same generation
Time Dimension	Between generations	National equity between generations	Global equity between generations

From this perspective, sustainable development has consequences for distribution along several dimensions: global within and between generations, and national within and between generations. Of these different dimensions, it is that of equity within each generation – in particular, social equity within our own generation in a global perspective – which has received least attention within the sustainable development discourse (Redclift, 1993).

We may still question, however, whether there is a 'logical' connection between social equity between generations and social equity within our own generation, as asserted in the report. No further grounds for the assertion is given, but a possible explanation may be that if the equity considerations oblige us to take future generations into account, it will be inconsistent if equity considerations are not to be found equally binding within our own generation. The fundamental question raised, therefore, is the normative-conceptual limits of the concept.

1.4   NARROWING THE NORMATIVE SCOPE?

A Norwegian economist, Carl Erik Schulz has specifically warned against trying to include too much in the idea of sustainable development, thereby rendering it no more useful than a plea for general welfare (Schulz, 1992:25). We prefer to turn the question around, however: What are the normative implications of *omitting* different elements from the definition in the Brundtland Report? This can be illustrated by a few examples.

In a report from a conference in Bergen, Norway on 'Sustainable Development, Science and Policy' (NAVF, 1990), it was established that sustainable development 'is about the fair treatment of future generations' (NAVF, 1990:233). Sustainable development was here defined as:

> development which allows all future generations to have a potential average quality of life at least as high as the average quality of life of the current generation. In this definition, quality of life is a measure of the average well-being of the members of a generation, and depends on traditional material consumption as well as on leisure, environment quality, and so on (NAVF 1990:233).

This definition differs from the one in the Brundtland Report in several ways. The definition itself does not take into account equity within the present generation. It claims, however, to include 'the fair treatment of members of this generation', although for a different reason. It is not linked to an objective for social equity, but to the fact that 'poverty itself leads to the destructive use of environmental resources' (NAVF 1990:233). The implication is thus the same as that of which the WCS report was accused: it is not poverty itself that is the problem, but the damage that the poor inflict on nature. Poor people undermine sustainable development for future generations.

According to Eirik S. Amundsen *et al.* (1991), sustainable development (as in the Brundtland Report), is primarily an equity concept, but it is seen as a *collective* equity concept that should be linked solely to the relationship between generations:

> Sustainability as we understand it, is a collective equity concept. It has nothing to do with the relationship between individuals, but between generations (Amundsen *et al.*, 1991:20).

The reason given is as follows: 'In general debate, it will probably ... be useful to reserve the concept of sustainability for generational conflict, because a dilution of the concept results in its meaning being less clear' (Amundsen *et al.*, 1991:21). From our reading of the Brundtland Report, it is not so obvious that the concept given here conveys a *clearer* meaning; but there can be little doubt that it conveys a *different* meaning.

The limitation of the concept is based on a supposition of separability between equity within a generation, and equity between generations. The authors are undoubtedly right in saying that this differentiation makes it 'easier to analyse important conditions of the concept of sustainability as applied to distribution between generations' (Amundsen *et al.*, 1991:21).

But if sustainable development is limited at the outset to the issue of distribution between generations, there will not be anything else to analyse about sustainable development except just that. In other words, the limitation restricts both the concept and the analysis. But there is an essential difference between limiting an analysis (to the question of distribution between generations), and limiting the concept of sustainable development itself (to the question of distribution between generations). The limitation is understandable as an argument for making a particular analysis more manageable, but it is problematic in the extreme when used as an argument for limiting and defining the basic idea.

Why is this so? The central issue is what emerges as a consequence of the delimitation. This understanding of the concept results in what the authors refer to as a paradox in so far as our actions may be sustainable, but still be unacceptable from an equity point of view. This becomes clear if one looks more closely at the definition of sustainable development which emerges: 'Development is sustainable if it is possible and if the living conditions of generations are non-diminishing throughout the development' (Amundsen *et al.*, 1991:21).

In this context, sustainable development may be consistent with extensive poverty, hunger and miserable living conditions for the majority of the world's population. The goals that are given first priority in the Brundtland Report – meeting human needs, and particularly the basic needs of the world's poor – are no longer the primary developmental goals. The central task as regards the Third World is no longer necessarily related to living conditions, hunger and poverty, but to ensuring that the poor do not damage the environment we are all dependent on. When the authors at the same time assert that, 'Still, the problems of equity within a generation are perhaps greater than those between generations' (Amundsen *et al.*, 1991:21), the proposed delimitation of the concept is presented in an ambiguous light.

More importantly, the idea of separability is in itself highly problematic even within the narrow context of analysis. The distribution of costs and benefits within our own generation influences the living conditions of both the next and future generations. Viewed as such, there is a 'logical' connection between equity within and between generations, as asserted in the Brundtland Report. More to the point, a definition that does not include equity within our own generation will not be able to address the fundamental normative questions: Whose common future is it? Whose children will have the possibility of reaching adulthood? In this connection the exclusion reduces sustainable development from being a normative concept about our common future to a normative concept about *our own* future.

1.5   EXPANDING THE SCOPE?

Instead of excluding elements from the definition in the Brundtland Report, the question is whether or not the concept should be expanded. Several writers have done so, and the following examples may illustrate what this implies for the understanding of sustainable development.

Even though Amundsen *et al.* and others limit the applicable domain of the concept, they nonetheless expand the definition by focusing on general living conditions rather than on basic needs. The living conditions of a particular generation are understood as the average living conditions of the generation's individuals, expressed as a measure of what is thought important for the good life. The baseline for living conditions is thus not only 'the level of consumption, the state of health and nature, but also culture, knowledge, freedom, legal protection, peace and the possibility for self-realisation' (Amundsen *et al.*, 1991:21). 'Living conditions' are, in this view, substituted for the concept of needs in the Brundtland Report in concrete terms.

The Brundtland Report itself encompasses basic needs such as jobs, food, energy, water and sanitation. This is thus less comprehensive than the concept of living conditions. However, the report is not consistent in its use of the concept of needs. It differentiates between two types of needs – general needs and basic needs.

Sustainable development requires 'meeting the basic needs of all' (WCED, 1987:44). Yet in the same sentence, it also says that sustainable development presupposes that all have 'the opportunity to satisfy their aspirations for a better life', which brings the concept more in line with the concept of living conditions. As Hanne Svarstad (1991) has pointed out, there is a major difference between these two goals. Hence, the conclusions that can be drawn with respect to the development goal are dependent on which of these objectives they are related to. At the same time there is a need to clarify what 'general' and 'basic' needs are.

David Pearce *et al.* (1990) define development as a vector of desired social goals, that is to say, it is a list of the objectives that society attempts to realise or maximise. According to Pearce *et al.*, the elements of such a vector (U) may include:

- increases in real income per capita;
- improvements in health and nutritional status;
- educational achievement;
- access to resources;
- a 'fairer' distribution of income;
- increases in basic freedoms (Pearce *et al.*, 1990:2).

Sustainable development in this context is defined as 'a situation in which the development vector D does not decrease over time'. Such a list may be more or less comprehensive and may include more than the concept of basic needs as defined in the Brundtland Report.

Raino Malnes (1990) has a far more stringent list of what are included as basic needs. He differentiates between 'needs of subsistence', 'the conditions of decent existence', and 'personal preferences or desires'. According to Malnes, needs of subsistence are the conditions for survival and normal function in the strict physical sense. These include 'nutrition, protection from the elements, medical care in case of illness, and rest. One may extend this list, but it will on no account be long' (Malnes, 1990:13).

Employment is excluded from Malnes's stringent concept of needs, in cases where having to work is not essential for survival. However, employment has a special status in the Brundtland Report. Not only is it defined as a basic need, it is also viewed as the most important of the basic needs: 'The most basic of all needs is for a livelihood: that is, employment' (WCED:54). By defining employment as a basic need, it follows that to combat unemployment becomes a central political goal for attaining sustainable development. Following this argument, the Norwegian Minister for the Environment, Thorbjørn Berntsen, defines employment as an explicit part of sustainable development: 'Social development is not sustainable if high unemployment prevails' (Berntsen, 1994:5).

The difference between 'essential needs for survival' and 'conditions for a decent life' is also central to Thomas Chr. Wyller's viewpoint. In Wyller's interpretation of the Brundtland Report, its goal is 'to save the world and more'. For Wyller this 'and more' is a fundamental weakness: 'There is a difference between threats to life and threats to the good life. To secure humanity's continued existence is one thing; to ensure equity and equality, freedom and quality of life, is another altogether' (Wyller, 1991:176).

Wyller's criticism amounts to a critique of the scope of the concept. The essence of sustainable development should, in this view, be nothing less than to save the planet. Everything else comes second: 'the biological conditions for existence of life (are) to begin with, consistent with both glaring social injustice and the hundreds of millions whose lives are empty' (Wyller, 1991:178).

The most important threat to life on Earth is, in this view, humanity's total consumption of resources: 'The crisis is a cumulative result of overtaxing the Earth'. Therefore, it refers to 'a relationship between humans and nature, and not *nota bene*, to the relationship between humans' (Wyller, 1991:176).

Wyller's criticism of the Brundtland Report focuses on three conditions: (1) that the report does not identify the factors that threaten life; (2) that it does not formulate a hierarchy of values, with mutual ranking and possible value conflicts; and (3) that it does not make any actual value choices.

One could argue that the extent to which one meets basic needs is, in many cases, about survival, and that such a prioritisation concurs with Wyller's own. Of the list of basic needs in the Brundtland Report, it is only employment (when there are other sources of income) that cannot be directly linked to survival. On the other hand, if one acknowledges a stringent concept of needs, it is an open question as to how many of the world's poor will be affected by sustainable development. One may be poor, but nonetheless survive. To combat poverty will be given priority in the attainment of sustainable development when poverty can be shown to be the cause of the destruction of the environment. In the Brundtland Report, reduction of poverty is both a means – 'a precondition for environmentally sound development' (WCED, 1987:69) – and an end in itself (WCED, 1987:8).

Wyller's criticism raises a range of fundamental questions regarding the understanding of the concept of sustainable development. To what extent can and should the concept be linked to the factors that threaten life? To what extent can the concept express a hierarchy of values, with mutual ranking, and possible value conflicts? To what extent can the concept reflect actual value choices? To answer these questions, we must look more closely at the relationship between the conditions for sustainable development and the development objective itself, that is to say, the relationship between 'the goal of development' and 'the prerequisites for sustainability'.

According to Pearce *et al*. (1990), the definitions of sustainable development are often confused with the conditions for sustainable development. For Pearce and others, these latter are of different magnitude, and must be treated separately. The definition and meaning of sustainable development are viewed as 'evident from the phrase itself' (Pearce *et al*., 1990:4). Looking at the Brundtland Commission's definition, the relationship between conditions and definitions is, however, more complex than is evident here. This can be illustrated by looking at the relationship between human needs and nature's carrying capacity.

1.6 THE CARRYING CAPACITY OF NATURE AND SUSTAINABLE DEVELOPMENT

The key question of this issue is the extent to which the various conditions for sustainable development form part of the development goal. In the Brundtland Report's definition of sustainable development, consideration for nature's carrying capacity is a minimum requirement: 'At a minimum, sustainable development must not endanger the natural systems that support life on Earth: the atmosphere, the waters, the soils, and the living beings' (WCED, 1987:44). Hence, not endangering natural support systems is both a goal in itself (a part of the development goal) and a condition for sustainable development.

But what are we to do if conflicts arise between the goal for social equity and the minimum requirement for sustainable development? To what extent is there a hierarchy of values in sustainable development? As Arne Næss (1991) interprets the concept of sustainable development, 'development is not sustainable if it is not ecologically sustainable' (Næss, 1991:37). The phrase 'ecological sustainability' should be understood as being synonymous with 'ecological maintainability in the long-term' (Næss, 1991:38). According to Næss, ecological sustainability, together with economic prosperity and a long-term perspective, constitute the key elements of sustainable development.

Following Næss, several other authors have made ecological processes and nature's carrying capacity an explicit part of the definition of sustainable development. The report, *Caring for the Earth. A Strategy for Sustainable Living* (1991), defines sustainable development as 'improving the quality of human life while living within the carrying capacity of supporting ecosystems' (IUCN/UNEP/WWF, 1991:10). This definition places great emphasis on ecological sustainability, and in that sense, is more precise than the definition found in the Brundtland Report. On the other hand, *Our Common Future* identifies political, social, economic and cultural threats to future development. The sustainability constraint, in other words, includes more than environmental sustainability, though many prefer to restrict the term for this usage (Meadowcroft, 1996).

None of the above definitions says anything, however, about how possible conflicts between the different goals should be resolved. Consequently, the definitions are not capable of establishing a hierarchy of values among the different goals. It could be argued, however, that this is exactly the intention: development is only sustainable when it takes into consideration *both* human needs and the carrying capacity of nature. The point then becomes specifically one of *not* establishing a hierarchy of values between the two dimensions, but of excluding development paths which do not take both into consideration. This is indicated in *Our Common Future* as follows:

... a new development path was required, one that sustained human progress not just in a few places for a few years, but for the entire planet into the distant future (WCED, 1987: 4).

Sustainable development requires that the adverse impacts on the quality of air, water, and other natural elements are minimised so as to sustain the eco-system's overall integrity. In essence, sustainable development is a process of change in which the exploitation of resources, the direction of investments, the orientation of technological development, and institutional change *are all in harmony* and enhance both current and future potential to meet human needs and aspirations (WCED, 1987:46).[4]

Does this mean that there is no hierarchy of values in sustainable development? Both yes and no. Even though one cannot draw clear conclusions about the mutual ranking of the various characteristics of the concept, sustainable development establishes a hierarchy of values above all other development paths. At the same time, it is natural to interpret the first of the two key concepts within sustainable development as an expression for mutual prioritisation: 'in particular the essential needs of the world's poor, to which overriding priority should be given' (WCED:43).

1.7   SOCIAL ORGANISATION AND SUSTAINABLE DEVELOPMENT

The issue of a hierarchy of values and the overall scope of applicability of sustainable development may also be raised regarding social organisation. To what extent should particular forms of social organisation form part of the developmental goal of sustainable development? Stephen Viederman's (1994) definition of the concept provides a point of departure for discussion:

Sustainability is a community's control and prudent use of capital – all forms of capital: nature's capital, human capital, human-created capital, social capital, and cultural capital – to ensure, to the degree possible, that present and future generations can attain a high degree of economic security and achieve democracy while maintaining the integrity of the ecological systems upon which all life and all production depend (Viederman, 1994:1).

The term 'capital' is here used by Viederman in a broad sense and also includes things that cannot be quantified, such as 'the aesthetic value of nature' and 'the spiritual purposes of humans'. As Viederman himself stresses, that which differentiates this definition from many others is that democracy becomes an integral part of the developmental goal of sustainable development. The

Brundtland Report is more diffuse on this point. It emphasises participation and democratic processes, and proposes, among other things, an increased use of referendums (WCED, 1987:63), but primarily as a means or strategy for attaining sustainable development, not as ends in themselves.

The question raised by Viederman's definition is whether the intrinsic value of democracy is not so vital as to be incorporated into the essential definition itself. It might then be contended that the Brundtland report sets limits on how much one may manipulate social organisation in the name of sustainable development. The consequence of excluding democracy from the concept would be that development could be viewed as sustainable even though one goes from democracy to dictatorship, or remains in dictatorship. A 'sustainable dictatorship' is, however, hardly within the normative scope of the Brundtland report.

This has not prevented at least one Norwegian author, however, from raising serious questions as to democracy's role in promoting sustainable development. Thomas Chr. Wyller (1991) forthrightly maintains that 'democracy (may) no longer constitute an absolute value, but should be assessed with respect to its necessity for overcoming the environmental crisis' (Wyller, 1991:179). 'What leads us to believe', he asks, 'that a system – created under quite different conditions and structured with quite different values from those of today, would be conducive to radical ecopolitical intervention?' (Wyller, 1991:180). Steinar Lem (1994), spokesman for Norway's second largest environmental NGO, goes even further: 'in a hierarchy of values, democracy is not the highest good. Right to life comes first.... Today, democracy can be considered terrorism against the unborn' (Lem, 1994:145–8).[5]

If democracy is defined as an integral part of sustainable development, the 'permissible' developmental paths are narrowed to an even greater extent. Development that does not take human needs and nature's carrying capacity into consideration, while maintaining democracy, is not sustainable. Again, the definition of sustainable development establishes a hierarchy of values that overrides all other development paths.

The same reasoning may be applied to human rights. However, this is of little use in solving possible contradictions between the various parts of the development goal. Wyller's criticism, as an internal criticism of the goals, still stands therefore. The Brundtland Report does not provide answers on how the value conflicts internal to the concept should be resolved. On the contrary, it appears to assume that value conflicts do not arise. Hence it avoids making further value choices which would come to the fore if it stressed possible internal conflicts. To a certain degree it emphasises different values by giving first priority to the world's poor. But to what extent should one take the needs of future generations into consideration if these are in conflict with the needs of the present generation? How, in other words, should one rank the various group needs within the same generation and between generations if these are in conflict?

The Brundtland Report provides little guidance on the issue. What 'development that meets the needs of today without compromising the needs of future generations' actually implies for development goals, therefore, has to be made more precise. Raino Malnes (1990) draws a similar conclusion when he states that: 'there must be an attempt to spell out competing considerations and gauge their relative force, and such cannot be found in *Our Common Future*' (Malnes, 1990:6).

1.8   MAKING THE SUSTAINABLE DEVELOPMENT CONCEPT OPERATIONAL

What we thus argue is that the Brundtland Report's definition of sustainable development establishes a hierarchy of values over *other* developmental paths. It provides general standards for what is necessary if development is to be sustainable. An operationalisation of the concept would involve a clearer stipulation of the central political goals required to realise these values, which in turn must be followed by steps for implementing the goals. While the goals are closely linked to the definition itself, the strategy for realising them is less dependent on the definition's content. We will here concentrate, therefore, on the question of central goals for environment and development policy which are implied by the sustainable development concept. First, the issue of growth.

Much of the criticism aimed at the Brundtland Report is directly related to the status of economic growth (Reid 1995). The report lists the following major goals (WCED, 1987:49).

- reviving growth
- changing the quality of growth
- meeting essential needs for jobs, food, energy, water and sanitation
- ensuring a sustainable level of population
- conserving and enhancing the resource base
- reorienting technology and managing risk
- merging environment and economics in decision-making

The debate on growth may be said to have two different but related dimensions. These correspond roughly to the differences between physical sustainability and sustainable development. The first is based on nature's carrying capacity, where the core of the dispute is whether continued global economic growth is physically or ecologically sustainable. This is primarily an empirical question. The other dimension is linked to the relationship between human needs and nature's carrying capacity. This dispute is both empirical and normative, and involves the question of the quantity of growth as well as the distribution of the benefits of growth in time and space.

1.9 ECONOMIC GROWTH AND PHYSICAL SUSTAINABILITY

The Brundtland Report prescribes minimum growth rates of 3 to 4 per cent for OECD countries,[6] and between 5 to 6 per cent for developing countries. For the OECD countries, this is seen as necessary if they are to play a role in the expanding world economy. As Stein Hansen (1992) points out, the report here presumes a kind of macro trickle-down effect, where it is presumed that in order to promote growth in poor countries, one must have certain minimum levels of growth in the rich countries (Hansen, 1992:183).

Table 1.1   Real growth in gross national product in OECD and developing countries since the submission of the Brundtland Report (annual changes in per cent)

	1988	*1989*	*1990*	*1991*	*1992*	*1993*	*1994*	*1995*	*1996*
OECD countries	4.3	3.2	2.6	1.0	1.6	1.2	2.9	2.7	2.7
Developing countries	5.2	3.9	3.9	4.9	5.9	6.1	6.3	5.6	6.1

Source: OECD and IMF.

Besides a revival of growth, the report prescribes a comprehensive redistribution of benefits, both through increased aid from North to South and through redistribution within individual countries. Another important condition for global economic growth is that the content or quality of growth be changed: 'Such growth rates could be environmentally sustainable if industrialised nations can continue the recent shifts in the content of their growth towards less material- and energy-intensive activities and the improvement of their efficiency in using materials and energy' (WCED, 1987:51). Gro Harlem Brundtland (1994) has later stressed this point: 'It is not the case that the lesser the economic or consumption growth, the more sustainable the growth is. It is the content of growth that is critical.'

As it appears that there is considerable agreement as to the problematic nature of the content of growth, one can then ask why the issue of growth rates remains so controversial. In P.A. Victor's (1991) classification of various economic schools of thought, there is one school in particular – 'the thermodynamic school' (connected with, for example, Kenneth Boulding, Nicholas Georgescu-Roegen and Herman Daly) – which is specifically addressed to this problem. The school gets its name from the second law of thermodynamics, or 'the law of entropy' (see Box 1.1). In Norway, the Nobel-prize winner Trygve Haavelmo and his colleague Stein Hansen (1992) are associated with this school, and Haavelmo (1971) was one of the first to use the entropy concept[7] in economic theory.

Herman Daly (1977, 1992a, 1992b, 1993) is also a leading representative of this direction.[8] His conviction is that the economy should be viewed as an open subsystem within a larger, but finite, closed and non-expanding eco-system. The Earth's ecosystems contribute a stream of natural low-entropy resources that are transformed in the economy by labour and capital (which does not itself physically form part of the product). All resources that go into the process also come out in one or another useful (products or recyclable waste) or non-useful (waste, pollution and so on) form – output which the Earth's various depository systems must then deal with (Hansen, 1992:19). The conversion of natural resources into necessary and luxury goods does not, however, eliminate anything. The economic process (production followed by consumption) is thus 'entropy-creating'. The amount of raw materials from nature that go into the production process corresponds to the amount of waste materials that finally returns to the same nature. There is, however, a *qualitative difference* between raw materials and waste materials, and entropy is a measure of that difference.

In this perspective, the scale of the human economy in relation to the finite, closed and non-expanding ecosystem is critical. According to Daly, the best index of this scale is the percentage of human appropriation of the total world product of photosynthesis. Net Primary Production (NPP) is the amount of solar energy captured in photosynthesis by primary producers, minus the energy used in their own growth and reproduction. NPP constitutes the basic food resource for all life on Earth not capable of photosynthesis:

> Vitousek, et al. (1986) calculate that 25 per cent of global (terrestrial and aquatic) NPP is now appropriated by human beings. If only terrestrial NPP is considered, the fraction raises to 40 per cent. Taking the 25 per cent figure for the entire world, it is apparent that two more doublings of the human scale will give 100 per cent. Since this would mean zero energy left for all non-human and nondomesticated species, and since humans cannot survive with-out the services of ecosystems (which are made up of other species), it is clear that two more doublings of the human scale is an ecological impossibility, although arithmetically possible (Daly, 1993:44).

The carrying capacity of nature and the relative size of the economy in rela-tion to ecosystems are thus closely linked. Even though nature's carrying capa-city is not static (it may rise with investments, technology and changes in social organisation), unwanted waste materials will begin to accumulate if the scope of global economic activities exceed the Earth's drainage and absorptive capacity. Hansen (1993) points out that there is every indication that 'it will be the global drainage and absorptive capacity of the soil, air and water that will finally determine the scope of global economic activities' (Hansen, 1993:19).

Box 1.1   *Entropy*

The first law of thermodynamics says that energy (or matter/energy) can neither be created nor destroyed. In other words, both the amount of matter and energy is constant. But to be able to bring about changes in the form of matter, we must make use of a special quality of energy, namely its ability to perform work (Daly and Cobb 1989 and Magnus *et al.*, 1979).

Entropy is a measure of the change in form of the energy. When energy loses its ability to perform work, entropy increases. In contrast with matter, energy cannot be used again or recovered. Energy use is a one-way flow; that is to say, a process where energy changes from one state to another, but not back again. The energy loses its ability to perform work, or entropy is increased. (Magnus *et al.*, 1979).

So as to maintain production and consumption processes, energy with low entropy must be supplied constantly; that is to say, energy that can perform work. Changes in the states of energy are encapsulated in a universal law, the second law of thermodynamics, or the entropy law: 'In the universe, energy is constantly changing from a state of being useful for work, to being unuseful for work', or 'In the universe, entropy is increasing constantly' (Magnus *et al.*, 1979).

This may be illustrated by the following example. When one burns a piece of coal, the energy in the coal is transformed into heat and ash. These are also forms of energy, and the amount of energy in the heat and ash corresponds to the amount that previously existed in the coal, the difference being that it is now more diffuse. The dispersed heat cannot be used again in the same way that it was used originally. In other words, when one burns a piece of coal, it is transformed from being a natural low-entropy resource to a high-entropy resource. It loses its ability to perform work. In practice, this implies that it is impossible to recycle something one hundred per cent (Daly and Cobb, 1989; Ophuls and Boyan, 1992; Turner 1993).

This is also the view of the Brundtland Commission. The ultimate limits to global development are viewed in the report as being determined by two things: the availability of energy, and the biosphere's capacity to absorb the by-products of energy use. These energy limits are assumed to be approached far sooner than the limits imposed by other material resources, because of the depletion of oil reserves and carbon dioxide build-up leading to global warming (WCED, 1987:58–9). For Daly, however, the greenhouse effect, acid rain, and depletion of the ozone layer are proof that we have already exceeded an acceptable limit with respect to the size of the macroeconomy (Daly, 1993:44; Paehlke, 1989; Turner 1993).

On this basis, Daly (1992b) differentiates between three different political goals which can all be related to the concept of sustainable development: *Allocation, distribution* and *scale*. These concepts are defined in the following way:

Allocation refers to the relative division of the resource flow among alternative product uses – how much goes to production of cars, to shoes, to
ploughs, to teapots, and so on.
Distribution refers to the relative division of the resource flow, as embodied in
final goods and services, among alternative people. How much goes to you, to
me, to others, to future generations.
Scale refers to the physical volume of the throughput, the flow of matter-
energy from the environment as low-entropy raw materials, and back to the
environment as high-entropy wastes (Daly, 1992b:186).

For Daly, the ecological component lies, first and foremost, in 'scale': 'It is
measured in absolute physical units, but its significance is relative to the natural
capacities of the ecosystem to regenerate the inputs and absorb the waste outputs on a sustainable basis' (Daly, 1992b:186). In Daly's view, it is absolutely
crucial that one can fix scale in an sustainable way, referred to as 'the concept of
optimal scale' (Daly, 1992b:187).

The core of Daly's thesis is that scale must be fixed before one can determine
distribution and allocation. At the same time, scale can only be fixed through
social choice; choice which must reflect ecological limits. These types of choices
must be based on estimates of carrying capacity or safe minimum standards
which determine the limits to the total global scope of pollution. Once this is
accomplished, it should be possible to provide for distribution according to
criteria for social equity. Only after having made social decisions regarding the
optimal scale and an ethically just distribution, 'are we in a position to allow
reallocation among individuals through markets in the interests of efficiency'
(Daly, 1992b:188).

This then raises the question as to whether there is a real conflict between
focusing upon the content and the size of growth. For both Brundtland and
Daly, it is crucial to reduce the physical through-put of natural resources and to
limit the amount of waste materials. Is the conflict over growth simply not
necessary, therefore?

When it comes to the significance of changing the content of growth, this
would seem to be the case. With regard to growth in Gross National Product
(GNP), however, there is real disagreement. Daly's argument is that it is simply
not possible to reduce the physical through-put in the economy to an adequate
extent without at the same time reducing the GNP. This is substantiated as
follows:

> While it is true that some activities are more throughput-intensive than
> others, it is not clear that these activities are always services, nor is it clear that
> the differences are very great once indirect effects are incorporated.... That
> most services require a substantial physical base is evident from causal obser-
> vation of a university, a hospital, an insurance company, a barber shop, or

even a symphony orchestra. Certainly the incomes earned by people in the service sector will not all be spent on services but will in fact be spent on the average consumer basket of both goods and services (Daly, 1977:118).

In this view, the content and size of growth are linked. To believe that sustainable development can be achieved by changing the content of growth alone is an illusion; what Daly refers to as 'a non-physical "angelicized GNP"'(Daly, 1977:118). The disagreement thus appears to be primarily related to whether the GNP will rise or fall if the physical through-put in the economy is reduced. While Daly believes that it will fall, others, including Robert C. Paehlke (1989), are of a different opinion: 'Daly's assertion is made without sufficient evidence. The expansion of human services, especially if they replace other forms of economic activity, is likely to positively affect the environment. Human services do not generally require much energy or material throughput' (Paehlke, 1989:131).

In Paehlke's perspective, the combination of environmental technology, energy conservation, and renewable energy production will allow for growth in the gross national product (GNP). In this view, reducing growth in GNP is in itself not necessarily beneficial. Reduced growth in GNP does not automatically reduce the physical throughput in the economy. If this is to be changed, the composition of the GNP must be changed. Even if one reduces the physical through-put in the economy, there will thus be room for continued economic growth in GNP. Paehlke's conclusion is that we should thus minimise the physical throughput in the economy, and maximise the Gross National Product.

John Pezzey (1992) draws a similar conclusion, asserting that 'economic growth is fundamentally a growth in the value of output, which does not necessarily require a growth in materials and energy use, since technical progress can reduce the materials and energy needed to produce a unit of value. On their own, thermodynamic laws therefore tell us frustratingly little about sustainability in simple, absolute terms' (Pezzey, 1992b:324; see also Jørgen Randers, 1994:20 for a similar view). Whether a given path of economic growth (measured in GNP) results in an increase in the physical through-put in the economy or not is thus an empirical question (Pezzey, 1992b:325). The same may be said as to whether global economic activity is on the verge of exceeding the Earth's drainage and absorption capacity.

1.10   ECONOMIC GROWTH AND GLOBAL EQUITY

The debate on growth, however – in terms of both content and size – takes a different turn when one brings in the question of equity. How are the benefits of growth to be distributed in both time and space? The Brundtland Report provides the following general criteria:

Living standards that go beyond the basic minimum are sustainable only if consumption standards everywhere have regard for long-term sustainability. Yet many of us live beyond the world's ecological means, for instance in our patterns of energy use. Perceived needs are socially and culturally determined, and sustainable development requires the promotion of values that encourage consumption standards that are within the bounds of the ecologically possible and *to which all can reasonably aspire* (WCED, 1987:44).[9]

This assertion raises a number of fundamental issues with respect to both continued economic growth and what actually constitutes an equitable distribution of goods. The permissible 'consumption margin' is here limited by two conditions. It requires that: (1) consumption standards are within the bounds of the ecologically possible; and (2) that consumption standards are so determined that everyone (in time and space) can reasonably aspire to them. But how is this to be understood? One plausible interpretation is that these principles, similar to John Rawls's (1972) principles of justice, are supposed to work in tandem. That is, they are interrelated and should be applied together.

It is clear, however, that these principles are not necessarily egalitarian principles: to aspire is not the same as to attain. The principles thus seem to open up the possibility of an unequal distribution of goods, both within and among countries. What the principles allow for, however, is a differentiation among different categories of 'goods'.

On the one hand, you have the class of goods which are necessary to meet human needs. Energy is, according to the report, one such need. It is our patterns of energy use which are used to illustrate the claim that many of us live beyond the world's ecological means. Since the need for energy is universal (that is, necessary for development), and numerous populations live under conditions where the need is not satisfied, the conclusion must be that some must reduce their consumption (the ones who live far beyond the world's ecological means) so as to give others the possibility of increasing theirs.

This is, of course, based on an assumption that energy is a limiting factor for global development. The report explicitly recommends, therefore, a low-energy scenario (over the next 50 years) with a 50 per cent reduction in primary energy consumption per capita in industrial countries, so as to allow for a 30 per cent increase in developing countries (WCED, 1987:173). This is understood to 'require profound structural changes in socio-economic and institutional arrangements and it is an important challenge to global society' (WCED, 1987:201). The Commission still views it, however, as the preferred alternative: 'The Commission believes that there is no other realistic option open to the world for the twenty-first century' (WCED, 1987:174).

A second category of goods could be said to fall outside the scope of the principles advocated in *Our Common Future*. Provided that everyone's basic needs are met, it would be perfectly possible to have an unequal distribution of all kinds of goods which do not create serious environmental problems, even if everyone should both aspire to and attain them.

A third category of goods, however, would be goods that are not necessary for meeting human needs, but which are nonetheless problematic from an ecological point of view should *everyone* either aspire to or attain them. It is clear that the report does not advocate an equal distribution of such goods. It does not argue that everyone should attain the same standard of living, but that everyone should have their basic needs met.

This links up with yet another perspective from *Our Common Future*. The distributional criteria which is supposed to solve the tension between aspiration and achievement is the principle of equal opportunity. The report applies this as a principle of justice both within the current generation (within and between nations), and between generations. The following can be seen as an equal-opportunity principle within and between nations: 'What is required is a new approach in which all nations aim at a type of development that integrates production with resource conservation and enhancement, and that links to both the provision for all of an adequate livelihood base and *equitable access to resources*' (WCED, 1987:39).[10]

And the following can be interpreted as an 'equal-opportunity principle' between generations: 'The loss of plant and animal species can greatly limit the options of future generations; so sustainable development requires the conservation of plant and animal species' (WCED, 1987:46). This same argument is used concerning non-renewable resources: 'Sustainable development requires that the rate of depletion of non-renewable resources should foreclose as few options as possible' (WCED, 1987:46).

Sustainable development not only demands, in other words, that present and future generations should have the ability to meet their own needs, but also that each generation should leave open as many options as possible for future generations. Thus the equal-opportunity principle should be understood as an inherent part of the concept of sustainable development, both within and between generations. It is an extension of the basic concept given by the core definition of sustainable development.

But does this allow us to speculate on what we *reasonably* can/should aspire to? The dilemma can be illustrated with reference to the annual report to Parliament by the Norwegian Minister of the Environment (Berntsen, 1994). The report prescribes an economic growth for Norway of 2.5 to 3 per cent per annum, in line with OECD projections. The reasons given for justifying such growth in terms of sustainable development are: (1) that this should place Norway in a better position to accelerate change in a more sustainable direction; (2) that it is necessary in order to maintain current welfare and living standards in Norway; (3) that it is necessary for the development of new methods for strengthening the cooperation with developing countries; (4) that it is necessary for increasing the efficiency of international development aid; and (5) that it is necessary to maintain a high level of foreign aid (Berntsen 1994:10).

The following arguments are put forward in opposition to a reduction in the level of economic growth: (1) It would imply that we were actually willing to reduce growth in total consumption and welfare goods; and (2) it would delay changes towards more environmentally friendly means of production (Berntsen, 1994:8). The Minister's point of departure is, however, very close to the two principles in the Brundtland Report:

> If the rest of the countries in the world try to achieve the same level of material welfare as in the industrialised countries, we will clearly exceed the limits of global sustainability. All individuals have the same inherent value and dignity and are entitled to a fully human life.... We must develop patterns of consumption which can be applied on a global basis.... If seven billion people – the expected population of the world in the year 2010 – are to consume energy and other material resources at the same level as the rich countries today, it won't be enough with one Earth – we need ten! (Berntsen, 1994:8).

This reasoning *seems* to imply that the present material welfare level in the OECD countries cannot be universalised out of concern for the Earth's sustainability and future generations. But what is in fact advocated is that the same material welfare level which is viewed as incapable of being universalised, both can and should be maintained, and even increased, in Norway. There is thus neither consistency in the actual presentation nor with respect to the basic principles and goals of the Brundtland Report.

The growth debate thus seems to go in two different directions depending on whether its starting point is *physical sustainability* or *global equity*. On the one hand, there is the prospect of continued economic growth with changed content or quality, where the question becomes one of *not* being able to universalise current standards of living in OECD countries; while, on the other, you have the option of a real fall in the total consumption of energy, and possibly in other material resources, which would require an absolute reduction in economic growth in the OECD countries, so as to make possible increased consumption in the lesser developed countries.

Must we choose between the one or the other? Or will technology solve the dilemma of both maintaining and eating cake? What the growth debate clearly illustrates is that an honest regard for social equity directly tied into the carrying capacity of nature may be much more difficult to reconcile than the members of the World Commission presumed.

1.11   SUSTAINABLE DEVELOPMENT: A USEFUL CONCEPT?

In this introduction, we have looked at several different definitions and interpretations of the concept of sustainable development. Even though their content and characteristics vary, they have several common traits. They are all aimed at the future; they are all normative in that they say something about how the future should be; and they admit 'permissible' development paths, depending on the scope of the definition.

Beyond this, the diversity of understanding is striking. But does this mean that the concept is not useful? The question is clearly not easy to answer, but Abraham Kaplan's (1964) approach to the nature of theoretical terms may provide some help. In his widely acknowledged *The Conduct of Inquiry*, Kaplan provides a general description of why concepts, regardless of how specifically they are defined, make usage uncertain. He refers to the problem as the 'openness of meaning' and differentiates between four types.

The first type is 'systemic openness', a property shared by all theoretical terms. This is because the specification of their meaning requires the context of the entire set of sentences in which they appear. Each sentential occurrence is 'a partial determination of meaning' (Kaplan, 1964:64). Further, the set of propositions that make up the theory is never complete: 'No single specification of meaning suffices for a theoretical term, precisely because no single context of application exhausts its significance' (Kaplan, 1964:64). Systemic meaning is, therefore, always open. The diversity of definitions in the Brundtland Report is thus partially a reflection of the concept's systemic meaning. In Kaplan's terms:

> There is a kind of pseudo definition in which a meaning is set down although the term is not in fact thereafter always used in accord with the 'definition'. The chances are, indeed, that a key term of this kind is 'defined' several times and in several different ways. This diversity does not necessarily mark a lapse either of logic or of memory, but the occurrence, rather, of systemic meaning (Kaplan, 1964:64).

In this light, diversity of meaning is something one has to live with. When the concept is used in contexts different from the original, its meaning is changed.

A second type of 'openness of meaning' is 'vagueness'. Here the problem arises with respect to the 'edges' or 'borders' of terms, where decisions must be made as to 'where to draw the line'. This problem cannot (according to Kaplan) be solved beforehand or once and for all: 'The point is that lines are drawn and not given; that they are drawn always for a purpose, with reference to which the problem is solved in each particular case; that our purpose is never perfectly served by any decision; and above all, that no decision can anticipate the needs of all future purposes' (Kaplan, 1964:66). As such, the ever-present possibility of the occurrence of borderline cases makes the meaning of every term vague, no matter how precisely the term is defined (Kaplan, 1964:65). Whether democracy is an essential characteristic of sustainable development or not is thus a question that has to do with the concept's vagueness.

But vagueness is not only about what the characteristics of the concept are. A third type of 'openness of meaning' is 'internal vagueness'. It is not, as with ordinary 'vagueness', concerned with the difficulty of deciding whether or not something belongs to the designated class. Instead, the question here becomes a 'matter of degree'. The defining properties of a term can always be partially fulfilled. One can talk of more or less 'freedom', more or less 'democracy' and so on. 'Internal vagueness' thus 'stratifies denotations, according to whether they are central or marginal cases or something between' (Kaplan, 1964:68). To what extent a specific policy represents sustainable development, is, in this context, not a question of 'either-or' (whether the characteristics of the concept are present or not), but a question of degree.

Clarifying internal vagueness can be an important tool for making the concept more precise. But even a clarification of the concept's internal and external vagueness will not prevent it from being given other meanings. Kaplan refers to his fourth property as 'dynamic openness'. No matter how exhaustive and complete the meaning of a term may seem, nothing can prevent it from being used in a very different sense because there are simply no terminal contexts of inquiry. This is not, however, necessarily a bad thing. On the contrary, this form of 'dynamic openness' can be seen as providing 'the leading edge of scientific terms, their permanent possibility of change in meaning' (Kaplan, 1964:69). In Kaplan's view, this property provides conceptualisations with the capacity for reaching out for a firmer grip on reality and it is this that make dynamic openness the leading edge of scientific terms. As such, it opens up for re-definition and the construction of new meanings and conceptualisations.

The concept of sustainable development provides every indication that it encompasses all four types of semantic openness. As a principle to provide guidelines, or as an ethical code for human survival and progress (Moxnes, 1989), the concept is on a par with other high-minded terms such as democracy, freedom, human rights, and so on. The 'openness of meaning' of these concepts can never be closed. The content of sustainable development is thus not fixed once and for all. Its fruitfulness is linked to continued political discourse on the concept's content and future goals; to continuing debates as to the instrumental implications of its normative aspirations.

The present work should be read as a contribution towards this end. The book is organised around our own understanding of the meaning of sustainable development as put forth in *Our Common Future*. The purpose is not to focus on disagreements, but to lay the foundation for greater consensus on the concept's content and implications. The stronger the consensus over content, the greater the possibility for an effective realisation of goals and values. The desired end is a more effective implementation of the UNCED programme, and the immediate means is a more focused and constructive discourse on the nature of the programme's key concept.

1.12   SUMMARY OVERVIEW

In Chapter 2, Jon Wetlesen takes up the issue raised in the Brundtland Report as to the *need for a global ethic*. What are the normative premises for substantiating the Brundtland Report's conclusions regarding welfare and social equity? As these premises are not adequately accounted for in the report, there remains a basic philosophical challenge to both clarify their nature and indicate how they can possibly be substantiated.

Human needs occupy centre stage in the Brundtland Report's definition of sustainable development. But how are we to understand and eventually operationalise the difficult concept of needs in this context? Wenche Håland takes on the task in Chapter 3 by highlighting central problems related to the concept and by making an initial attempt to differentiate the idea in a manner conducive to more practical application and evaluation.

Social equity within our own generation is another central aspect of the developmental goal, and the Brundtland Report assigns first priority to the basic needs of the world's poor. In Chapter 4, Andreas Føllesdal defends this emphasis in the report and argues that if conflicts arise between the basic needs of the world's poor and the environment, it is the former which must come first.

Social equity between generations is another key element of the developmental goal, but how can responsibility to future generations be understood and eventually enacted? Per Ariansen takes up this issue in Chapter 5, discussing how the notion can be meaningfully elaborated so as to pave the way for more effectual procedures and future-oriented consequences.

Chapter 6 can be seen as a transitional chapter, since it moves the analysis from the goals of development to the 'proviso' of sustainability. Nils Christian Stenseth moves the discussion from the realms of ethics, values and goals to the more determinative realms of biology and ecology. His concern is to elaborate two of the most central ideas of the Brundtland concept: the *carrying capacity of nature* and *threats against biodiversity*.

Another central variable conditioning the prospects of sustainable development is the so-called 'key concept' of *social organisation*. It is a basic premise of the entire idea that social change can, in fact, be steered and controlled; a premise which – as Oluf Langhelle demonstrates in Chapter 7 – warrants considerable analytical scrutiny. What are the grounds for either optimism or pessimism with respect to the normative project, and what role does democracy play in the plan?

Jon Birger Skjærseth continues the investigation of the conditions affecting change when he turns, in Chapter 8, to the question of *international political cooperation*, more specifically the limitations set by the principle of the right to national self-determination for effective and binding international agreements as well as for implementing institutional reforms.

In Chapter 9, Geir B. Asheim presents the first of two economic perspectives on the problem, looking most specifically at the issue of *economics and generational obligations*. How can we conceptualise these obligations within current economic discourse, and how can we be sure that we have found effective ways to fulfil the obligations?

This cross-generational analysis is then followed up by Stein Hansen in Chapter 10 with a comprehensive problematisation of *the gap between rich and poor countries*, and an action-oriented discussion of the strengths and weaknesses of various developmental strategies aiming towards closing the gap.

In Chapter 11, Ingunn Moser addresses the very complicated and critical issue of *technology*, focusing on what she perceives to be an ambivalence in the Brundtland Report as to the nature of technology as both 'problem-solver' and 'problem-creator' in relation to sustainable development.

Finally, in the concluding chapter, the editors return to a more general conceptual analysis, building on the perspectives presented, to probe deeper into the consistencies and conflicts in the Brundtland Report, so as to see how these can be related to existing policies and priorities. An attempt is made to show that, despite a considerable degree of internal 'vagueness', the concept of sustainable development provides adequate normative-conceptual grounds for external application and evaluation. Though it is difficult to determine internal priorities and unambiguous guidelines for action, it is nonetheless clear that the path of sustainable development is distinguishable from other paths of development, and that the key to its distinction lies in a normative insistence on the dependence between environmental sustainability and developmental justice.

NOTES

1. As pointed out by Karl-Gøran Mäler (1990), this diversity in definition and usage is also present in the Brundtland Report. For a summary of various definitions of sustainable development, see Pezzey (1992a) and Pearce *et al.* (1989). The various definitions found in the Brundtland Report are also listed here. It must be added that although there are different definitions to be found in *Our Common Future*, there are fewer actual definitions than are listed by Pezzey and Pearce *et al.* In these lists, three out of seven 'definitions' are in fact about the requirements of sustainable development. Two of them do not even qualify as definitions or requirements. This leaves two actual definitions in the list, and these are entirely consistent.

2. There are also other interpretations of what is meant by development in the Brundtland Report. Jon Wetlesen (see Chapter 2), interprets it rather differently from the way we do here. According to Wetlesen, the Brundtland Report has a neutral concept of development.

3.   The WCS Report, however, emphasises the need for a 'strategy of combatting poverty' (WCS, 'Introduction', 8). For a discussion of World Conservation Strategy (WCS), see Adams (1990:46–51).
4.   Our italics.
5.   For a thorough discussion of the relationship between democracy and the environment, see William M. Lafferty and James Meadowcroft (eds.), *Democracy and the Environment. Problems and Prospects*, London: Edward Elgar, 1996.
6.   *Our Common Future* used the traditional term, industrialised countries, while we prefer (the more precise) OECD countries as a collective term for the 'rich' part of the world.
7.   Entropy – (actual) relationship between a quantity of heat and the absolute temperature.
8.   Thermodynamics – part of physics that deals with dynamics where temperature plays a critical role.
9.   Our italics.
10.   Our italics.

2 A Global Ethic of Sustainability?

Jon Wetlesen

What is implied by a global ethic if it is to provide the normative premises for sustainable development, and how sustainable is such an ethic in relation to moral opinion, nationally and internationally? This essay is an attempt to contribute an answer to this question. It takes its point of departure from the report of the World Commission for Environment and Development: *Our Common Future*, also called The Brundtland Report. This report provides strong recommendations for sustainable development both in OECD countries and in developing countries. But how are these recommendations substantiated? According to the interpretation that is suggested here, we can distinguish between two types of premises: the normative that concerns a global ethic, and the descriptive that concerns empirical hypotheses on the conditions for sustainable development. The normative premises involve some strong presuppositions on welfare and social justice for all humans in the present and in the future. The report hints at these normative presuppositions, but it makes no attempt to clarify them in more detail. It is a philosophical challenge to clarify what they imply, and how they can possibly be substantiated convincingly. The issue is discussed in connection with John Rawls's theory on social justice, and a radical interpretation of it concerning international relations.

2.1 THE BRUNDTLAND REPORT AND GLOBAL ETHICS

The term 'sustainable development' was coined in 1980 in the *World Conservation Strategy*.[1] The Brundtland Commission's report *Our Common Future* of 1987 adopted this as a central term and strongly contributed to its acquiring currency in the international political debate. The Brundtland Report argues that sustainable development should be a central and major concern for political decisions, both internationally and nationally. It provides various reasons for this, some of which are strategic, with regard to the self-interests of individual states, while others regard humanity's common welfare and social justice. At one place in the report, these moral concerns are described as a global ethic:

> We have tried to show how human survival and well-being could depend on success in elevating sustainable development to a global ethic (WCED, 1987:308).

30

One question that can be raised in this connection is this: how does the Brundt-land Report interpret the relationship between 'sustainable development' and 'global ethics'? Does it assume that the moral concerns in a global ethic are defined into the concept of sustainable development, such that it is true per definition that sustainable development involves a global ethic? Or does it assume that this is not true by definition, but rather that this is an empirical hypothesis concerning a necessary condition for the realisation of a global ethic? The report is not entirely clear on this point, and both these interpretations are possible. William M. Lafferty and Oluf Langhelle, in Chapter 1, support the former interpretation, whereas I prefer the latter.

The latter interpretation may be summarised as follows: the thesis to be justified is normative. It prescribes that political decisions should be compatible with concerns for sustainable development, both nationally and internationally. This is substantiated by two types of premises, normative and descriptive. The normative premises prescribe an overriding goal for the policy. It should be aimed at welfare and social justice for all people in the present and future. The descriptive premises clarify the empirical conditions for the realisation of this goal, for instance with regard to our consumption of natural resources, our pollution and our social organisation. Here, what is required is that processes of change in economy and society are kept within the bounds of sustainability, so that development does not undermine itself.

This provides the basis for understanding the relationship between sustainable development and global ethics. The global ethic relates to the normative assertions. These are concerned with, first of all, the general premises relating to welfare and justice, and secondly, the more special normative conclusions that can be drawn from the normative premises when these are combined with the descriptive premises. In this way, sustainable development pertains, first and foremost, to the descriptive assertions, that is, the empirical assumptions of a scientific and social type, about which conditions have to be fulfilled in order to realise welfare and justice for all people over many generations.

2.2 NORMATIVE PREMISES OF WELFARE AND SOCIAL JUSTICE

Let us look closer into these normative and descriptive premises. The normative premises concern welfare and social justice.

> The satisfaction of human needs and aspirations is the major objective of development (WCED, 1987:43).

The report interprets 'welfare' primarily as the satisfaction of human needs, and secondarily as the satisfaction of other expectations. Here, it implies the fundamental human needs for, for example, primary goods like food, water, clothes, housing, work, and so on, and other legitimate expectations for a good or better life. That these expectations are legitimate presumably means that in all likelihood they can be justified in light of the concern for equitable distribution, such that ideally all parties involved can agree with them. On this understanding it is reasonable to interpret 'welfare' in the report, primarily in an objective sense, as being concerned with conditions and standards of living. Secondarily, however, it may also be interpreted in a more subjective sense, so as to include the experienced quality of life as a legitimate expectation.

In view of these goals it appears as if the World Commission presupposes some kind of teleological ethics oriented toward the common welfare. If it assumes a utilitarian ethic, this may be understood as a question of maximising the welfare in sum or on average, perhaps without requiring that it be distributed in any particular manner. The report, however, is also concerned about the equitable distribution of welfare, oriented especially towards the least advantaged. This concern is clearly expressed in the report, and it may imply that it is rooted in one or another form of deontological ethics, based on duties or rights, rather than on teleological ethics:

> The essential needs of vast numbers of people in developing countries – for food, clothing, shelter, jobs – are not being met, and beyond their basic needs these people have legitimate aspirations for an improved quality of life. A world in which poverty and inequity are endemic will always be prone to ecological and other crises. Sustainable development requires meeting the basic needs of all and extending to all the opportunity to satisfy their aspirations for a better life (WCED, 1987:43f).

Moreover, it is assumed that this distribution should take place not only between generations but also within each generation. This is how the report understands social justice, as an equitable distribution within each generation and between generations:

> But physical sustainability cannot be secured unless development policies pay attention to such considerations as changes in access to resources and in the distribution of costs and benefits. Even the narrow notion of physical sustainability implies a concern for social equity between generations, a concern that must logically be extended to equity within each generation (WCED, 1987:43).

The last sentence in the above quotation needs to be commented on. Here, it is said that an equitable distribution of welfare is a prerequisite for sustainable development. The idea seems to be that if the national and international social conditions are inequitable, these will cause crises that can jeopardise sustainable development. The question is whether this contradicts the interpretation above that assumes the opposite direction of causation, that is, that sustainable development is a prerequisite for social justice. I believe that there is no contradiction here, but that it is a question of two different stages in the train of thought. On one hand, sustainable development is a prerequisite for an equitable distribution between generations. This means that each generation must keep within the bounds of the conditions for sustainable development. Otherwise, previous generations will ruin it for later generations. On the other hand, equitable distribution within each generation is a prerequisite for sustainable development. Otherwise, it will cause crises that will jeopardise such a development.

If this is a correct interpretation, the text must be said to be misleading when it asserts that concerns of social justice between generations and within each generation are 'logically' covered by the idea of sustainable development. According to the interpretation above, these conditions are understood to be empirical causal conditions, and not as logical conceptual conditions. On the other hand, the alternative interpretation is also a possibility to be considered. This is the interpretation maintained by William M. Lafferty and Oluf Langhelle. It must be admitted that their interpretation appears to gain some support in the passage last quoted. As I see it, the drawback of their interpretation is that it makes all the assertions on the relationship between sustainable development and global ethics true per definition, and hence, to a certain extent, trivial. The first interpretation avoids this.

We may sum up the normative concerns of the interpretation proposed as follows: the main purpose of a global ethic is to promote the common welfare for all people and to distribute it in an equitable manner between generations and within each generation.

2.3 DESCRIPTIVE PREMISES OF THE CONDITIONS FOR SUSTAINABLE DEVELOPMENT

Let us then look at the descriptive premises. According to the interpretation assumed here, the point of these premises is to clarify how the economic and social development should be managed in order to realise the objectives of global ethics. The main point is that development must be sustainable.

Let us first look at what the report implies by 'development'. In the text, we find the following statement:

> the term 'development' being used here in its broadest sense. The word is often taken to refer to the processes of economic and social change in the Third World....Development involves a progressive transformation of economy and society (WCED, 1987:40 and 43).

Here again, we are faced with the question of interpretation mentioned previously. Are the normative concerns of welfare and equity built into the concept of development by definition, or do these moral concerns come in as additional presuppositions? Lafferty and Langhelle interpret the text as stating that the moral concerns lie within the concept of development itself. For my part, I agree that the concept of development has built into it an orientation towards some sort of purpose or other, but not necessarily the purposes that are characteristic of a global ethic. One could, for instance, imagine that a certain state went through a development that maximised its own welfare, without taking humanity's common welfare into consideration. It did not even need to take into consideration an equitable distribution of welfare within its own borders. Nonetheless, it could make sense to say that such a state developed more or less in relation to the goals which were adopted. I believe that the Brundtland Report uses the term 'development' in this broad sense. In addition, however, it assumes that development should be steered on the path of a global ethic. This presupposes that development is steered in such a way that it becomes sustainable. Let us look at how the concept of sustainable development is introduced at the end of Chapter 1 and the beginning of Chapter 2 of the report:

> Sustainable development is development that meets the needs of the present without compromising the ability of future generations to meet their own needs. It contains within it two key concepts:
>
> - the concept of 'needs', in particular the essential needs of the world's poor, to which overriding priority should be given; and
> - the idea of limitations imposed by the state of technology and social organisation on the environment's ability to meet present and future needs (WCED, 1987:43).

When one interprets this descriptively, as I do, sustainable development must be understood as an economic and social process of change which can be maintained over many generations without undermining itself. The sustainable factor in this interpretation is primarily the fact that it can last. This descriptive component comprises hypotheses on the causal conditions that have to be fulfilled for this to be possible.

I assume that the concept has its primary application in the use of renewable resources. If they are going to be utilised in a sustainable way, they must not be overtaxed, that is, they must not be used more per time unit than they are capable of renewing themselves. This concerns, for example, the harvesting of populations of animals or plants. The concept can also be used in an analogical sense with regard to non-renewable resources. They must be used in such a way that some of what is taken out is invested into finding alternatives to this resource, so that in the future, one has other means of attaining the same goals. The concept can also be applied to the use of the natural environment as a recipient of waste from human production and consumption. This implies that one must not discharge into the environment more than it is capable of absorbing without becoming polluted. Finally, the concept can also be applied to the organisation of society. It must be organised in such a way that it does not create serious social conflicts resulting in the breakdown of society, as we have discussed earlier.

It may be objected to this descriptive interpretation that it does not take into account the first of the two key elements of the definition of sustainable development above: that it should cover the needs, in particular the basic needs of the world's poor, who should be given overriding priority. This is clearly a normative element, and it is explicitly covered by the concept. I do not think that this is a crucial objection, however. At most, both the normative and descriptive interpretations are reasonable. It shows that the passage can be interpreted normatively and in that case the concept of sustainable development has built in a concern for social justice when it comes to the distribution of welfare. This becomes a part of its conceptual content. On the other hand, the passage can also be interpreted descriptively. In that case the elements covered by the concept of sustainable development are understood as necessary empirical conditions for fulfilling the goal of equitable distribution of welfare. On this second interpretation the statement in the text becomes a non-trivial assertion, namely that it is necessary to have sustainable development in order to cover the basic needs of all people, in the present and future, particularly those of the poorest. And the normative conclusion is that this is given overriding priority. That it should be given overriding priority is not a consequence of the conceptual content of sustainable development, but follows from an overriding concern that forms part of the normative premises for the whole theory of sustainable development.

2.4 DO WE HAVE A DUTY OF JUSTICE TO PROMOTE SUSTAINABLE DEVELOPMENT?

We have now distinguished between descriptive and normative premises for the normative conclusion that prescribes sustainable development. These normative premises are linked to the idea of a global ethic and include fairly strong assumptions about what sorts of duties we are bound by, and they are not likely to gain the adherence of everyone without further ado. Some will challenge the assumption that people who are relatively well off today have direct moral duties to the least advantaged people in our generation, nationally or internationally, and even less so to future generations. They may concede that it would be morally good and praiseworthy if they refrained from causing harm, and perhaps even provided help to these people, but this would not be a duty of justice, nor even of charity, but a supererogatory action, beyond the call of duty. Others may agree that we have a duty not to cause harm to the least advantaged, but not to offer help to them. In this case too, positive help would be supererogatory. Others, again, assume that we have a direct duty in both respects, but that the negative duty not to harm is a perfect duty, being correlated with the claim-rights of the other party, whereas the positive duty is only imperfect, without any correlated claim-rights. The negative duty would then be conceived of as a duty of justice, while the positive duty would be conceived of as a duty of charity or of beneficence.

The Brundtland Commission appears to take it for granted that we have duties of justice in both regards. This is a strong assumption, and it is an open question what kind of theory of justice would have to be presumed to meet this expectation. We shall return to this question.

2.5   IS THIS AN ANTHROPOCENTRIC ETHIC?

So far we can safely surmise that the normative foundation of the Brundtland Report is anthropocentric: it assumes that it is for the sake of human beings that we shall adopt a sustainable use of natural resources and the environment; in other words, it is for the sake of people living now and in the future. In this perspective, nature is ascribed instrumental value in relation to human needs and other interests. The report has much to say about natural resources, both renewable resources in the form of populations of animals and plants, and non-renewable resources of minerals and fossil fuels. These resources contribute towards setting limits for a sustainable production of goods and services needed by the present and future generations, and for the environment's limits for absorbing wastes. In one or two places, however, the report appears to allude to a non-anthropocentric perspective, for instance in the following passage:

> If needs are to be met on a sustainable basis the Earth's natural resource base must be conserved and enhanced. Major changes in policies will be needed to cope with the industrial world's current high levels of consumption, the increases in consumption needed to meet minimum standards in developing countries, and expected population growth. However, the case for the conservation of nature should not rest only with development goals. It is part of our moral obligation to other living beings and future generations (WCED, 1987:57, also compare 13).

Here it is said that we have a moral duty, or even an obligation, not only to humans living in the present and the future, but also to other living beings. If the report contends that we not only have indirect duties, but direct duties to non-humans, the possibility opens for a non-anthropocentric ethic. This may be an individualistic ethic for the protection of animals or other singular organisms, or it may be a holistic ethic for the protection of supra-individual systems such as species or ecosystems. These possibilities are formulated in several different ways in the environmental ethics of our time, and this may be the reason that the report indicates the possibility. However, this is not the main thrust of the report. In the main, the report has an anthropocentric orientation. Since the report is a political document, the Brundtland Commission may have had good reasons for arguing from anthropocentric premises. These premises are presumably adhered to by a broader section of the global audience they address than the alternative non-anthropocentric views, and therefore they are probably more suitable as points of departure for a convincing or persuasive argument.

2.6 SUSTAINABLE DEVELOPMENT AS A SOURCE OF MORAL LIMITS

A global ethic seeks first of all to regulate actions which probably will have far-reaching consequences in space and time, and which therefore affect very many, or even all, human beings in the present and in the future. We shall return to the question presently of the kind of norms that are central to a global ethic. But let us first note that with regard to the interpretation and application of these norms to concrete cases, much will depend on the empirical hypotheses one accepts, for instance about how natural resources are to be exploited, or about how much pollution nature is able to tolerate, in order to satisfy the basic needs of all human beings now and in the future.

In global ethics it is important to distinguish between basic and derived norms. Basic norms are supposed to be universal and binding for all moral agents in relation to all moral subjects, so that they will act in ways that are compatible with respect and concern for these subjects. Derived norms, on the other hand, may be particular and adapted to local contexts. The norms of sustainable development, for instance, will be contingent on what kinds of resources are available and what they allow of extraction or harvesting. The norms for sustainable fishing, hunting, agriculture, and forestry, for example, will vary according to local conditions, and the knowledge of these conditions will depend on the experience that has been gained over the centuries in local traditions. There is no reason why a global ethic should be in favour of standard solutions which are applied in the same way everywhere.

The main task for a global ethic is presumably not so much to find particular solutions for what ought to be done in concrete situations in different areas, as to outline certain limits that ought not to be ignored. This is particularly important with regard to the use of natural resources and the disposal of waste. This type of limit-setting is morally relevant in the sense that if these limits are exceeded, harm which could be avoided will be inflicted on other moral subjects, while it will also be in conflict with the moral duties that the moral agents are bound by to avoid such actions, and hence to protect the subjects against such harm.

For example, if one generation extracts too greedily of the Earth's finite resources of minerals and fossil fuels without developing substitutes for them, there will not be much left for later generations. Once consumed, always consumed. If these resources are to be distributed in an equitable manner between different generations who are interested in using them, there have to be limits on each generation's use.

Or if one generation harvests renewable resources, like certain stocks of fish, wild animals, timber, or other populations of animals or plants, in a manner that is not sustainable, these species will be endangered, or become extinct. Once extinct, always extinct. It is similar for problems of deforestation, depletion of ground-water, soil erosion, salination, desertification, and so on. Species of animals and plants are also endangered from intrusion into their natural habitats in ways which make it impossible for them to survive there. The restructuring of landscapes by agriculture is another example; construction of cities, suburbs, roads, railroads, airfields, and ports are other examples.

The same thing goes for waste and pollution, whether it be the pollution of the soil, rivers, lakes or the seas, or the atmosphere, by acid rain, herbicides,[2] pesticides,[3] oestrogens, industrial wastes, new chemical substances which are potentially toxic, substances which may affect the genes, carcinogens, especially in connection with nuclear wastes, and so on. These and other factors involve considerable risks to the health and lives of great numbers of humans, both now and in the future, and often into the far future. Nuclear wastes, for instance, imply risks – not least genetic risks – for humans and their environment for hundreds of thousands of years. In addition, there is the risk of climate change caused by CO_2 emissions; that is, the greenhouse effect due to the combustion of fossil fuels, and the growing risk of cancer caused by ultraviolet radiation as a result of the CFC emissions, due to the depletion of the protective ozone layer.

In particular there are two reasons why a global ethic has become more urgent in our time than before. First, we have developed much more powerful technologies than those used in earlier societies. During the hunter-and-gatherer societies over the last one hundred thousand years and earlier, and during the agricultural societies over the last ten thousand years, the main sources of energy were the three Ws: wind, water and wood, in addition to the muscle power of humans and domesticated animals. After the industrial revolution, some 250 years ago, fossil fuels were also used, together with hydroelectric power and nuclear power. Information technology and biotechnology are not blameless either with regard to the impact on nature and the environment, and the pace of technological innovation is continually increasing. Second, the population explosion in itself has a major impact on nature and the environment. At present, the global population is increasing at a rate of ninety million people per year, that is, a quarter of a million per day.

2.7 UNIVERSALIST ETHICS

The kind of global ethic indicated by the Brundtland Report, must, to a great extent, be a universalistic ethic. We may distinguish between three dimensions in such an ethic. It sets up certain moral norms that obligate:

1. all moral agents in relation to
2. all moral subjects, and the validity of these norms will presumably pertain to the fact that there is agreement on them among
3. all affected parties, in any case to the extent that they are moral agents that fulfil certain conditions for impartiality. This is of course, a difficult requirement, and there is no opportunity to go deeper into it, except for a few comments.

Let us take a closer look at these three dimensions. But first, some comments concerning the kinds of norms being discussed. Some of these norms are anchored in the respect for other moral subjects and their self-determination and freedom. Norms of truthfulness and honesty can probably also be counted in this group. Other norms are anchored in care for other moral subjects and their welfare. Here, it may concern negative norms, in particular the prohibition against causing avoidable harm to another moral subject, as well as positive norms; for example, the obligation to hinder an avoidable harm being inflicted on another subject, or to alleviate the harm that has been inflicted, or to promote the other's welfare in other ways. These norms are quite general. When they are issued and applied to concrete cases, they can be specified in diverse ways, as they actually are in daily morality within different societies and moral traditions.

The first dimension relates to the class of moral agents; that is, those who are bound by the norms in a global ethic. This concerns not only individual agents, but collective agents also, and not only the private but also the public, at the local, regional, national, international and transnational level.

More specifically, this concerns everyone who can be attributed responsibility for specific actions that affect other moral subjects' interests and inflict harm on or give benefits to them. If one agent causes an avoidable harm to another moral subject, he or she can complain and raise an accusation against the offender. This accusation should be directed against someone who is able to defend himself or herself, which presupposes that he or she is an accountable moral agent. This opens the way for an adversarial procedure, as it is called in law; that is, for a procedure by accusation and defence prior to a final verdict. The accused party can try to provide a defence for his actions, either in the form of a justification warranted by valid moral norms, or in the form of an excuse. If this is not achieved in a convincing manner before the general public, the accusation may be confirmed as a moral judgement.

The second dimension in a global ethic relates to the class of moral subjects: that is, those who are directly protected by its universal norms. This concerns a class that has been ascribed moral status. It is a controversial question how extensive this class is. According to particularistic positions, this class comprises some, but not all humans; but according to universalistic positions, it comprises all humans, or even non-human beings, as we mentioned above in connection with non-anthropocentric interpretations.

The third dimension in a global ethic concerns the question of who must accept and agree on the universal norms in order that they shall be morally valid, and therefore binding. Whether this dimension is applicable depends on the kind of meta-ethical theory about the conditions for morally valid norms that one accepts. First and foremost, it is relevant if one includes recognition and consensus theories on moral validity, particularly the type that presumes that there must be a well-based impartial consensus among all the affected parties for a norm to be morally valid. Modern discourse ethics lean towards this direction; something similar applies to John Rawls's theory of justice (1971). I shall go deeper into this by bringing up some characteristics of Rawls's theory.

There are, however, other types of recognition theories which are not based on universal consensus. This concerns, for example, theological validity theories that assume that norms must be recognised by God and be sanctioned by His superior will, to be morally valid. On the other hand, theological theories are dependent on the revelation of God's will, and the interpretation and application of these revelations. Hence, a context of understanding is assumed, with its distinctively acknowledged meanings and acknowledged authority within a hermeneutic tradition. This leads one back to a recognition theory of validity, but not to a consensus theory like the modern theories mentioned above.

Moreover, there are other types of theories about validity that are not based on recognition or consensus at all. This concerns different variants of meta-ethical moral realism which assumes that validity of moral norms concerns their truth.

I assume that recognition and consensus theories are more convincing in a multicultural world where there exist a plurality of comprehensive views on what an adequate basis of moral validity is. If it is possible to come to an agreement on which norms are accepted as valid, and hence binding, independently of particular controversial comprehensive views, then it may be sufficient with a recognition or consensus theory of validity. This does not imply that one should reject comprehensive doctrines as untrue. One need neither accept nor reject them; the question of their truth value may remain open.

The problem is then to find some form of recognition or consensus that will be able to provide the basis for the validity of the type of universal norms that are indicated in the Brundtland Report's global ethics. I suggest that we look closer into certain characteristics of Rawls's theory of justice in this connection.

For one thing, Rawls has proposed a theory of the conditions that should be ful-filled for an impartial defence of the differences in the distribution of welfare. This theory has particular relevance for the most disadvantaged party, which, according to the Brundtland Report, 'should be given overriding priority'.

Against this it may be argued that Rawls's theory is not relevant to the Brundtland Report, because the difference principle that Rawls formulated is limited in scope, covering only sovereign nation-states. According to Rawls himself, it does not apply to international justice. On this point, however, others have recommended a more radical revision of Rawls's theory, so that the differ-ence principle is also applicable internationally. I shall go into Thomas Pogge's (1989) suggestion in this connection. There is reason to believe that the Brundt-land Report's indications of social justice will require a radical theory of this kind. Finally, I shall go into the objections raised by Rawls against such a radical interpretation of his theory. First and foremost, these concern the fact that they will hardly get any particular support, and hence, they lack political realism.

2.8   RAWLS'S IDEAL THEORY OF JUSTICE IN A SOVEREIGN NATION-STATE.

In *A Theory of Justice* (1971), John Rawls proposed a theory of justice as fair-ness. Rawls developed his theory of justice as fairness within a wider framework of assumptions about justice as a natural duty (Rawls, 1971:108–17). Justice as fairness is an institutional obligation, binding on those who explicitly or tacitly agree to take part in social co-operation and the sharing of burdens and benefits that have been mutually agreed upon. This obligation is mutually binding on all who participate in the institutionalised co-operation. Justice as a natural duty, on the other hand, is binding to all moral agents in relation to all other moral subjects (agents, persons), independently of any institutional consensus. Rawls assumes that all agents have natural duties of non-maleficence, of beneficence, and of justice. We have, for instance, a natural duty to support and comply with those just institutions which have been established, and to contribute to the establishment of new just institutions where required, when this can be done within the confines of reasonable costs.

The theory of justice as fairness can be understood as a theory adapted to the task of framing the basic institutions of a just society. Rawls prefers to start with an ideal theory of one just nation-state, and then goes on to a theory of interna-tional justice (Rawls 1971:4, 8, 457), whereas some of his more radical followers prefer to start with a theory of global justice. In either case, however, it is pos-sible to use some of the devices Rawls has proposed, notably his notion of the original position and the veil of ignorance.

Rawls's theory starts with a hypothetical contract situation called the original position. This is outlined as a kind of supposition. The task here is to choose a set of basic norms of justice from an open list of alternatives taken from the most promising candidates in the current philosophical discussion, both tele-ological and deontological. These norms are to be general, universal, public, ordered according to rank, and final; and they are to be chosen under circum-stances which promote an impartial choice without bias or prejudice (Rawls, 1971:130–6).

Once chosen, these basic norms of justice are to function as a frame of refer-ence within which other norms may be concretised in a step-by-step sequence: first the constitutional norms (constitution) of a sovereign nation-state, which defines the division of power between the legislative, the executive and the judi-cial authorities; then the norms set by the legislative authorities; and finally the administrative decisions and judicial decisions made by the executive and judi-cial authorities. All of this defines institutions in the public domain, and in addi-tion come private decisions by individuals, corporations, organisations, and so on, within this framework (Rawls, 1971:195–201).

A major point in Rawls's theory is his concern with impartiality. He outlines the circumstances of justice as a situation where different parties have a conflict of interest due in part to scarcity of resources, and in part to limited mutual altruism.[4] Justice as fairness may be understood as an attempt to find an impar-tial procedure for the resolution of such conflicts.

Rawls contrasts his procedure with that of classical utilitarianism (Rawls 1971:183–92). According to the utilitarian procedure, collective decisions of action should be made in the same way as individual decisions by a kind of cost/benefit analysis. In a decision situation one needs to be adequately informed about the alternatives of action, their probable consequences with regard to how they affect all parties concerned, either positively or negatively. The impar-tial spectator must use his powers of empathy and feel how each party will prob-ably be affected by the consequences of the different alternatives of action. In a sympathetic way, he must feel their sorrows and joys, or their dissatisfactions and satisfactions, and then he must sum up the net benefits and costs in welfare for all parties concerned, and arrive at a general conclusion with regard to which alternative will maximise the common utility in total or on average. With this theory it would not only be morally right to sacrifice the interests of individu-als or minority groups if this would serve to maximise common utility, but those who are sacrificed would even have a moral duty of benevolence to let this happen.

Rawls's objection to this procedure is that it conflates all desires and interests into one system, and thus fails to respect persons and their different interests. Therefore it gives inadequate protection to individual persons whose vital interests may have to be sacrificed for the abstract common utility of all. In this way it mistakes impersonality for impartiality. By contrast he proposes his own theory of justice as fairness as an alternative procedure for reaching impartial decisions. Instead of defining impartiality from the standpoint of a sympathetic observer who responds to the conflicting interests of others as if they were his own, he defines impartiality from the standpoint of the litigants themselves.

The device which Rawls proposes in order to make this work is the veil of ignorance in the original position (Rawls, 1971:136–42). This is done with a supposition. We shall imagine a hypothetical contract situation where people in ordinary life (let us follow Hare's proposal (1976), and call them POLs) are represented by free, equal and rational people in the origin position (POPs). These POPs are supposed to be adequately informed about the alternative sets of basic principles of justice, and also about the general features of those societies which would be constituted if one or the other of these sets of principles were chosen. Some principles would give a foundation for more egalitarian societies, others for more hierarchical societies with greater differences in the distribution of primary goods.

One piece of information would be withheld from each POP, however, and that is, which position he or she would end up in in each case. This information would be disguised by the veil of ignorance. They would not know the probability of ending up in any position, for instance as man or woman, white or black, belonging to some religious group or political party rather than another, being well endowed or poorly endowed with natural assets and abilities, being healthy or frail, and so on. In fact, Rawls also assumes that they do not even know in which generation they will be born (Rawls, 1971:284–93).

So we have a situation where the POPs are going to choose basic principles of justice without knowing how they themselves will be affected by the principles they choose. The veil of ignorance prevents them from tailoring the principles to their own particular interests, and this is the reason why it enables them to make an impartial decision. Rawls assumes that it is rational when making decisions under this kind of uncertainty, to follow the maxi-min principle. This principle prescribes that if one is to make a decision between alternatives which possibly have both good and bad consequences, and one does not know the probabilities of these consequences, then one ought to look at the worst consequences of each alternative, and choose the alternative which has the best of the worst consequences. Applied to the present case, this implies that one should compare the consequences of adopting the different principles of justice with regard to how they affect the least advantaged party. And then one should choose the set of principles which maximises the interests of the least advantaged party with respect to the distribution of primary goods.

There is some affinity between Rawls's approach and the utilitarian approach in this area, especially rule-utilitarianism. Both choose rules (or general norms, principles) in view of their consequences, provided they are generally followed. The difference is that utilitarians choose rules in view of their consequences for the common utility of all parties concerned, while Rawls chooses rules in view of their consequences for the utility of the least advantaged party.

Rawls supposes that free and equal rational beings will agree that there is a presumption of an equal distribution of all social primary goods – liberty and opportunity, income and wealth, and the basis of self-respect, unless an unequal distribution of any or all of these goods is to the benefit of all, which means that it must be to the advantage of the least favoured as well (Rawls, 1971:61, 303). He supposes that the presumption of equality will be indefeasible in the case of primary goods relating to freedom, and that it may be defeasible in the case of primary goods relating to welfare. This is the basis of his two principles of justice:

> First: each person is to have an equal right to the most extensive basic liberty compatible with a similar liberty for others. Second: social and economic inequalities are to be arranged so that they are both (a) reasonably expected to be to everyone's advantage, and (b) attached to positions and offices open to all (Rawls, 1971:61, 303).

Rawls's first principle of justice can be interpreted as approximately covering the same field as the civil and political human rights, and the second principle of justice as approximately covering the economic, social and cultural human rights. The second principle permits a difference in distribution of welfare, but only on the condition that it is to the benefit of the least advantaged. This is the famous difference principle of Rawls. It implies a duty of redistribution from those who receive a greater share to those who receive a smaller share.

There is a difference, however, between Rawls's principles of justice and the principles of human rights. According to Thomas Pogge, we may say that Rawls distinguishes two sessions in the original position: a domestic justice session and an international justice session (Pogge, 1989:240–80). In the domestic session, the POPs are supposed to represent the individual citizens of one nation-state, and Rawls argues that in so far as the POPs are free and equal rational beings, they will agree on the two principles of justice, including the difference principle. In the international session, however, the POPs are not supposed to represent individuals but rather the states in international society. The principle of equality is reinterpreted here so as to ascribe equal rights to independent peoples organised as states, in analogy to the equal rights of citizens in a constitutional regime. The principal task of the POPs in this session is to choose the fundamental principles to adjudicate conflicting claims among states. At this point Rawls argues for some central principles of international law, such as the principle of self-determination, non-intervention, self-defence against attack, defensive alliances, that treaties are to be kept, *jus ad bellum* and *jus in bello* (Rawls, 1971:378f). These can be characterised as principles of international non-aggression, as quite distinct from principles of international redistribution.

It seems correct to say that the principles of international justice which Rawls seeks to justify are closely related to the civil and political rights, but not to the economic, social and cultural rights. According to Rawls himself, neither the second principle of justice nor the difference principle has an application in international justice. One implication of this is that there is no presumption of equality of persons in international society, and the difference between rich and poor countries need not be justified in terms of maximising the utility of the least advantaged persons. In this way, Rawls's version of the theory of justice as fairness has only quite moderate implications for international justice. On the other hand, one should not forget that Rawls (1971:114 and 1993b:76) also assumes that there exist natural duties in addition to the institutional ones, and that the relationships between states are bound by a natural duty to justice and mutual aid. This, together with considerations for human rights, hence provides the rich countries with a moral duty towards the poor countries. And this is considered to be a duty of natural justice, and not only a duty of beneficence, or even a supererogatory exhortation.

2.9 RADICAL INTERPRETATIONS OF RAWLS'S POSITION

Others, however, have proposed more radical interpretations of the original position and the veil of ignorance. Following Thomas Pogge once again, we can say that the tendency of these interpretations is to suppose that there is only one session of the original position: a global session. Here, it is assumed that the POPs represent individual humans in international society, without limits in space or time. The veil of ignorance conceals from the POPs which national state they will be born in, as well as which generation they will be born into.[5]

If Rawls's assumption is correct, that free and equal rational beings would choose the two principles of justice in the domestic session of the original position, then it seems that they would do the same in the global session, provided the veil of ignorance is extended in this way. In that case, there would be a universal ideal consensus on the basic principles of international as well as intergenerational justice. With regard to the second principle of justice, it would have the further implication that there is a presumption for an equal distribution of primary goods in the world and over the whole series of generations, unless an unequal distribution could be justified as being to the benefit of all parties concerned, including the least advantaged.

If this proposal is found convincing, one would have to ask: How much of the present world order could be justified in terms of these criteria? Probably not very much. Then one would have to ask: What kind of reforms would have to be made in order to rectify the situation? Quite obviously, the answers would be rather radical, implying strong duties of justice on the part of the richer part of the world in relation to the poorer part, and on the part of both in relation to future generations, involving monetary and trade reforms, debt cancellation, massive development aid, strict regulation of multinational corporations, and so on. Thomas Pogge's proposal for a global resource tax is highly relevant in this context (Pogge, 1994:195–224).

Based on a radical interpretation of the original position, the POPs would be regarded as representatives not only of moral agents, but more generally of moral persons. In this way, moral consideration would be extended to moral persons who are not moral agents, thus including all or most marginal cases of human beings: foetuses (at least after the first trimester of the pregnancy), children, the highly mentally retarded, the highly brain-damaged, the highly senile, and so on. Or at least, this could be argued along the lines we suggested above.

Some radical interpreters of Rawls have proposed that we should go even further than this, and extend the model of the original position and the veil of ignorance into the non-anthropocentric domain. We might suppose that the veil of ignorance concealed from the POPs whether they would be born as humans or non-human living beings.[6] True enough, in order to be POPs they have to be rational beings, but this does not entail that they must be born as rational beings in real life. They might be born as domesticated animals, or as wild animals, or as other kinds of living beings. When the POPs consider this possibility, which principles would they agree on, pertaining to the ways humans should treat non-humans? What kinds of norms would they agree on with regard to the use of animals in science, commercial animal husbandry, commercial and sport hunting, trapping, fishing, zoos and so on? It is most likely that these norms would impose strict restrictions on human actions in these areas.

2.10   ARE GLOBAL ETHICS SUSTAINABLE?

We have taken as the point of departure the Brundtland Report's recommendations on sustainable development, and investigated some possible justifications. In view of the interpretation that has been proposed, the recommendations are substantiated partly by normative premises for a global ethic, and partly by descriptive premises for empirical conditions for sustainable development. The normative premises concern universal norms that bear on the common welfare for all people, and an equitable distribution of welfare within each generation and between generations, particularly with respect to the most disadvantaged parties. It is a strong assumption when the Brundtland Commission requires that such norms should be valid, and hence, binding on all moral agents. But is this, by itself, a sustainable assumption?

If moral validity has to be grounded in a factual overlapping consensus, nationally and internationally, there does not seem to be a strong case for the claim that these norms are morally valid. It may well be that Rawls's reservation against those who interpret his theory of justice more radically is based on a recognition of this fact. Rawls's own thinking on international justice has taken a steadily more moderate course in recent years.[7]

Suppose that we wish to hold on to a radical theory of justice, and that we assume that its moral validity must be somehow grounded in consensus. If we believe it is valid, we must assume that it is grounded in a hypothetical or counterfactual ideal consensus. The drawback with this is that we are left with a fairly speculative theory of justice. Moreover, it will compete with several other speculative theories of justice, some of which may be far less universalistic and egalitarian than the one we have been considering. This indicates that the adherents of a radical theory of justice should be somewhat circumspect when they make claims for the validity of their theory. And yet, who knows, perhaps, they are right. May be they belong to the vanguard in the development of a sustainable moral consciousness?

NOTES

1. IUCN/UNEP/WWF (1980). See also the follow-up report, IUCN/UNEP/ WWF (1991).
2. Herbicide – weed killer.
3. Pesticide – agent that protects plants from harmful animals, insects and other organisms.
4. Altruism – thought and action that is motivated by a concern for the well-being of others.
5. Interpretations along this line have been proposed by, among others, Bryan Barry (1973, 1979), Peter Danielson (1973), Robert Amdur (1977), and Charles R. Beitz (1979).
6. Donald Van De Veer (1979) and Bryan Norton (1989).
7. Over the last 15 years, Rawls has revised his earlier theory in the direction of a political liberalism based on overlapping agreement. This is summed up in Rawls 1993a and further elaborated upon in Rawls 1993b.

3 On Needs – a Central Concept in the Brundtland Report

Wenche Håland

Chapter 2 of the Brundtland Commission's Report, *Our Common Future*, begins with the following:

> Sustainable development is development that meets the needs of the present without compromising the ability of future generations to meet their own needs. It contains within it two key concepts:
>
> - the concept of 'needs', in particular the essential needs of the world's poor, to which overriding priority should be given; and
> - the idea of limitations imposed by the state of technology and social organisation on the environment's ability to meet present and future needs (WCED, 1987:43).

Further on, it says:

> Sustainable development requires meeting the basic needs of all and extending to all the opportunity to satisfy their aspirations for a better life (WCED, 1987:44).

Thus, a central concern for the World Commission is the needs of all contemporary and future human beings. Furthermore, meeting people's basic needs and their aspiration for a better life is desirable.

In my opinion this statement makes it all the more important to discuss the concept of needs and its use. Such a discussion might be of help in trying to find out more about whether sustainable development is a realistic possibility or whether it is sheer utopia. Or perhaps we might paradoxically call it a 'realistic utopia'? Given the attitudes and actions of men in the present world, and given the course we are following today, it may seem utopian to reach the goal of sustainable development as described by the Commission. However, the Brundtland Report shows with remarkable clarity the disastrous consequences to all people in the world, if attitudes and actions are not changed in order to attain sustainable development. Viewed from this perspective, the seemingly utopian becomes perhaps the *only* realistic course of action.

As is mentioned in Gro Harlem Brundtland's foreword in the report: if we do not succeed in getting our message of urgency through to today's parents and decision-makers, we risk undermining our children's fundamental right to a healthy, life-enhancing environment. Unless we are able to translate our words into a language that can reach the minds and hearts of people young and old, we shall not be able to undertake the extensive social changes needed to correct the course of development (WCED, 1987:xiv).

3.1   THE USE OF THE CONCEPT OF NEEDS IN THE BRUNDTLAND REPORT

The Brundtland Report uses the concept of need in many different ways and on different levels. Thus, the content of this core concept in the commission's definition of sustainable development is relatively imprecise. How it will be possible to give priority to basic needs *and* 'people's aspiration for a better life' will also impact on the extent to which further development will be sustainable.

Some examples of the report's use of the concept of needs may be clarifying : basic needs include the needs for food, shelter, water, hygiene and health care, and so on; the most fundamental need is that of a means of livelihood, that is to say, work (WCED, 1987).

A citation from A. Katoppo asserts that:

- Their basic needs include the right to preserve their cultural identity, and their right not to be alienated from their own society, and their own community (WCED, 1987:31).

The Commission puts forward its view that:

- Sustainability requires concepts of human needs and well-being that incorporate such non-economic variables as education and health enjoyed for their own sake, clean air and water, and the protection of natural beauty (WCED, 1987:53).

Furthermore:

The common theme throughout this strategy for sustainable development is the need to integrate economic and ecological considerations in decision-making (WCED, 1987:62).

According to the Commission, 'our perceived needs are socially and culturally determined', but it nevertheless assumes that the need for equality and for a 'dominance-free dialogue' (Habermas) is general, in asserting that:

The sustainability of ecosystems on which the global economy depends must be guaranteed. And the economic partners must be satisfied that the basis of exchange is equitable; relationships that are unequal and based on dominance of one kind or another are not a sound and durable basis for interdependence (WCED, 1987:67).

Human need for meaning and for self-confidence is, likewise, touched on indirectly on p. 113, and to some extent, touches on the theme of conflicting needs:

At the heart of the issue lies the fact that there is often a conflict between the short-term economic interest of the individual nations and the long-term interest of sustainable development and potential economic gains of the world community at large (WCED, 1987:160).

The theme is implicit in the following statement:

Given the large disproportion in per capita energy consumption between developed and developing countries in general, it is clear that the scope and need for energy saving is potentially much higher in industrial than in developing countries (WCED, 1987:196).

Also, the conflict between arms production and sustainable development is touched on:

the potential threat to the environment from war, the greatest need is to improve relations among those major powers capable of deploying weapons of mass destruction. . . . Successful negotiations would contribute significantly to stemming the spread of nuclear weapons as the major nuclear-weapon states would deliver on their promise of nuclear disarmament. Such progress is consistent with the basic needs of our times and the right of humanity to have the spectre of nuclear destruction removed from the face of the Earth (WCED, 1987:304).

Even though some conflict areas are mentioned, it seems nevertheless that the Brundtland Commission generally avoids discussing the issue of conflicts between sustainable development and growth ideology. For example, we read that:

Industry is central to the economies of modern societies and an indispensable motor of growth. It is essential to developing countries, to widen their development base and meet growing needs.

Many essential human needs can be met only through goods and services provided by industry. The production of food requires increasing amounts of agrochemicals and machinery. Beyond this, the products of industry form the material basis of contemporary standards of living. Thus all nations require and rightly aspire to efficient industrial bases to meet changing needs (WCED, 1987:206).

If the most important goal is to meet basic needs, one may well question the wisdom of 'cultivating' new and changing needs, if this will be at the expense of the central goal.

Even though the Brundtland Report mainly discusses human needs, it also says that:

At a minimum, sustainable development must not endanger the natural systems that support life on Earth: the atmosphere, the waters, the soil, and the living beings (WCED, 1987:44).

Furthermore:

There is still time to save species and their ecosystems. It is an indispensable prerequisite for sustainable development. Our failure to do so will not be forgiven by future generations (WCED, 1987:166).

As formulated, it has the character of an indispensable moral requirement to recognise the interdependence between all living beings, and that long-term survival is the most basic need, both for mankind and for all life on Earth. But as I see it, it is precisely in relation to such a categorical declaration on the overriding goal, that the report does not sufficiently tackle the issue of the goals it otherwise prescribes.

3.2 SOME PEOPLE MUST RENOUNCE THE FULFILMENT OF THEIR NEEDS

As a political document and a declaration of intent, the Brundtland Report is, nevertheless, an important and useful document. As one often experiences with this type of political document, the lack of clarity and precision has probably been a condition for obtaining consensus among the Commission members. It is therefore all the more important that the document is regarded as a basis for further work aimed at obtaining an optimal basis for action to promote sustainable development. For example, we may start with the statement: 'Sustainable development requires meeting the basic needs of all and extending to all the opportunity to satisfy their aspirations for a better life.'

Particularly the latter part of the sentence needs to be both more precise, and perhaps above all, modified. One may wonder if the Commission is afraid to state plainly that sustainable development will also require that many people will have to renounce the fulfilment of some of their needs. If we are to have a chance of meeting the basic needs of everyone, it is evident that the distribution of the world's resources will have to be different from the present one. Thus, sustainable development will presumably require that quite a few of the needs that people in rich countries have regarded as a matter of course be fulfilled, will no longer be fulfilled. Hence, it is important to elaborate on such relationships, and to expect that people – when understanding the seriousness of the situation – are both able and willing to sacrifice some benefits to preserve life on Earth. We know that man is able to show heroism, to live up to extremely difficult demands in extreme situations. In Churchill's famous appeal to the British people during the Second World War he promised 'blood, sweat, toil and tears'. People's willingness to sacrifice at that time was caused by the common experience of a concrete threat, and a common belief that if only everyone was willing to sacrifice, it would be possible to meet and overcome the threat. Thus, the psychological need to survive as a nation took precedence over strong, individual needs.

This example illustrates that human needs, and above all, the ranking of needs, are not static, but are dependent on several factors in the interplay between individuals and the cultural context. Even the need for survival individually may be subordinated to the survival of the group, nation or species.

It is essential to further elaborate and clarify the fundamental conditions for sustainable development and the inherent distribution problems. To reach a deeper understanding of the interplay between people and between nations, and the interplay in a wider ecological context, is going to be a great challenge. Such an understanding may make possible a gradual change in people's perceived needs – especially the ranking of needs in the richer part of the world – which may bring the satisfaction of needs into accord with ecological requirements.

3.3   TO PRESERVE LIFE – A BASIC NEED

Let us therefore begin with the most basic need of all, that of the preservation of life. In phylogeny, a diversity of 'ingenious methods' exists to adapt to the environment and to secure the propagation and survival of the species. Survival is dependent on access to food and water, as well as the ability and possibility to protect offspring from natural forces and 'natural enemies'. In small, local units, 'natural enemies' are relatively easy to localise, and it is relatively easy to understand what is needed to maintain the balance between species. The

interplay and balance in the total ecosystem on Earth is so difficult to comprehend that our understanding so far is minimal.

3.4   HUMANS – A SPECIAL SPECIES?

Humans as a species have long secured their survival through an ability to adapt
to and master the different conditions of life in more flexible ways than other
species.

This means, among other things, that humans have been capable of satisfying
their basic needs in very many different ways. They have been able to adjust to
extreme differences in climatic conditions, and they have met their nutritional
needs in a great variety of ways. A crucial difference between humans and other
species, is that humans have not only been adjusted to the conditions of nature,
but have, to a very large extent, secured their basic needs, 'made themselves
independent', by mastering their surroundings, and by trying to subdue nature.
They have been so successful in their efforts over a long period of time, that they
have had the 'surplus' to develop and meet many differentiated and varied
needs. But one may also speculate on the long-term consequences of human
'arrogance'; the fact that man regards himself to be master over nature, with the
right to exploit it, and use it for his own purpose, with a never-failing faith in his
ability to master possible problems through the development of steadily new and
better technology. Our growth ideology and our difficulty in taking its negative
consequences seriously enough may be seen as a result, among other things, of a
lack of modesty and understanding of mankind's place within a larger, ecological context. The enormous man-made ecological problems facing the world
today, have caused a dawning realisation of the fact that humans are also a part
of nature, and that respect for and identification with nature are perhaps fundamental to our understanding of it. Accordingly, the key words in creating long-
term security seem to be interdependence and balance – not dominance over
nature.

As is evident from the above, I assume that the greatest challenge of today is
perhaps the understanding of the relationships and interactions between
humans and the rest of nature. It is also my contention that our view of human
needs will not only be dependent on the culture we are a part of, but also on our
view of man in general. The challenge is great, and it is necessary to approach it
with a high degree of modesty and an effort to understand our own limitations.

It will be essential to analyse and face the challenge of conflicting needs, and
to try to see the connection between general basic needs and the many diver-
gent and culture-dependent shaping of needs.

Given the point of view that needs are flexible, it is also, as previously mentioned, essential to discuss how human needs can be influenced in directions
which may further a sustainable development.

3.5 DIFFERENT APPROACHES IN DISCUSSING THE CONCEPT OF NEED

Needs may be discussed from different points of departure. One of the Brundt-land Commission's approaches in discussing the concept of needs is in the form of human rights: to what degree may the fulfilment of basic needs be considered a human right? What moral obligations rest on all of us for a distribution of benefits which will secure that these human rights are fulfilled? What will we have to do to make it possible to further interaction and co-operation between individuals, organisations and nations, which will enable us to fulfil such moral obligations? To push it to extremes, how do we proceed from understanding the universal need for survival to morally binding actions, in a complicated area where understanding of connections, of interactions is very difficult indeed? One point of departure is to discuss the concept of needs, and assumed connections between basic needs and secondary needs.

The ethnologist Konrad Lorenz (1966) has studied in detail the survival strategies of different species, the basis for what we usually call instinctive actions, what basic needs these actions fulfil, and in which ways environmental factors effect them. For instance, he describes the ways in which the survival of a species is secured through a readiness for action: fights between rivals, fights over territory, and the protection of offspring. Very often, there is a very fine balance between the protection of the offspring and the heightened aggression directed against those who may represent a danger to the offspring. Under very special circumstances, this aggression may be directed against the offspring, and lead to its death. In other words, even instinctively rooted needs may, under very special conditions, release (self-)destructive actions.

It is usual for psychological research to regard needs as biologically rooted bases for action, and survival as its fundamental goal. The concept of needs is supplemented with the concepts of drive and motive, to stress the connection between needs and actions. It is also usual to assume a hierarchical connection between fundamental, biologically rooted needs and secondary, culturally rooted motives and actions.

In this chapter, I shall limit myself to a short description of A.H. Maslow's model.

3.6 MASLOW'S MODEL OF NEEDS

According to Maslow (1962), a hierarchical system of needs is the basis of man's motivations and actions. The most fundamental needs are the physiological needs for food, drink, and protection from pain, cold and heat. If one of these needs is unsatisfied, it will, according to Maslow, totally dominate actions and mental processes. The next step in the hierarchy is the need for safety, which will dominate when the most fundamental needs have been satisfied. The third step in the hierarchy consists of social needs: needs for contact with others and for self-assertion. The final step, which may dominate man's actions after the satisfaction of the more basic needs, is the need for self-actualisation, that is, the need to grasp one's possibilities, develop one's gifts and personality. Creative, intellectual and aesthetic needs also belong here. The people he calls 'self-actualising' are the most mature and mentally healthy among us.

Maslow's theory has been under discussion for many years. Many colleagues have disagreed with his strictly hierarchical model of needs. The way he stresses the need for self-actualisation and the criteria he uses for inclusion in his group of self-actualising people has also been regarded as elitist thinking.

However, his model may be used as the point of departure for a further discussion of the distinction between basic/secondary needs, and the distinction between universal/culturally instigated needs. The conception of this may vary, depending on cultural background and on one's concept of man. It seems to me that discussing and delimiting basic needs is rather important. This concept is central to the Brundtland Report. Essential in Maslow's theory is, in my view, his idea that unfulfilled needs may come to dominate an individual's thoughts and actions completely. This becomes especially important seen in connection with all the different ways man's needs may be 'shaped' within different cultural contexts.

3.6.1 The Need for Attachment – a Basic Need?

A special challenge in the discussion of need lies in trying to throw light on needs which are difficult to quantify, and which are rarely listed among basic needs, but which according to recent research, should be regarded as fundamental. The need for attachment, which emerges in the earliest phase of life, is indeed one such very important need.

Until some twenty to thirty years ago, researchers in developmental psychology assessed the basic needs of infants to be the needs for food, milk, warmth and care. Empirical research in later years has, however, shown very clearly that interaction and reciprocity with the significant others are also fundamental from birth onwards – and for the further development of the child intellectually and emotionally (Trevarthen, 1975). According to the social scientist John Bowlby (1988), attachment behaviour has survival value, and its origin is biological. He puts it rather strongly, emphasising that 'it would be biological folly' if this were not so. Because of the human infant's total dependence on the significant others through many years, the psychological attachment to them, including sensitivity to others and the ability to learn from them, are central criteria for survival. A feeling of security, predictability and an emerging sense of mastery are closely connected to attachment to the significant others. In other words, the need for, and the drive towards attachment to others is very strong from the beginning of life, and neglect may have very serious consequences. René Spitz's pioneer study from 1946 of a group of children who for different reasons had been taken away from their mothers at six months of age, and who were staying in a nursery home where they were physically well attended to, but with very little attention and psychological care, showed that some of the infants reacted with what Spitz called 'anaclitic depression' because of lack of mothering. They were sad, introverted and unable to have contact with others. The mortality rate was also higher than normal.

There is not much reason to doubt that the need for attachment in different forms continues to be basic throughout life. One study pointing in this direction is Dag Hareide's study from 1991. He asked 1000 people in the county of Hedmark, Norway, what for them made life worth living. The most important answers were in the following hierarchical order of importance.

1. To be loved by somebody, to mean something to others, human consideration and sense of community.
2. Good health.
3. Unspoiled nature, nature experiences.
4. Meaningful work.
5. To have enough money, a certain standard of living.

Under different cultural conditions, the ranking of the answers might have been different; among other reasons, because unfulfilled basic needs supposedly would be dominant (see Maslow), while fulfilled needs may remain 'invisible' and to a certain degree unacknowledged. One of Hareide's conclusions is that using the trend in violence, crime, alcohol-abuse and suicide as measures of the quality of human relations, a clear deterioration seems to have taken place in Norwegian society during the last 30 years. One explanation of the ranking in his study may therefore be that his subjects feel these values are being threatened. Another indication that such a point of view may be right, is that people who have had near-death experiences, very often will declare that the need for attachment to their significant others is their most important and valued need. Material values become less important, while relations to others gain in value (see Ring, 1988).

Data from psychotherapeutic research have shown that a salient problem for many people in western culture is that their need for security and attachment early in life has been neglected (see Håland, 1986). For all of them, this has had a negative influence on their self-image and for the development of their capacity for loving – for some of them, to the extent of not daring to seek closeness to others. Instead they have in various ways tried to hide and to compensate for their lack of basic trust and lack of experience in feeling close to others. Some of them have developed strong needs to control others, to dominate others, and a strong need for 'one-upmanship' – at worst, to be violent to others and to destroy others. Characteristic, then, is the treatment of others as objects rather than equals. Others may have developed other types of 'compensatory needs', like different kinds of greed. For instance, they may develop a pronounced consumer attitude – they can never get enough, be it consumer goods or favours. Different combinations of the above-mentioned compensatory needs may of course be developed.

The knowledge we have today about the neglect of children's attachment needs gives reason to believe that a number of people having this type of problem live their lives without gaining the understanding and insight necessary for again daring to experience and act constructively to satisfy their need for attachment. On the other hand, there is reason to believe that the fact that competition, consumption, admiration for the 'winner' and not least, admiration for material wealth, are highly valued in our society, supports and contributes to maintain what I have called compensatory needs.

However, the compensatory behaviour cannot satisfy the underlying basic needs. The tragedy is that, this not being acknowledged, one is doomed to failure, while all the time strengthening the compensatory behaviour (see Maslow's point of view about unsatisfied needs which may completely dominate behaviour).

The long period of dependency early in life makes children receptive to their culture's values through their parents' attitudes and actions. This may contribute to the shaping of needs in unfortunate directions mentioned above. When needs have been shaped in specific directions, 'functional autonomy' may be the result. This means that the connection back to the underlying basic needs is no longer acknowledged. The secondary, compensatory needs will be experienced as the 'real' ones, and accordingly, the needs one will seek to fulfil.

More than 30 years ago, Erich Fromm criticised western society for being production-centred and commodity-greedy. He stressed the importance of radical changes in the social structure. He ends his book *The Art of Loving* in the following way:

> Society must be organised in such a way that man's social, loving nature is not separated from his social existence, but becomes one with it . . . any society which excludes, relatively, the development of love, must in the long run perish of its own contradiction with the basic necessities of human nature. . . . To have faith in the possibility of love as a social and not only exceptional-individual phenomenon, is a rational faith based on the insight into the very nature of man (Fromm, 1957:133).

Seen in the light of the discussion on compensatory needs, it seems reasonable to assume that Erich Fromm is right in his reasoning about the future of man – for two reasons:

1. It is difficult to believe in the survival of a society which does not fulfil 'the basic necessities of human nature'.

2. If the compensatory nature of human greed is not acknowledged, it will
    probably only increase.

To the degree that a sustainable development depends on both the will to
share the necessities of life between rich and poor countries in a different way
from what is done today, and a will to reduce some of the demands which are felt
to be both necessary and self-evident by people living in abundance, this is going
to put great demands on people in our part of the world. Changes in this direction presuppose deep insight – including self-insight and changes in attitudes.
Not least, it presupposes that society has leaders and 'trend-setters' who are
emotionally secure, confident and generous people – not greedy and exploit-
ative. There is reason to believe that the Brundtland Report represents *one* salient point of departure for an action-oriented discussion of values.

Research in Norway and other Western countries has shown that people's
awareness of, and interest in ecological problems have been growing during the
last decade (see Jensen [1989]; Strumse [1991]). A growing number of people
also wish to give priority to environmental considerations rather than to further
industrialisation. For instance, in a Norwegian study in 1990, a majority of the
subjects said they would give priority to environmental considerations more
than to further economic growth (see Strumse, 1991).

Research results like these indicate that a 'climate' for political decisions
which does not only favour economic growth, is beginning to emerge. A certain
degree of optimism may be justified – especially if further growth in people's
awareness and understanding of relations and connections takes place.

3.6.2   A Theory of Physical Health and Autonomy as Universal Basic Needs

A great challenge in meeting the problems of global distribution is to find ways
of discussing the fulfilment of basic needs in ways that will lead to a globally
manageable operationalisation. This is precisely the ambitious goal of Len
Doyal and Ian Gough's *A Theory of Human Need* (1991). Their goal is to develop a theory of need which is neither as relativistic as many of the definitions
in Western society nor as paternalistic as those of eastern European societies
under communism. 'Human needs', they argue, 'are neither subjective preferences best understood by each individual, nor static essences best understood
by planners or party officials. They are universal and knowledgeable, but our
knowledge of them, and of the satisfiers necessary to meet them, is dynamic and
open-ended.'

Doyal and Gough wish to develop a theory defining universal needs, which
may function as a basis for a comparison between the nations of the world in fulfilling the basic needs of their populations. They want to find out more than just
the statistical mean for each country. More important, perhaps, is the distribution within each country, especially if one wants to find out – which they do –

under what social preconditions, political, economic and ecological, the basic needs of all members of a certain society have hitherto been closest to fulfilment. This seems to me to be very important also because the Brundtland Commission claims that a sustainable development requires meeting the basic needs of all.

Doyal and Gough's book provides, in my opinion, an important contribution to a further operationalisation of the concept of need which may provide wider possibilities for action. I will therefore, with the reservation that a short rendering of the contents of the book hardly will be fair to the authors, try to discuss some salient points. The authors describe basic needs as follows:

> Basic human needs stipulate what persons must achieve if they are to avoid sustained and serious harm (Doyal and Gough, 1991:50).

And they claim that:

> since physical survival and personal autonomy are the preconditions for any individual action in any culture, they constitute the most basic human needs – those which must be satisfied to some degree before actors can effectively participate in their form of life to achieve any other valued goals.
>
> To be autonomous in this minimal sense, is to have the ability to make informed choices about what should be done and how to go about doing it. . . . A person with impaired autonomy is thus someone who temporarily and seriously lacks the capacity for action through his agency being in some way constrained (1991:53).

However, Doyal and Gough claim that physical survival is not sufficient; to survive with one's health intact is a basic need. Therefore the two basic needs in their definition are physical health and autonomy. An optimal level of physical health, then, means as long a life and as little illness as possible in relation to genetic potential.

Their concept of autonomy is rather inclusive, to the extent that it is dependent on the level of self-understanding, understanding of culture, the psychological capacity to formulate options and the objective opportunities to act accordingly. Furthermore, a connection exists between the level of autonomy, self-respect and mental health, and these are linked to relations of altruism and generosity. One might say that a salient feature in their concept of autonomy is a general need for sufficient freedom of action to be a participant more than a recipient, a freedom to participate in 'creating the good society'. Contrary to the way autonomy is often defined, theirs is a *relational* definition. It seems fair to say that the need for attachment is included in their concept of autonomy. In other words: we constantly live with the paradox that the realisation of individual autonomy is dependent on others.

It seems reasonable to ask: is Doyal and Gough's view of man naive, or does it seem reasonable to assume that such a basic need exists? (See the need for attachment, and see Erich Fromm, quoted earlier.) Anthropological literature describes isolated, so-called primitive societies, in which relations and attachment are given higher priority than individualism and separation, and giving and sharing higher than having and owning (Nilsen, 1989). This may be yet another indicator that the need for autonomy, the way Doyal and Gough define it, is a basic need.

The highest possible degree of autonomy is what the authors call *critical autonomy*, which includes political freedom and real influence on the rules and norms of one's culture, and the ability to transcend them. In my view, there is reason to believe that critical autonomy is particularly important for solving international conflicts.

Interaction with others is, of course, fundamental in order to fulfil one's basic needs. Doyal and Gough's reasoning goes on as follows. Essential features in all societies, be they ever so different in other respects, are: all cultures must have a material production. It is necessary somehow to procure food, shelter and other satisfiers for its members. All societies have an implicit social contract subject to perpetual testing and re-negotiation: about division of labour, the sharing of the amenities and pleasures of life, the demands and requirements of the dominant individuals or groups. Rules regarding the exchange and distribution of goods emerge, which of course vary among different cultures according to their moral beliefs about the justice of whatever degrees of inequality are tolerated. Whatever their normative details, however, they all aim at levels of production which are sufficient at least for group survival. To the extent that members of the group accept and internalise the existing system of distribution and find it 'natural', one might say that the factual has acquired normative force (Ofstad, 1971), that is to say, the way it functions is also the way it ought to function. For forms of life to exist over time, their modes of production must also provide the material foundation for successful biological reproduction and socialisation. Infant care and socialisation in their turn are salient features for society's survival.

Production, reproduction, cultural transmission and political authority (backed up by sanctions) are referred to by Doyal and Gough as 'structural activities which any minimally successful mode of social life must be able to carry out'. They stress the interdependence between individual need-satisfaction and the social preconditions, and they claim that they 'are not adopting the sort of abstract individualism which is often exhibited by utilitarian writers and politicians'. The main focus of the book is, however, basic needs which exist independent of the *form* of society, but which are individually shaped in interaction with the specific surrounding culture in ways which give members of the society scope for their abilities *and* the protection inherent in mutual control and moral obligations followed by the members of society.

If we make our perspective more inclusive and focus on the principle of sustainable development, the interaction perspective, in my opinion, becomes all the more important. For instance, what and how much will people in the rich part of the world have to renounce, if we are to fulfil the indispensable moral obligation formulated by the Brundtland Commission? How do we move from rhetoric to action? What is the best policy for reaching an optimal satisfaction of needs within the limits set by sustainable development, and hence, the best way to redistribute income and wealth?

To state what *ought* to be done is only the beginning. With operationalisation, the difficulties and conflicts of interest truly emerge. If the privileged people of the world are not willing to share, is it desirable or even possible to force them? And who should have the power to use what kind of force?

According to Doyal and Gough, informed and critical discussion is essential in the effort to find possible solutions to the immensely difficult problems inherent in sustainable development and redistribution. They lean on Habermas's view of man: his 'belief in the basic goodness of ordinary people and their potential to live, work, create and communicate together in harmony and to use practical reason peacefully to resolve their disputes and to optimise their need-satisfaction', and his belief in the value of what he has termed 'dominance-free dialogue'.

Doyal and Gough also refer to Rawls's *A Theory of Justice* (1972). Rawl envisages a debate on justice 'under the veil of ignorance' (that is, the partakers in the debate not knowing what will be their own position, the result for themselves personally of the decisions made by the group). This set-up might be regarded as an attempt to make it possible in a rational way to empathise with the less privileged. The drawback in Rawls's thinking, they find, is that it presupposes a society of unavoidable social class differences and with competition and incentives as virtues. They also find Rawls's theory lacking in depth as regards the discussion of participation and democracy, and they find that he neglects the problem of global justice.

A reallocation of goods and services is, in their opinion, a prerequisite for making it possible to establish an appropriate system of international political authority which will be able to provide for a legal regulation of potential threats to future generations' possibilities to fulfil basic needs.

In moving from rhetoric to action, a first step is to find ways to operationalise, to measure the level of satisfaction of basic needs, using cross-cultural measures. The choice between what is possible to operationalise and degree of universality is difficult, but progress has been made in this respect. Doyal and Gough find it important to elaborate on characteristics in the way needs are satisfied. Some may be expressed through universal measures. For example, the number of calories per day for a specified group of people has transcultural relevance, likewise, shelter from the elements and protection from 'disease-carrying vectors'.

The following way of reasoning is salient in their struggle to systematise:

Satisfier characteristics are a subset of all characteristics, having the property of contributing to the satisfaction of our basic needs in one or more cultural settings. Let us now subdivide this set further to identify universal satisfier characteristics: those characteristics of satisfiers which apply to all cultures. Universal satisfier characteristics are thus those properties of goods, services, activities and relationships which enhance physical health and human autonomy in all cultures (Doyal and Gough, 1991:157).

These universal satisfier characteristics thus provide the crucial bridge between universal basic needs and socially relative satisfiers, and therefore Doyal and Gough name them *intermediate needs*. Their list of intermediate needs includes the needs for:

Nutritious food and clean water
Protective housing
A non-hazardous work environment
A non-hazardous physical environment
Appropriate health care
Security in childhood
Significant primary relationships
Physical security
Economic security
Appropriate education
Safe birth control and child-bearing.

The only criterion for inclusion in their list is whether or not any set of satisfier characteristics universally and positively contributes to physical health and autonomy. The authors are well aware that their list may not be complete and that their 'labels' may be ambiguous. Their reason for not including sexual needs for instance, is that some people live healthy and autonomous lives without having sexual relations. Given sexual relations' fundamental role in creating the next generation, and thus for long-term survival, one might question such an omission. Even though the list may not be all-inclusive, it gives the possibility of comparing already existing statistical material, to make a comparison between the nations of the world, and of the distribution within a specific country. The list also makes it possible to get an overview of the quality of existing statistical material, that is, the areas where reliable material exists, and the areas where further research is needed. As a standard against which to compare need-satisfaction, Doyal and Gough have chosen an optimum. This optimum is the existing conditions in the countries of the world having the highest standard in health and autonomy, as measurable through existing data regarding satisfaction of 'intermediate needs'. Two of their tables are reproduced in the Appendix to this chapter so as to illustrate their way of systematising existing data regarding 'intermediate needs' (Tables 3.1 and 3.2).

Even though available statistics have their limitations and elements of uncertainty, the main tendencies are clear. Enormous differences in the satisfaction of basic needs exist between rich and poor countries (see Appendix). However, great differences exist also among the low-income countries and among the rich countries as regards the distribution of goods. Available data on the income-shares of the poorest 20 per cent of populations also show that it is among middle-income Third World countries that inequalities in income and need-satisfaction are greatest. There is also a regional effect, revealing the Latin American countries as the most inegalitarian (see Doyal and Gough 1991:263).

Among the rich countries, the Scandinavian welfare states are those which most closely approximate optimum need-satisfaction at the present time – both in standard and in distribution. It is interesting to note that according to the UNICEF report *The Progress of Nations* (1994), the Scandinavian countries are contributing twice as much per capita as France, Germany and Canada, three times as much as Britain and six times as much as USA to the developing countries. The value of solidarity, which is salient in the Scandinavian welfare states, is – it seems – also reflected in their attitudes towards international society.

Available data show that the relation between mean income and need-satisfaction is not a simple and linear one. The question of distribution, be it between men and women on the household level, within a nation, or on the international level, represents the biggest challenge, especially in relation to renewable/non-renewable resources.

The United Nations' Development Programme (UNDP) started publishing a yearly *Human Development Report* in 1990. The 1994 edition shows clearly the effort to steadily develop more comprehensive and differentiated definitions and measures of need-satisfaction and development than GNP (Gross National Product). I see this also as an attempt, long overdue, to change the hierarchy of values inherent in the indexes commonly used to compare the state of affairs in the nations of the world. The index used by the UNDP is what they call Human Development Index (HDI), intended as a measure of people's potential for a long and healthy life, for communication and participation in their community and to have enough resources for a decent life. The report is concerned with developing a less commodity-based index than the GNP – an index taking care of human dignity, possibility for participation and choices: in short, an index based on values and ways of thinking having much in common with Doyal and Gough's relational thinking.

HDI is constantly improved and corrected, based on the experience with the weaknesses of the index, and on input from researchers and decision-makers. One kind of improvement is that not only average figures for the individual countries are used, but also figures showing distribution between the poorest and the richest, and between women and men. In addition to the literacy rate, the number of schooling years is included. The threshold value for income is changed from 'the poverty line in industrial countries' to the current world average for real GNP per capita. This enables the population and their govern-ment to evaluate progress over time and to set criteria for political intervention. It also provides the possibility of instructive comparisons of the development of different countries.

It does sound promising to me that it seems to be more widely understood than before that basic needs include psychological and social needs as well as physiological needs, and that an interaction between these needs exists throughout life. This kind of insight does not make the practical work for a more even distribution of goods more easy than before, but in my opinion it is an insight which is fundamental also for the goal of a sustainable develop-ment. I see this as a signal that a concept of reality based on a 'rationality of care' and an understanding of global interdependence is gaining influence also in the United Nations. I also agree with the point of view put forward in UNDP's report, that if too much weight is put on the material we may be easily tempted to divide the world into contributors and recipients – which would be reductionist and unfruitful. Perhaps even more unfortunate is the fact that such points of view are part of a value hierarchy with the rich countries at the top of the hierarchy. If we are to have any chance of creating sustainable development, it is essential to question the rich countries' prioritisation of values. If 'the world is ready for more comprehensive and nuanced develop-ment goals', as claimed in the 1994 UNDP report, then also for this reason, it is good news.

Doyal and Gough claim that the need for autonomy (meaning freedom to participate) is fundamental. Modern development psychology describes the fundamental meaning of attachment. The understanding of human psycholo-gical needs (and we may add, the human tendency to develop compensatory needs if their basic needs are not met) is also essential to the UNDP's way of describing human development. Such an insight appears to be fundamental for arriving at long-term strategies for optimal fulfilment of material needs through a better understanding of relationships.

Doyal and Gough also draw conclusions on the relationship between indi-viduals and state power which deserve attention and further discussion. Put very simply, their conclusions may be summarised as follows.

The optimal relation between individual freedom and state control will vary. A strong state control seems to be necessary to change distribution in the poor part of the world. It is, however, very important to find out how and where in the process towards a more just distribution the state control will have to be loosened to prevent the control of the inhabitants becoming a goal in itself, developing into abuse of power instead of functioning as a means to secure an optimal fulfilling of the needs of the population. Whether such a process will succeed, is of course dependent on the international community's understanding and approbation of different ways and means towards a better distribution. This appears to be essential if destructive interference is to be avoided, and sufficient international support is to be secured.

If Doyal and Gough's contention is valid, it would indeed be difficult to develop sufficient communication, empathy and understanding between nations and between individuals to help the poor countries of the world to reach an optimum of distribution and need-satisfaction, close to what the Scandinavian welfare states have achieved. The challenge lying ahead of us is, however, even more difficult and demanding. As mentioned, there is a demand for developing and deepening our self-understanding and our understanding of global interdependence. If it is not possible to maintain the rich countries' level of need-satisfaction, we will have to find out what we will have to renounce among the benefits that we take for granted. And we will have to find out how it is going to be possible to change our value-hierarchies in order to accomplish such a difficult task. Among other things, this means understanding the psychological connection between the idea of man as the master of the rest of creation, economic superiority and wealth as the highest value, competition and ever more industrial development as an unavoidable necessity. Not least, it means questioning the assumption that the problems created by such development will always be solved through further technological advances.

Today, we witness an emerging understanding of the dimensions of the challenges facing the world, and of the mutual dependency which makes it impossible to 'resign'. One challenge is also to try to find out how to release man's capacity for heroism on a large scale, with the aim of realising a more just distribution, fulfilment of needs and sustainable development.

A realistic view of the dimensions of the problems we are facing also demands a willingness to take part in an ongoing discussion and assessment of the relation between freedom, regulation and control in our part of the world, if and when drastic changes become necessary.

APPENDIX

Table 3.1   Suggested indicators of intermediate need-satisfaction

Universal satisfier characteristics	Social indicators
1. Food and water Appropriate nutritional intake	Calorie consumption below FAO/WHO requirements[a] Other nutrients consumption below requirements[b] % lacking access to adequate safe water[a] % suffering malnutrition/deficiency diseases[*a] % low birthweight babies[*a] % overweight, obese[*b]

Table 3.1 (*contd.*)

Universal satisfier characteristics	Social indicators
2. Housing Adequate shelter Adequate basic services Adequate space per person	% homeless[b] % in structures that do not protect against normal weather[b] % lacking safe sanitation facilities[a] % living above specified ratio of persons per room[b]
3. Work Non-hazardous work environment	Incidence of specified hazards[b] Incidence of job tasks undermining emotional cognitive/autonomy[c] Deaths/injuries from work accidents[*a] Deaths/illness from work-related diseases[*a]
4. Physical environment Non-hazardous environment	% experiencing concentrations of pollutants[b] > specified levels: air, water, land, radiation, noise
5. Health care Provision of appropriate care Access to appropriate care	Doctors/nurses/hospital beds per population < specified levels[a] % without access to community health services[a] % not fully immunised against specified[a] diseases
6. Childhood needs Security in childhood Child development	% of children abandoned, abused, neglected[c] % lacking stimulation, positive feedback, responsibility[c]
7. Support groups Presence of significant others Primary support group	% without close, confiding relationship[c] % with no/very low social contacts[b] % with nobody to call on when in need[c]
8. Economic security	% in absolute poverty[a] % in relative poverty (participation standard)[c] % with poor protection against specified contingencies[b]
9. Physical security A safe citizenry A safe state	Homicide rates[a] Crime victim rates[b] Victims of state violence[b] War victims[a]
10. Education Access to cultural skills	Lack of primary/secondary education[a] Years of formal study < specified level[a] Lack of specified qualifications [b] Lack of higher eduction[a]
11. Birth control and childbearing Safe birth control Safe child-bearing	Lack of access to safe contraception and abortion[a] Maternal mortality rate[*a]

Notes
a Reasonably reliable universal or near-universal data
b Data for few countries only, but where there is a clear idea of operationalisation
c More speculative suggestions for indicators
* Indicator of health or autonomy related to a particular universal satisfier characteristic

Table 3.2   Substantive need-satisfaction in the Three Worlds

	Third World				Second World	First World	World
	China	India	Other, low income	Other, medium income			
1. Pop., 1986 (m)	1 054	781	663	1 230	396	742	4 885
2. GNP/head, 1986	300	290	242	1 330	(2 059)	12 964	2 780
3. GDP/head ppp, 1980	–	573	(760)	(2 594)	–	9 699	(3 879)
Survival/Health							
4. Life expectancy, 1986	69	57	50	61	72	75	64
5. Infant MR, 1985	36	105	119	66	23	9	61
6. Under-5 MR, 1985	50	158	193	108	27	12	94
7. Low birth weight (%)	6	30	24	12	6	6	14
Autonomy							
8. Literacy, 1985 (%)	69	43	46	73	(c.100)	(c.100)	70
Intermediate needs							
Water/nutrition							
9. Safe water, 1983 (%)	–	54	33	59	(c.100)	(c.100)	–
10. Calories, 1982	111	96	92	110	132	130	111
Housing							
11. Overcrowding, 1970s (%)	–	–	–	(61)	13	2	
Health services							
12. Pop/phys., 1981	1.7	3.7	11.6	5.1	0.34	0.55	3.8
13. Access, 1980–3 (%)	–	–	49	(57)	(c.100)	(c.100)	–
Security							
14. War dead, 1945–85 (%)	0.2	0.1	1.0	0.4	0.0	0.0	0.3
15. Homicide, 1987	–	–	–	(8.3)	1.9	3.8	(4.6)
16. Poverty, 1977–84 (%)	–	48	(55)	(33)	–	–	–
Education							
17. Adults: sec. ed. (%)	16	14	(9)	10	42	30	16
18. Adults: post-sec. ed. (%)	1.0	2.5	(1.4)	4.8	(8.9)	11.7	3.7
19. Students: sec. ed. (%)	39	35	23	47	92	93	51

Table 3.2 (contd.)

	Third World				Second World	First World	World
	China	India	Other, low income	Other, medium income			
20. Students: post-sec. ed.(%)	–	–	3	14	20	39	19
Reproduction							
21. Contraception, 1985 (%)	77	35	21	50		66	50
22. Maternal MR, 1980–7	44	340	510	130		10	250

Notes

The definition of 'low' income, 'middle' income and 'industrial market' economies follows the World Bank (1988, p. 217). However data for the state socialist countries have been recomputed to include eight countries; Albania, Bulgaria, Czechoslovakia, German Democratic Republic, Hungary, Poland, Romania and the USSR. Four high-income oil-exporting nations in the Middle East are excluded from these country groups, though they are represented in the global averages. There are many problems in equating 'development' with income per head (Thirlwall, 1983, ch. 1), but the organisation of world statistics makes it difficult to present the data organised according to some other variable. Countries in groups are weighted by population except where noted. Numbers are in brackets when data is available for fewer than half the countries in that group.

Since there are well-known problems in comparing per capita incomes across nations, two separate measures are provided. Row 2 shows average GNP per head in $US at current exchange rates, whereas row 3 shows average GDP per head (unfortunately only for 1980) in $US at 'purchasing power parities' which reveal differences in national real incomes, more accurately (World Bank, 1987, pp. 268–71). Unfortunately this information is not yet available for all nations.

– = not available

Definitions and sources
(by row numbers)

1. Total population, 1986, millions (World Bank, 1988, Table 1).
2. Gross national product per head in 1986 in $US using average exchange rates for 1984–6 (World Bank, 1988, Table 1).
3. Gross domestic product per head in 1980 in $US at 'purchasing power parities' (World Bank, 1987, Box A.2).
4. Life expectancy at birth in years, 1986 (World Bank, 1988, Table 1).
5. Infant mortality before one year of age, per 1000 live births, 1985 (UNICEF, 1987, Table 1).
6. Mortality of children under 5 years of age per 1000 live births (UNICEF, 1987, Table 1).
7. Proportion of babies weighing under 2500 gm (UNICEF, 1987).

8. Percentage of persons aged 15 and over who can read and write, 1985 (UNICEF, 1987, Table 1).
9. Access to drinking water, as defined by WHO, 1983 (UNICEF, 1987, Table 3).
10. Daily calorie supply per head as percentage of requirements, 1983 (UNICEF, 1987, Table 2).
11. Percentage of housing units with more than two persons per room, various years 1970s (UN, 1987, Table 4.5).
12. Population (thousands) per physician, 1981 (World Bank, 1988, Table 29).
13. Percentage of population with access to health services as defined by WHO, 1980–3 (UNICEF, 1987, Table 3).
14. War deaths between 1945 and 1985, as percentage of population in 1986 (UN, 1987, Table 9.11).
15. Homicides per 100 000 population (WHO, 1989, Table 10).
16. Percentage of population with incomes below that where a minimum nutritionally adequate diet plus essential non-food requirements is affordable, as estimated by World Bank (UNICEF, 1987, Table 6).
17. Proportion of adults who have ever entered secondary education; various years between 1970 and 1982 (UNESCO, 1989, Table 1.4).
18. Proportion of all adults who have entered post-secondary education; years between 1970 and 1982 (UNESCO, 1989, Table 1.4).
19. Number of secondary school pupils of all ages as percentage of children of secondary school age (generally 12–17 years), around 1985 (World Bank, 1988, Table 30).
20. Number of students enrolled in all post-secondary education, schools and universities, divided by population aged 20–4, around 1985 (World Bank, 1988, Table 30). Details of coverage are given on p. 303.
21. Percentage of married women of childbearing age who are using, or whose husbands are using, any form of contraception, whether traditional or modern methods (UNDP, 1990, Table 20).
22. Annual number of deaths of women from pregnancy-related causes per 100 000 live births (UNDP, 1990, Table 11).

Source: Doyal & Gough, 1991

4 Sustainable Development, State Sovereignty and International Justice

Andreas Føllesdal

4.1 INTRODUCTION

The right to development gained broad attention in the mid-1980s: the UN recognised a human right to development in 1986,[1] and the World Commission on Environment and Development presented its conclusions regarding sustainable development in 1987.

The Commission, chaired by Gro Harlem Brundtland, declared that sustainable development is an overriding requirement for national and supranational institutions. We must promote 'development that meets the needs of the present without compromising the ability of future generations to meet their own needs' (WCED, 1987:43). The Commission goes on to address conflicts between the claims of today's poor and tomorrow's environment. To be sure, the environment often improves with the eradication of poverty: 'Poverty reduces people's capacity to use resources in a sustainable manner; it intensifies pressure on the environment' (WCED, 1987:49). But sometimes these goals appear to conflict, and people have different views: citizens in richer countries give priority to conserving the environment rather than to promoting economic development in other states.[2] On the other hand, the governments of China, Brazil and India and many developing countries claim that they must give priority to their economic development, above environmental considerations. The Commission holds that in conflicts between the basic needs of the world's poor and environmental concerns, basic needs should be given priority.

Another area of conflict arises between environment, development and traditional conceptions of sovereignty. In exchange for accepting the Montreal Protocol's requirement for removing ozone-damaging substances, developing countries have demanded economic support from other countries.[3] Such claims may merely be requests for side-payments in the bargain, but they may perhaps also be well-founded claims within a more just world order: that there are international obligations of aid to alleviate conflicts between human rights and development.

The present chapter seeks to elaborate and justify these claims of priority of basic needs over environment and sovereignty. It also holds that development

70

strategies should secure the basic needs for today's poor through respecting human rights – if necessary at the expense of protecting the environment. Moreover, such development strategies may require international aid with ties, contrary to traditional conceptions of state sovereignty.

Some might claim that the concept of sustainable development is diluted by mixing it with considerations of global justice (for example, Amundsen *et al.*, 1991:7). Two responses are in order. Firstly, if sustainable development is to serve not only as one of several conflicting ideals, but as an overriding requirement for legitimate regimes and national policies, the norm must be specified in a defensible way which warrants its priority. Not to do so leaves the application of the slogan open to intuitionist weighting, both in day-to-day politics and in administration and adjudication. Secondly, if sustainable development is indeed to be put forward as an overriding requirement, the argument presented here insists that such policies must secure the basic needs of all. It is inconsistent with the equal worth of all humans to advocate sustainable development to the detriment of individuals' survival, or to accept that people alive today should be sacrificed for the sake of future generations. This is unacceptable when there are alternatives – namely that existing inequitable regimes and social institutions must be changed.

Section 4.2 outlines aspects of a theory of justice providing a systematic perspective for addressing these concerns. Section 4.3 defends the Primacy of Human Rights for development strategies. Section 4.4 addresses the conflicts between human rights and development, while Section 4.5 discusses conflicts regarding human rights and sovereignty. Industrialised countries have obligations towards developing countries where necessary for ecologically justifiable development strategies that also respect human rights. But international aid need not be unconditional: it may be necessary to influence internal conditions in developing countries through economic pressure. Section 4.6 reflects on some principled objections against the Primacy of Human Rights. We consider an alternative, *the Primacy of the Environment*, sometimes argued by deep ecologists, which holds that environmental concerns should be of primary importance in the choice of development strategies, and if necessary at the expense of today's poor. A complete rebuttal of this view is beyond the scope of this chapter. The aim is rather to identify the issues of disagreement.

4.2   ON JUSTICE

Political authorities regulate, directly and indirectly, many of the factors that influence both our lives and those of future generations. The conflict between those starving today and the environment of tomorrow arises within specific social institutions and global regimes. Indeed much starvation could have been avoided with other laws and regulations for the distribution of property and political power within developing countries, to remove the extreme poverty there. And other ground rules for international trade could have also secured the basis of existence for the poor:

> In the context of basic survival, today's needs tend to overshadow considera-
> tion for the environmental future. It is poverty that is responsible for the
> destruction of natural resources, not the poor (Geoffrey Bruce, in WCED,
> 1987, 127).

The rules that govern today's practices are under some control at state and international levels, even though they are badly co-ordinated. It thus seems appropriate to clarify both whether alternative institutions and regimes are politically viable, and how such institutions should distribute benefits and burdens so as to reduce the burdens of protecting the environment on the poor. Such assessments require a comparison of the consequences for all affected parties.

4.2.1   Equal Worth

Equal worth of all is a basic norm in the political culture of democracies. All cit-izens should count, and be regarded as equals, for certain political and legal purposes. This requirement of equal worth entails at a minimum that the inter-ests of all are taken into account. The use of state power must therefore be jus-tifiable to all affected parties. To address issues of distributive justice across borders and generations, we apply the same perspective to regimes and social institutions – and to the state system itself. They must take due consideration of all affected parties, including unborn future generations. The current disasters of famines and armed conflicts underscore that the present world order falls far short of this requirement.

Given that the *status quo* is not legitimate, an important task is to determine principles for transition to better arrangements. Many important dilemmas of sustainable development and today's poor require precisely such principles of transition from non-ideal situations. What does the commitment to equal worth imply for the choice of development strategy?

One might hold that a just society – and a just global society – should maximise the average quality of life. However, utility maximisation does not ensure equal worth, because the distribution of benefits is ignored. For instance, the average quality of life may be maximised by letting a few starve, so as to improve the well-being of many others. Others insist that such strategies do not give enough weight to the equal worth of all. The Brundtland Commission seems to endorse this when it holds that development towards a legitimate world order must be sustainable, and secure the basic needs of today's people. This conclusion may be justified by the more fundamental normative position of Liberal Contractualism (Rawls, 1971; Scanlon, 1982).

Institutions are legitimate only if they can be justified by arguments in the form of a social contract of a particular kind. All individuals must be served by the social institutions: the interests of every individual must be secured and furthered by the social institutions as a whole. This commitment is honed by the notion of possible consent, allowing us to bring the vague ideals of equal dignity to bear on pressing questions of legitimacy and institutional design. The principles of legitimacy we should hold institutions to are those that the affected persons would unanimously consent to – under conditions which secure and express their status as appropriately free and equal. The set of social institutions as a whole thereby secures the interests of each affected party to an acceptable degree, including our interests in, for instance, peace, stability, basic needs and shares of goods and powers.

4.2.2 Pluralism

The equal worth of all implies that the demands we make on development strategies should take seriously the plurality of conceptions of the good. Even though all may endorse the norm of individuals' equal worth, we have different views and opinions about the worth of nature and about what makes life worth living. Some are ascetics, others not; some regard nature as valuable because it is useful, or because it provides them with good experiences or a sense of larger meaning of their life, while others believe that plants and pristine nature have a value all of their own, independently of whether humans value them or not. We thus assess many life situations and possibilities differently because we have different views on what the good life consists of. This pluralism makes it all the more difficult to find reasoned principles of legitimacy among all affected parties. Many claim, for example, that not only humans count as involved parties: moral status is also attributed to animals, plants, species or ecosystems.[4]

The equal worth of all requires us to heed the fact that many of us have partly incompatible though plausible views about the good life. This pluralism is a further challenge in determining how social institutions and regimes should be arranged. We cannot expect agreement about who should count, and which interests should count in arguments about social institutions.

The following sections develop and defend sustainable development from a liberal contractualist position where all humans, and only humans, count as affected parties for the issue of legitimate institutions. Many otherwise incompatible world-views which endorse the norm of equal worth of all humans also accept this starting-point.

4.3 THE CASE FOR HUMAN RIGHTS

Human rights are requirements that individuals' vital basic needs should be institutionally protected against specific threats caused by the state and the global order (Føllesdal, 1991, 1995). From the point of view of liberal contractualism the Primacy of Human Rights is to be preferred over the Primacy of the Environment, which would maintain that tomorrow's environment should be secured even at the expense of today's poor.

The contractualist interpretation of the norm of equal worth requires that alternative principles are compared in light of the difference they make for affected individuals, including future generations. This evaluation must consider development strategies as they are likely to work in practice, with incentive effects, and with attendant risks of misjudgement and abuse. Hence we must rely on empirical data about the possibilities and hazards of alternative development strategies.

I shall argue that even though the Primacy of Human Rights incurs some risk of losses, the Primacy of the Environment entails even larger risks.

4.3.1 Basic Needs

Human rights aim at protecting certain needs against specific threats in a world order of sovereign states. Vital basic needs must be secured, through such means under political control as food, water, shelter, analgesics and vaccinations.[5] All these needs must be met if individuals are to survive. Hence claims to these goods and their priority over all other claims should command assent regardless of otherwise incompatible views of the good life.

Minimum levels of income and political rights are also basic needs in states characterised by a monopoly on the use of force, an extensive division of labour, and the use of institutional mechanisms for distribution. Thus where food is distributed through markets, all households must have money either through wages or through income compensation. Under such social conditions, we may say that individuals have a basic social need for money, or for gainful employment or income substitution – as well as for legal safeguards for distribution of food within the household. This fits well with the Commission Report, which includes work as a basic need.

Access to democratic decision-making procedures is also necessary for securing vital basic needs. The allocation of such options and control to others than the individuals themselves constitutes a serious threat to their basic needs. Freedom of the press, freedom of speech and political rights protect individuals' options, and ensure that the authorities take the individual's basic needs into consideration. Thus democratic rule, including freedom of the press and political parties, protects against acute famines in India (Sen, 1988). Note that this argument for political rights is not based on the more contested view that individuals have a central interest in autonomy, which pluralism rules out as grounds for claims.

Vital basic needs justify most of the human rights contained in international documents. However, this account diverges at some points from the Commission: some components of living conditions cannot be justified by appeals to basic needs. Moreover, the Commission maintains that a legitimate goal must be to ensure for all the 'opportunity to satisfy their aspirations for a better life' (WCED, 1987:42). The satisfaction of aspirations implies that institutions should be stable and clearly defined. Surely people must be able to plan for tomorrow, confident that their efforts will be rewarded as expected. These concerns seem legitimate: the satisfaction of reasonable expectations seem to be an important interest across many conceptions of the good life (Føllesdal, 1996). But the satisfaction of aspirations does not constitute further substantive claims on distributive shares within such stable institutions. Our subjective sense of well-being and our preferences are largely dependent on our aspirations – but we create these aspirations in light of the expectations created by the social institutions themselves. Satisfaction of aspirations is simply unsuited as a criterion for evaluating social institutions, since we are too adaptable (Erikson, 1993:78). So we should not demand of just institutions simply that all parties are satisfied, lest politicians should be tempted to adjust our aspirations instead of adjusting the background institutions.

We may also note that considerations of basic needs do not justify a requirement for equal distribution of benefits in general. Hence, this account deviates from the Commission's standpoint, when it contends that:

Living standards that go beyond the basic minimum are sustainable only if consumption standards everywhere have regard for long-term sustainability. Yet many of us live beyond the world's ecological means ... sustainable development requires the promotion of values that encourage consumption standards that are within the bounds of the ecologically possible and to which *all can reasonably aspire*. (WCED, 1987:44, my emphasis)

Considerations of basic needs cannot justify the claim that all should have an *equal* consumption level in both time and space. Nonetheless, basic needs can justify some limitations in permissible inequality. For instance, unequal distribution of many instrumental benefits, like income and political influence, should be limited when relative purchasing power and influence determine the distribution of goods.

4.4 THE PRIMACY OF HUMAN RIGHTS OVER SUSTAINABLE DEVELOPMENT

A sovereign state, and the ground-rules of the state system, can secure the basic needs of the inhabitants – including their basic social needs. But state power and international regimes also constitute threats to the basic needs of individuals. Human rights serve to prevent many of these threats.

This account of human rights requires, for each right, a detailed account of the social needs, damages and protection that pertain to each basic need. Justifications for freedom of the press, political rights and the right to work were sketched above, and similar arguments must be presented for each human right. These rights require a variety of institutional mechanisms that protect individuals, and hold the state and the states system internationally responsible for having such mechanisms.

Some human rights require certain outputs – obligations of result; others put constraints on the shape of legitimate institutions; while yet other rights require that particular institutions must be in place. For example, the human right to adequate nutrition may be satisfied if social institutions ensure that agricultural strategies, market mechanisms, and employment policies secure the basic social needs (and hence basic needs) of all to the extent possible – leaving the details open.

The right to development and other so-called third-generation rights raise new problems. What interests are at stake, and which threats are averted by such rights? I submit that the right to development, and in particular to sustainable development, should be understood as a protection against certain development strategies. The Primacy of Human Rights excludes certain development strategies that will be allowed by the Primacy of the Environment. The latter allows development strategies that sacrifice some people's basic needs, while the Priority of Human Rights disallows such choices. Respect for the equal worth of the existing poor implies that such sacrifices cannot be justified as long as harm of such magnitude can be avoided by choosing other development strategies consistent with the Priority of Human Rights.

The Priority of Human Rights for development strategies does not allow development strategies that sacrifice any of today's population to the advantage of tomorrow's individuals and their environment. The argument in favour of this view rests on considerations of risks tied to the two competing allocations of authority. The need for an environment–human rights trade-off is doubted on empirical grounds, and the power to disregard human rights risks that the interests of neither present nor future generations will be protected.

Some of the most compelling justifications for environmental protection appeal to the impact on future generations.[6] Some go as far as to maintain that the basic needs of future generations are at stake if the primacy of human rights for development is followed. On this line of thought someone's basic needs must be sacrificed in any case, as the basic needs of present and future generations cannot be satisfied irrespective of regimes or social institutions in place.[7]

However, this claim is highly questionable on empirical grounds. Many starve to death in the present world order, and other basic needs are not met today. And future generations may also die of hunger and lack of essential medical aid.

But these tragedies are not due to lack of resources: more than enough food is produced to feed everyone today, and population growth can be affected by political measures. The cause of hunger today is first and foremost an uneven distribution of resources within each country and between countries on a global basis. There are no grounds for believing that development strategies that satisfy the Primacy of Human Rights must sacrifice the environment and the basic needs of future generations. We have no convincing reason to believe that a world order ensuring a more even distribution of food and medicine cannot be stable and yield enough over time, given the population growth of the future.

There is no evidence for the claim that the goals of human rights and environment are incompatible in practice, either in the short or long term.[8]

Furthermore, we should be particularly sceptical in allowing authorities to inflict great suffering on present populations out of concern for future generations and their environment.[9] If the right to sustainable development was given priority over human rights, this right can easily become a government excuse for not meeting the people's basic needs (see Donnelly 1989:146). Thus even if development were sometimes to require the disregard for human rights, such licence opens up even greater risks. Thus governments should not be accorded the authority to make priorities for long-term development at the expense of today's poor. Non-democratic systems of government are notoriously unreliable for ensuring development, sustainable or otherwise. And if the Primacy of the Environment is made the basis of development strategies and international interventions it may simply open the way for a new imperialism (Guha, 1989).

In contrast, strategies allowed by the Primacy of Human Rights require changes in the national and international distribution of benefits. The national and international ground rules affect standards of living and hence the survival possibilities; development strategies must ensure that the ground rules secure the basic needs of all.

4.5 THE PRIMACY OF HUMAN RIGHTS OVER SOVEREIGNTY

The needs of individuals are threatened both by their own authorities, and by the state system. The state system limits the individual state's options, and hence the state's scope of real autonomy. Basic needs remain unmet today both because of unjustified inequality within each individual country and because of the economic world order: the effects of international markets, investments and lending institutions.

It is particularly troubling if governments of rich, developed countries are allowed to respond to environmental problems of their own making by regulating and limiting the development opportunities in the poorer countries – incurring poverty as a result. Instead international regimes must be changed so that such tragic choices do not arise. But are there institutional mechanisms that can protect needs against such national and international threats, particularly under policies of economic development? Some changes in regimes are called for, to comply with the Primacy of Human Rights.

It is not clear that some new economic world order is the only or the best way to secure more equitable conditions for international trade.[10] It is also unclear whether better regulations for multinational companies can be found, and whether they can be enforced (Dunning, 1993: Chapter 21). Others maintain that international trade in emission permits may take care of many important considerations (Westbrook, 1991). In addition to these important empirical issues, several troubling issues within political theory must be addressed.

Developing countries sometimes claim that they must damage the environment for the sake of pressing basic needs. Such claims, if true, are difficult to dismiss. If a government is actually faced with such a difficult choice – leaving that an open question – the Priority of Human Rights imposes responsibilities on other countries to further sustainable development. Such responsibilities may include economic and technological aid to poorer countries if necessary. The primacy of human rights for development hence limits the state's sovereignty by establishing certain obligations across international borders. Thus, if the state system is to be morally legitimate, the international community must be obliged to provide aid in certain situations. Such aid may consist of the transfer of benefits or know-how, international political support to secure conditions of trade that ensure a fair division of profits, training in negotiation strategies for the poorer countries against multinational companies – and international pressure to secure an equitable redistribution of income and influence internal to the countries that struggle to meet their basic needs.

An alarming objection to accepting such a right to development is that a government may excuse its own violation of human rights by appealing to others' breach of the right to development assistance. But this excuse is not valid as it stands: the right to food, for example, does not require a government to feed the citizens, but instead requires the authorities to develop and implement an agricultural and nutrition policy with a view towards basic needs, in light of available resources (Alston and Quinn, 1987). Thus even though international breaches of the right to development reduces resources, the government should still develop and implement development strategies based on the available resources.

A more fundamental objection is that the Primacy of Human Rights limits state sovereignty. Human rights imply obligations for the state and the state system, and we must consider whether this is an acceptable limitation of state sovereignty.

Individual states invoke two kinds of sovereignty.[11] The government asserts internal sovereignty over the citizens, with monopoly on the legitimate use of force, regulated by a statutory framework and the courts. The government is superior to all other parties within the territory of the state. Secondly, the government enjoys external sovereignty, not subject to external parties. The state's external sovereignty shields it from intervention and international demands. However, the Primacy of Human Rights as a requirement of sustainable development clearly limits the state's legitimate claims to internal and external sovereignty. A legitimate regime may include obligations of economic aid from richer countries via international financial institutions. And such aid may at least in principle be conditional, requiring that environmental concerns and human rights should be respected. Consequently, such ground rules allow other states – or in any case, international organisations – to intervene in a country's internal affairs. These prospects certainly conflict with the general norms of state sovereignty.

In response, first note that this is not yet an objection: the role of human rights and the Primacy of Human Rights is precisely to restrict state sovereignty, laying out the conditions of legitimate sovereignty of governments, clarifying under what conditions their claim to rule should be respected. An objection to such constraints must provide a normative justification for unbridled state sovereignty, which has yet to be provided.

Two further aspects may be mentioned in defence of the Primacy of Human Rights. From the point of view of international law, these alleged conflicts between sovereignty and human rights seldom occur, because in fact many states have consented to human rights treaties. In addition, interference is limited: human rights, including the right to development, should not replace the national culture, or replace global trade regimes, but instead constrain and prune those cultures and regimes, laying down limits on how individuals should be treated.

Many of the conflicts between development, human rights and the environment may be avoided by fulfilling international human rights obligations. When the environment of the future is threatened by the claims of today's poor, the solution will not require hard choices between the two, but rather require changes in regimes and social institutions to eradicate present poverty. It is hardly justifiable to maintain existing regimes simply because they secure the interests of citizens of rich states – far beyond their basic needs – when these trade patterns and allocation of power are detrimental to the most vulnerable. Citizens of rich democratic states have important political tasks at the national and international levels to ensure that international ground-rules take care of the concerns of both today's poor and tomorrow's environment.

4.6   OBJECTIONS

Finally, certain further objections must be considered against the Primacy of Human Rights. Several contributors to environmental political theory have advocated the significance of animals, plants, species or ecosystems for arguments for sustainable development. Liberal Contractualism and some other anthropocentric normative political theories are sometimes regarded as inadequate. These issues warrant consideration far beyond the space available here, but some comments may be of relevance when determining whether these theoretically important matters affect the Priority of Human Rights.

It is in principle possible that animals, species and ecosystems have inherent value beyond that of the values ascribed to them by humans, and that such values have implications for the proper design of social institutions and global regimes. However, a brief survey of the literature seems to indicate that the Priority of Human Rights is not at stake. Important theoretical issues arise regarding the scope of the political and about who has moral standing, but it is unclear whether available theories are at odds with liberal contractualism, or otherwise challenge the case for the Priority of Human Rights.

In support of this tentative conclusion, I first consider to what extent liberal contractualism is limited in its recognition of non-anthropocentric bearers of value, as compared to environmental theories. Secondly, I sketch some of the claims that alternative theories must support in order to challenge the Priority of Human Rights.

Some authors, for instance in the deep ecology tradition, hold that there are values which do not enjoy appropriate recognition within liberal contractualism. To clarify the issue we may distinguish three ways in which animals and non-sentient parts of nature may be accorded value within contractualism.

(a)   Contractualism is concerned to take account of all parties affected by alternative rules, the notion of 'affected' to be spelled out in terms of interests. In principle it would appear to be an open question – itself to be illuminated by normative theory – whether such interests need be consciously held, or whether only those who can speak and argue for their interests are properly considered to be parties (see Ackerman 1980:70). Thus, even though the theory laid out here has not made such claims, the sentient capacity of animals may place them in the domain of beings whose interests should be considered – the weight of these interests relative to other beings' left undetermined. However, it is less clear that other living things, and entities such as species can, without controversy, be said to have interests in virtue of which their lives go better or worse for them.

(b)   Parts of nature can have instrumental value for parties with moral standing, thus goods needed for consumption and satisfaction of interests have instrumental value.[12]

(c)   Parts of nature can also have a value for individuals which is not instrumental. For instance, an individual can take an interest in natural landscapes for their own sake, rather than for some purpose separable from the landscapes. Thus many individuals seek to be part of a larger context fixed by the external world.[13] Such intrinsic values can play an important role in answers to fundamental questions of why our lives matter. On this account parts of nature, such as species and landscapes, have value, and intrinsic value, but still only in relation to parties and their interests.

This taxonomy does not include all conceptions of value. For instance:

(d) Parts of nature can be said to be of intrinsic value which grounds claims independent of their role in sentient beings' interests and self-conceptions.[14] Some contributors to the 'deep ecology' tradition would appear to hold such views.[15] Assessing these claims requires an overall assessment of the plausibility of the political theories of which they are part, and this falls beyond the scope of this chapter.

Secondly, we must ask how such values may support the Primacy of the Environment, rather than the Primacy of Human Rights. The task may be illustrated by Katz and Oechsli's claim (1993), that an anthropocentric ethic cannot provide answers to the conflicts between the environment and basic needs in the Third World because important values come into conflict with each other. Katz and Oechsli hold that the conflict may be resolved, and may *only* be resolved, by also ascribing value to the natural environment. There would appear to be other strategies for resolving the conflict, such as the one offered above. Nevertheless, three questions emerge about such a strategy.

Firstly, Katz and Oechsli fail to show how their assumption, that the natural environment has intrinsic value, contributes towards resolving the conflict.

Secondly, the natural environment – or non-human sentient beings, for that matter – would have to be accorded greater value than humans, for such arguments to be accepted. Views in the (b) category cannot be expected to allow the value of the means to override the value of the individuals whose means they are. And such views along the lines of (a) or (c) or (d) have yet to be made plausible. Thus several authors who endorse (a) will still accept and insist on the Primacy of Human Rights.[16]

Thirdly, the norm of equal worth implies that the pluralism of world views must be taken seriously. This challenges views of type (a) and (c) (as well as d). How do non-anthropocentric theories handle the fact that they are based on premises that we cannot expect agreement on among all the affected parties? It seems quite unobjectionable to have a conception of the world that accords intrinsic value to the natural environment – for example, along the lines of (c) or (d) above – but it does not follow that this conception of the good – or of the world – should determine regimes and institutions, as long as reasonable people appear to hold alternative, equally sensible views.

Thus Goodin's clear explication of a green political theory rests on the claim that:

People must be able to see some sense and pattern in their own lives if they are to be able to see sense or value in any other more specific project they might pursue as part of their larger life plans. And that in turn presupposes that their lives form part of something outside of themselves, individually or collectively (Goodin, 1992:42).

The natural world – products of natural processes – provides one such setting. However, two challenges must be addressed: firstly, why the furtherance of such impersonal values is properly within the scope of what regimes and institutions should do, and secondly, how such values should be furthered under pluralism. There are different, plausible views about the centrality of such an interest of being part of something larger, and there are several settings – natural and social – that may satisfy this fundamental interest.

4.7 CONCLUSION

The Brundtland Commission asserts that if conflicts arise between the basic needs of the world's poor and environmental concerns, basic needs should be given first priority. This chapter has defended this requirement, the Primacy of Human Rights, for development strategies.

Development strategies should secure the basic needs of today's poor, by respecting human rights – if necessary at the expense of protecting the environment. Today's poor may not, and need not, be sacrificed to secure tomorrow's generation. Development strategies must improve the domestic and international distribution of benefits, by changing the ground rules so that the basic needs of all are met. Anything else is incompatible with the equal worth of all people.

The Priority of Human Rights does not require that democracy is replaced by philosophers' rule.[17] The normative political theory sketched above is a contribution to citizens' reflections, where improvements must come through public arguments and the voting booth to obtain more legitimate institutions. Our politicians should work towards changing the inequitable regimes and social institutions that allow such difficult choices to be presented as unavoidable. By this standard, the Brundtland Commission has provided an extremely valuable contribution.

NOTES

1. G.A. Research. 41/128 (1986). See also Schachter (1985) and Alston (1988).
2. Steidlmeier (1993); Gallup Poll: Public Opinion 1990 (Wilmington, Del.: Scholarly Resources, 1991), 38–43; Schramm and Warford (1989).

3. See, for example, Bryk (1991) and Steidlmeier (1993), whose references have been most helpful for the present chapter.
4. See, for example, Johnson (1991), (Nash 1989), Næss (1984), Wetlesen (1993) and, for an overview, Oelschlager (1991).
5. Though not health services in general, as this need has no clear cut-off point of satisfaction (see Føllesdal, 1991).
6. See, for example, Norton (1982) and Brown Weiss (1990).
7. For some Malthusian arguments to this effect: see Hardin (1974) and Ehrlich (1972).
8. See Beitz (1981a and 1981b), Alston (1989), Donnelly (1989), Goodin (1979) and Olson (1993).
9. Sohn (1982:48), van Boven (1979) and Donnelly (1985:506) note this danger.
10. See Gilpin (1987: 298ff) and Cornia *et al.* (1987) for a discussion on what this might involve.
11. See Bull (1977) for more detailed discussions on the state system.
12. See Goodin's discussion (1992:24) of 'consumer value'.
13. What Goodin calls 'natural resource based theory of value' (1992: 24–41).
14. Admittedly, the distinction is too blunt to allow easy classification of sophisticated views thus Dworkin's thought-provoking reflections (1993) on the sanctity of life and other 'detached' and sacred values might appear to straddle between (c) and (d). But see also Scanlon's illuminating review (1993).
15. Næss (1989), Sylvan (1985). And see Goodin (1992: 42–45) for helpful elaborations of this distinction between (c) and (d).
16. This concerns, among others, Rodman (1993), Baird Callicott (1993), Heffernan (1993), Marietta (1993) and Wetlesen (1993).
17. For such views see Walzer (1981) and philosophers discussed by Anker (1997).

5 Sustainability, Morality and Future Generations

Per Ariansen

Environmental philosophy has brought two topics to the forefront of philosophical discussion. One is the anthropocentrism / non-anthropocentrism debate in ethics, and the other is the question of obligations towards future generations. The deeper motives for focusing on these issues are, of course, intimately tied to the fact that the present generation may well be on its way to introducing practically irreversible and catastrophic damage to the global ecosystem. For the first time, one has to acknowledge that the global system does not have an infinite capacity to repair itself and provide humans with limitless new opportunities for a fresh start.

5.1 SUSTAINABILITY – A MORAL CONCEPT?

The familiar diagnosis of the situation is that cultural activity has not managed to develop within the confines of sustainability. Consequently, considerable attention and effort are now devoted to examining both the meaning of this key concept and its implications for policy. The concept has its origin in the science of ecology, where sustainability designates the ability of the whole or parts of a biotic community to extend its form into the future. When this concept is applied to human development, the question of moral or political bearings becomes urgent (The Brundtland Commission, *Our Common Future*, 1987). Exactly what kind of society or which parts of the community and of its environment ought to be sustained into the future?[1] Can the answer be found in the ecological concept of sustainability itself?

One reason why one may, *prima facie*, consider the concept to have a moral and not merely a descriptive technical content is that in accepting the requirements of sustainability, one seems by implication to accept responsibility towards future generations. However, the technical sense of the term really does not warrant such an implication. If a state of sustainability is interpreted so as to allow us to take some measures to secure sustainability of specific systems,[2] then one could well suggest that sustainability can best be secured if humans are removed from the ecosystem. There is, furthermore, no sufficient guidance in the concept itself when it comes to forming the political direction of the policy. All sorts of inter-human regimes are compatible with human

84

sustainable development in the ecologically technical sense that major traits of the ecosystems will hold without collapsing. Certainly, slavery would be compatible with sustainable development in this sense. A not so remote possibility would be a meritocracy of an ecologically enlightened elite. (See the reference to Garret Hardin below.)

In fact, the concept of sustainability is neutral in relation to political values. Even from a biological viewpoint, there is nothing in the concept that indicates any preferences for whatever system that is desirable or advantageous in the future, other than those that are relative to other systems chosen as points of reference. Seen from the viewpoint of human society, the concept of sustainability neither obliges us to care for future generations of humans, nor indicates what kind of social regime we should instigate among humans. Granted, the commitment to sustainability may rule out some kinds of social arrangements, and even prohibit some that are presently widespread, but the requirements of sustainability do not rule out a great variety of regimes that are compatible with it. Some of these regimes are definitely repulsive, from a moral point of view.

Nevertheless, the terms 'sustainable' and 'development' are conventionally and tacitly taken to suggest some sort of morally just arrangement, both locally, globally and over time. The requirements of development seem to have at least two dimensions: development in material standard (or possibly in the quality of life) and development in the moral sense – a progress in fairness, justice and general moral behaviour. The moral component cannot, as we have shown, be derived from the concept of sustainability, but technical premises for sustainability may be supplemented with normative, moral-political premises.[3] In their turn, these must be linked to an ethical theory that specifies who are the morally affected parties and which moral obligations and moral rights apply. Suppose that the coming generations are considered as morally affected parties, then sustainable development becomes an obligatory means to reach the moral goal of fair distribution. Sustainable development becomes the conclusion of a practical syllogism.

5.2 RESPONSIBILITIES FOR FUTURE GENERATIONS – SOME CENTRAL PROBLEM AREAS

With the basis we have outlined, three problem areas emerge:

- What moral theory or moral platform should we use as the basis?
- Do in fact future generations count as morally affected parties?
- Which political deeds or institutions would comply with both sustainability and our moral responsibilities?

I shall try to elucidate some aspects of the answers to these questions below. It will be necessary to deal with the question of the moral status of future generations first, as the answer to this question may be decisive both for the choice of moral platform and for the demands of sustainability.

In considering the moral status of future generations, we should distinguish between arguments which aim at questioning whether future generations have moral status *at all* and arguments which aim at pointing out particular difficulties pertaining to the moral status of future beings as beings that at the same time, are not with us. Further, one should make it clear whether one would consider present and future non-humans (animals or plants), as well as humans to have relevant moral status.

5.3   WHO ARE MORALLY AFFECTED PARTIES? DO WE HAVE DIRECT MORAL OBLIGATIONS TO FUTURE NON-HUMANS?

To address the issue of whether we have to speak about the obligations to future living beings rather than to future generations of humans, the moral status of non-human beings must be clarified. My conclusion is that direct moral duties go exclusively towards other humans or towards human arrangements, although there are obligations which make non-humans beneficiaries of inter-human duties. I shall argue for this below.

To defend an anthropocentric standpoint, one has to be able to prove the presence of at least one ethically relevant factor allegedly inclusive and exclusive to humans. In my opinion, this factor is the ability to understand ethics as a an intersubjectively sustained 'game' of self-legislation. I believe it is only in the recognition of morality as a 'game' that one can explain why, for example, wilful coercion of other humans is morally relevant, and that some occurrences of pain are ethically relevant and others are not. Animals cannot make the distinction between morally relevant coercion and pain and occurrences of the same induced by natural phenomena.[4] By implication, the idea of moral responsibility is exclusive to humans. Further, the fact that we do not hold animals morally responsible for their actions is a recognition that they are unable to see the point of morality. The day we find convincing grounds for changing our views on this point, then animals will have to be given direct moral status. Correspondingly they will have to be held morally responsible for some of their deeds.

The fact that a human can be offended morally implies that humans comprehend that their actor status with respect to the 'morality game' has been slighted. One may cause animals pain, but one cannot offend them. Nevertheless, it is clear that certain forms of inflicting pain are relevant in relation to ethics. In a world where no one experiences pain or loss, the inter-human moral norms will lose their meaning. Technically speaking, one could lie by stating the case wrongly, but such lies would be uninteresting because they had no value (sorrow or joy) significance. When a lie is perceived as morally relevant, it is because the lie can be directly or indirectly linked to displeasure. Hence, ethics presupposes a fundamental respect for the suffering of others. In this perspective, animals are possible beneficiaries of a moral consideration through the fact that they can suffer and they can be hindered and disturbed in their life development. Moral norms against animal mistreatment is of course linked to distaste for the suffering of animals. To perceive that animals suffer is, however, only necessary for, but not sufficient to make the case morally relevant. It is only when one's actions are determined by respect for the inter-human arrangement of self-imposed norms (an arrangement that is based on a general respect for suffering) that the case concerns morality. Also where it concerns relations to other humans, it is the respect for the scope of morality that counts, rather than the amount of suffering involved in each case. Hence, it is morally reprehensible to steal in cases where it is technically impossible for the theft to be discovered. I will try to further elucidate these views below.

At this point it is necessary to address a traditional argument (Regan, 1979) directed against anthropocentrism in ethics. Anthropocentrists are challenged to find a criterion of moral status which subsumes all humans and only humans. If anthropocentrism is to be upheld, the challenge will be to find a criterion which does not exclude so called 'marginal cases' of humans (infants, senile persons, unconscious persons, and so on). The hypothesis on the part of the critics of anthropocentrism is that if the criteria are chosen so that marginal cases are included, one would by the same criteria have to include some non-humans. The criterion I have indicated, that is, the ability to 'take the point' of morality, seemingly excludes both infants and the senile. Part of the response here is to point out that the criterion does not demand that moral awareness has to be actualised in the individual all the time. Sleeping and unconscious people still have full moral status. Furthermore, my response will be that we have good reasons to give humans the benefit of the doubt in cases where ethical awareness is not manifest. A senile human being may, for all we know, still retain some ethical awareness without being able to communicate it. Or the person may regain ethical awareness in the future.

One may well ask whether the benefit of the doubt should be extended to animals. When it comes to animals, however, one does not have the same grounds for extending to them the benefit of the doubt. There is no 'normal animal' where the moral status is indisputable. It is, therefore, never possible to determine whether a wounded or marginal animal is similar to such a 'normal animal' in this respect. Hence, there is a good reason to apply the proposed criterion (with a clause on extending the benefit of the doubt to marginal cases) to all humans and only humans. This means that direct moral obligations towards future generations will only concern generations of humans. As we have seen, it is however clear that we have indirect obligations – not only with regard to perceptible suffering among animals (also in the future), but also with regard to their life development. In addition, there are benefit-oriented anthropocentric or religious arguments for the cautious management of living and dead nature.

5.4   DO WE HAVE OBLIGATIONS TOWARDS POSTERITY?

A more drastic position to hold would be that beings which belong to the future are for this very fact, beyond the bounds of moral obligation. Putting such a position to the test, one could argue that members of future generations do not exist at present, and that it would be absurd to have obligations towards something which does not exist, just as it would be absurd to consider these non-entities to be rights-holders. In fact, one could say, maintaining the contrary would be like complying with alleged demands of ghosts and spirits. Obligations to future persons may be considered even more absurd: ghosts and spirits *may* exist at present. Future beings most certainly do not. One might attempt to circumvent this kind of argument by drawing an analogy between space and time, and arguing that since mere distance in space is morally irrelevant, the same goes for mere distance in time (Gregory Kavka, quoted in Attfield, 1983). For one thing, it may not necessarily be the case that distance in space is morally irrelevant. Secondly, the being who is spatially far away is at least co-existing with oneself in time and can in principle complain if unjustly treated. So let us find a stronger argument to refute the position that co-presence is a necessary condition for obligation.

Consider the following scenario: I wilfully deposit some toxic agent in a place where there is no one at present. Suppose that I can monitor the area, discovering in due time if anyone is approaching. Suppose further, that I see someone coming and commit suicide seconds before this being is harmed by the toxic substance. It is highly unreasonable that the fact that I am not a contemporary with this person at the time of the harm should clear me of responsibility also during the time period when this person was on a certain track towards harm – but before the harm was a fact. As a dead person, I may not be reproachable, but my dying cannot make my action while I was alive morally neutral. Correspondingly, we cannot absolve ourselves from responsibility for the future consequences of our actions by leaning on the fact that we will be dead when the harm is inflicted. What is critical for present responsibility is that there is a probability that someone in the future will be harmed as a result of our actions, who has not consented to being exposed to the harm. The probability of such harm occurring in all such cases may be debatable, but the outcome will only contribute towards determining the degree of responsibility, which presumes that we admit that responsibility is not precluded.

Let us finally address another argument which seems (almost) to rule out responsibility for future generations altogether. The argument, or rather its stunning conclusion, has been referred to as Parfit's paradox.[5] The argument brings to attention the fact that large-scale policy implementations not only affect the welfare conditions of future beings, but also determine which particular individuals will be born in the future. Consider that most people born after 1945 would not have existed had it not been for the war. The general social framework of the war situation clearly had an impact on such details of life as who came to mate with whom and at what moment. Had policies been different, then other couples would have procreated or at least the same couples would have done so at a different point in time, thereby producing individuals different from those that actually were born. Suppose our descendants inherit an Earth with markedly more depleted resources and a markedly more toxic environment. *Prima facie* one should think that the people affected were worse off, thanks to our misdeeds.

On second thought, according to the argument, they are really not worse off than they would have been had we conducted a more future-responsible policy. Had we done so, then these individuals simply would not have existed. So long as the people of the future on the whole find life worth living, they are actually better off as a direct result of our inconsiderate policies. All in all they should, from our point of view, really be grateful that we did not shift to a more environmentally sound policy.

The flaw in this argument is that it treats the two alternatives, *to exist* and *never to come into existence*, as if they were ordinary alternatives for an individual to evaluate and choose between. Normally, one evaluates by asking oneself whether one likes a given alternative better than another. No one can, however, evaluate whether one would like never having come into existence. If this were the state of the world, one would not be present to judge the advantages or drawbacks of this or that. It is meaningless to bring such a situation into a personal utilitarian weighing of preferences. It is like trying to apply preference utilitarianism in an area where it cannot be applied. Nevertheless, when presented (in a supposition) with a choice of this kind, the respondent will most likely distort the alternatives. The respondent will consider the imagined loss of given situations in the person's life *and* the events in one's life that led up to them. One is led to think that if one had never existed, one would have been without this or that pleasant experience. However, the unconceived cannot suffer any kind of loss. So, there is nothing that never having come into existence can be worse than – or better than.

It seems, consequently, that there are no sound arguments to rule out obligations towards future generations merely on the basis that these persons do not exist at present and will not exist until some period of time in the future. However, even though obligations are not ruled out, it may still be the case that the futurity of the beneficiaries of our acts induces special difficulties in assessing our obligations. Again we find that this problem cannot be addressed until another clarification has been made. We have to give some indication of the kind of obligations we have towards other people in general before we look for any particular difficulties stemming from the fact that moral patients are located in the future. Contractualism, as we suggested earlier, would bring up insurmountable difficulties, while on a communitarian platform, the fact that the other party is a late descendant may not make much of a difference at all.

5.5 SKETCHING A MORAL PLATFORM

Space does not permit a broad discussion of the wide-reaching issue of finding the proper platform for a moral commitment, so let me merely indicate my position, which has already partly emerged in my discussion of anthropocentrism above. The idea, of Kantian origin, that morality has derived part of its central meaning from the idea of a project of self-legislation is, in my opinion, the core of the element of *obligation* in ethics. It is essentially the imperatives of self-imposed ethical restraints which lay the ground for what we might call truly *moral pride*. We may act in compliance with moral prescriptions for a number of non-ethical reasons: we may feel that it is strategically smart not to lie in order that we may not be lied against later (contractualism), we may fear alienation and disaffection from others if we disobey the conventional taboo against lying (communitarianism), or we may simply be moved by a feeling of compassion not to lie to someone (compassionate ethics). The motivations mentioned are based respectively on shrewdness, fear and sympathy. None of them form a meaningful basis for feeling moral pride for not lying. The only motivation that does that is where one freely chooses to respect the discreet game of morality. This 'game' involves an obligation to continue to play the game even when it would be advantageous for one to stop playing.

The Kantian idea of self-legislation gives, in my opinion, a good anchoring point for what is called liberty-rights in ethics. These imply, among other things, the duty to not lie or deceive. The essence of these rights are subsumed under the fundamental respect for the game itself. For the game to be upheld, the participants must be respected as players. Their freedom must be respected, agreements relevant to the game must be kept, and information on the game must not be distorted. If any breach is allowed to occur, the game will break down. This is the essence of the Kantian imperative that the *Humanität* of each person be unconditionally respected.

However, even though self-legislation may be one of the constituents of morally relevant obligation, it may not provide an adequate explanation why this kind of obligation is *moral* – an inadequacy which sows doubt on the whole point of a self-legislation game. Consider again a world with rational beings where sensations of joy and sorrow are non-existent. As explained, in this world, it would be technically possible to tell a lie, but impossible to explain the ethical relevance of lying.[6] So, it seems that ethics needs another footing besides the idea of self-legislation. Further, this other footing is clearly connected with the dimensions of joy and sorrow, and it must somehow be involved with a willingness to alleviate suffering and bring joy to others, by some amount of self-sacrifice. This links morality to compassion. The source of compassion and self-sacrifice is not found in the morality game. These generic feelings are older than all culture. They are most likely linked to instincts that we have in common with animals, but with humans they can be the object of will and resolve.

It seems that morality stands on two legs: respect for the freedom and rational integrity of the agent/player of the 'game' of self-legislation and concern for the well-being of others. These correspond to the traditional division in ethics between the so-called perfect duties to respect liberty rights and the imperfect duties to respect the principle of beneficence. It has been a long-standing difficulty in ethics to integrate liberty rights and welfare claims/duties.

The solution, in my view, is to abandon all attempts to derive compassion from ethical principles of freedom and liberty and instead look upon compassion as something which is already there, coming from within, so to speak, ready to be rationalised by integration into some scheme of self-legislation. Compassion is not originally of an ethical nature. It may flow freely, following the emotional moods of the individual, it may be guided by conscious particularistic preference, it may be integrated in the common cultural myths of a society, or it may finally emerge as a constituent of ethics when it is rationalised by 'surrendering' to the discipline of universalistic maxims. In the latter case, compassion will no longer be merely particularly directed towards family, friends, or groups with a common cultural heritage, but be extended on a universalistic basis. Universalism arises from the condition that compassion operates under rules that apply to each 'player' who is located in one of the positions of the 'game'. When compassion operates under universalistic principles, it is disciplined by the call to comply with the central principle for all games that are rule-oriented: that equal cases should be treated equally. Since universalistic rules essentially hold for an unlimited time span, this type of rules will naturally aim to encompass future persons as well as present ones. However, the target of rationalised compassion is not a particular friend of ours, but rather the ideal type of the universal person, a general placeholder.

Only compassion which is administered on this level, is essentially ethical. Joy and sorrow take on their moral relevance only in the light of rationalisation. Most of the other kinds of particularistic compassion come under the label of kindness, a virtue which, of course, may well be laudable, but not on ethical grounds.

If it is right that ethics rationalises a practice that is already in place, we may expect that specific interaction situations will be rationalised with respect to the type of rules appropriate to the situation. In this light, emotional bonds and pre-ethical compassion are only two of several interaction relations that already exist. The distribution of benefits and burdens triggers rules of equity in ethics. Promises of aid or appeals for loyalty trigger ethical rules of honesty. The situation where we all often act based on others' statement of the case triggers rules of truthfulness, and so on. This points in the direction of an ethical pluralism – not in the sense of tolerance for various ethical systems, but in the sense that there does not exist a sweeping rule that clarifies ethical dilemmas concerning all themes, from freedom to distress.

One may well ask what the ultimate motive for self-legislation is. Rationalisation will, of course, give predictability as a bonus. This may well be part of the motive, whether acknowledged or not. However, the aim of the game goes beyond that. The bonus of playing the game is what we have called moral pride. The rationalised game of truthfulness, freedom and beneficence, is in a sense its own reward. Pride is linked not to the bonus each individual gets out of morality in the form of personal freedom or welfare, but to the condition that we uphold a game of obligation. This is the essence of the Kantian idea that the ultimate duty is towards the moral law itself. In a sense, obligation is not primarily directed towards people, but towards the particular web of universalist morality which is upheld by collective commitment. This is why we can see individuals as *placeholders* in the game. Obligations are directed towards single positions and also towards systems or patterns in the web of sociality. An individual has obligations towards anyone entering into a morally potent position in this web. The deeper meaning of the game is nevertheless linked to the condition that the game mediates over living people who feel joy and sorrow. It is the reason that the rules of the game sometimes have to yield when the game generates too much suffering.

What then is the conclusion concerning the right moral platform for the relationship to future generations? Since future generations are not accessible for mutual negotiations, contractualism is excluded as the basis for obligations. The same goes for any ethic based on so called enlightened self-interest – with the not-quite-relevant exception that we may have a self-interest in seeing to it that our children have the capacity to be of assistance, should we need it in old age. A promising approach within the framework of enlightened self-interest might be an elaborated Rawlsian approach, where the veil of ignorance also conceals which generation we belong to. The Rawlsian arrangement suggests a savings policy based on the maxi-min principle, which in turn is taken to be the principle most favourable to rational self-interest. However, the arrangement of the original position does not in itself explain or give reasons for non-egoistic commitment. It merely prescribes a method of making decisions once a commitment to the universalist approach is established. There is nothing in the original position in itself which explains why anyone should want to apply this particular kind of counter-factual deliberation. The mechanics of the original position is for people who are already committed to a non-egoist stance.

What is left is an ethic based on self-legislation, which is the most appropriate with regard to obligations towards future generations. We have already pointed out that the game of ethical self-legislation secures a set of freedom-rights (Nozick, 1974) for each moral agent. Normally, freedom rights are understood to be rights not to be coerced or interfered with. Knowing that they have us safely placed in our graves, future generations need not fear that we directly hinder their exercise of freedom. From a different perspective, freedom for future generations is indeed the responsibility of the present generation. A legacy of tyranny from our generation will undermine the prospects for self-legislation in the future. Since there is no end to the game of self-legislation, securing the basis for continuing the game also for future players is a prime obligation of the game itself.

The dominating topic of responsibility has nevertheless been tied to the question of the welfare of future people. Welfare responsibilities which oblige us to give up something are far more difficult to substantiate than obligations that secure freedom for others, since they entail something beyond the duty to not intervene in their lives. We have argued for the fact that welfare obligation is also a fundamental component of a Kantian-inspired ethic. Others have tried to link welfare obligations with freedom obligations by asserting that a certain level of welfare is a prerequisite for any placeholder, now or in the future, for practising freedom. This is a fruitful and commendable approach. However, this brings us inevitably into the realm of consideration and compassion which cannot be solved through freedom-rights, not least because this 'solution' implies that one must interfere with the freedom of those with freedom-rights. The amount of welfare necessary to exercise freedom will involve an estimation of a culturally acceptable level of welfare beyond which the individual has nothing to complain about or beyond which there is no need to feel sorry for the person. This brings the issue of the rationalisation of compassion into focus again. As opposed to duties of freedom, which appear to be absolute, it will always be difficult to determine the extent of the welfare obligations we have towards others – either present or future persons.

It is a legitimate concern for ethics to discuss which level of non-particularist obligation one ought to have for one's neighbour, both on the personal and on the social level. This discussion will have to unfold within the frameworks of various cultural settings, and therefore necessarily retain a strand of particularism. A society's dominant myths, narratives or ideals will bear the interpretations of the extent of universalism in obligations. If we focus on compassion as the basis for self-sacrifice – and ignore all variants of enlightened self-interest – then there are several possible bases for such compassion. If the basis is love of one's own descendants, there is not much universalism involved. If the concern is for safeguarding a whole group of descendants within one's own culture, the obligations will not extend to 'the others', unless they convert to the 'right' culture. This is particularly true in cases where one believes that one's own culture has a specific historic task. There is the universalistic duty to not wilfully inflict harm on anyone within a certain causal closeness to one's actions. But then, it is duty rather than compassion that is the dominating motive. And finally there are obligations which are not only linked to suffering, but also to the possibility of the exercise of freedom or autonomy. This is a particular blend of rationality and compassion that, in my view, is the central core of ethics.

In reality, these factors are at work all at once in a culture, both separately and interwoven into one another. Also, the issue has further complexities: compassion is not merely a feeling we have as a matter of fact, it is also a feeling which the project of rationalisation – with its drive towards universalism – tacitly urges us to cultivate.

5.6 PARTICULAR DIFFICULTIES IN ASSESSING OBLIGATIONS TO FUTURE BEINGS

When the debate leaves the fundamental philosophical discussion and comes down to questions of what kind of savings arrangement we ought to have, a further set of problems pertaining to the fact that the beneficiaries are located in the future will have to be dealt with. I will not attempt to work on answers to these questions, but merely try to present them.

One of the problems concerns the uncertainty as to the resource and needs situation of the future. Another is the uncertainty connected with the fact that savings in the present may have to go through the hands of several generations before they can be cashed in. We have normally no secure control of our savings in the intermediary generations. Finally, there is the question of which myth to refer to when it comes to defining the quality of life or what are the basic needs of people, as understood in the present.

The first of these problems indicates that we ought to single out for saving those resources which, to our best knowledge, are irreplaceable. This would certainly include the cultural heritage in the form of art, literature and information in general, engineering monuments, architecture and the like. Further, it would be reasonable to preserve biodiversity and some areas of natural, uncultivated landscapes, preferably so that the diversity of nature is represented.

Preservation is one thing – responsibility for future damage another. As indicated earlier, we have an indubitable responsibility for future harmful effects of our actions – corrected for the probability that the damage actually occurs and that one, in the meantime, has not lost interest in the object that we fear might be harmed, such that the effects of our actions are neutral, valuewise. Nuclear power is a paradigmatic example, where future damages and problems with nuclear waste can be predicted with almost 100 per cent accuracy. Despite the attractiveness of using nuclear power as an energy source, concerns of harm to future generations have stigmatised this form of technology. Climate problems and that of an increased greenhouse effect are based on less clear probability estimations, but here, the damage will be so extensive if they occur, that a 'look before you leap' strategy would be rational.

The second problem has the potential to create a challenging dilemma. If we want to secure something for future generations, we may have to safeguard it from the present and future generations applying means that are questionable from the point of view of the self-legislating ethical project itself. Garret Hardin (1994) points to historical examples where people were being forced to starve to death, rather than being allowed to consume the seed stock of grain saved for the future. An additional sinister aspect of the situation is that in order to safeguard scarce resources for posterity, one must consider, according to Hardin, raising an elite of guardians and also protect (at least relatively) the elite group from any effects of general shortage, in order to prevent the guardians from shifting their allegiance away from future generations. Hence, concern for future generations may have to be weighed against our democratic and egalitarian ideals.

The third problem stems from the fact that one cannot fight for the interests of a given group without some political vision of what the good life for this group should be. This is the stuff politics is made of. In the field of politics, within a sustainable framework, a certain kind of obliqueness occasionally seems to occur. The restraints of sustainability are intended to rule out some lines of action or some policies. However, as we have discussed above, the restraints of sustainability do not provide sufficient information to determine one particular vision as the commendable policy. Sustainability is in fact silent on the question of the quality of life, as illustrated by the Hardin examples. Consequently, when calling for a change of policy, one should attempt to distinguish between that part of one's political programme which pertains to the technicalities of sustainability, and that part which contains one's vision of the good life.

There is another side to this problem. For those who want to speak on behalf of future generations, there are two particular problems to address. First there is the problem of estimating the political weight of demands on behalf of posterity. In an imagined voting procedure, would the spokesmen for posterity have an infinite number of votes? Secondly there is the question of how to deal with the ordinary political struggle between visions of the good life on behalf of people who cannot voice their opinion. The fact that one party claims to speak on behalf of future generations does not in itself contribute to the validity of the particular vision of life one defends and wants extended. When speaking on behalf of future generations, one will not so much convey the requests of posterity as one will actually be recommending a life-style. My personal quest would be for an open, egalitarian society with room enough for social experiments, varieties of cultural expression and justice and compassion as cultural ideals.

NOTES

1. Christopher Stone points out that the present–future axis in the debate quickly turned into a North–South axis (Stone, 1994). One suspects that the question of what sort of society shall be continued is not so relevant as long as one regards the problem as a pure generation conflict. 'The future generations are "like us", the only difference being that they come after us in time.'

2. The so-called technical meaning of the term is further muddled by the failure to specify which system one would like to see sustained. By natural processes species die out, and evolution sees to it that others emerge. In this larger system no subsystem is sustained over long (say, geological) periods of time. It is therefore conceptually quite possible to let the meaning of the concept imply that nature should take its course. If one further considers human activity as 'natural' as well, the concept of sustainability will totally dissolve.
3. 'Technical' premises for sustainability are never purely technical, but also contain a political component. See the end of this chapter.
4. There exist forms of 'disappointment' in the animal kingdom, as when 'friendship' turns to 'hostility'. Such cases do not indicate morality, but at most, lie within an emotive 'love horizon'.
5. See Norton (1982). The point in question has been stated independently by Robert M. Adams, Derek Parfit and Thomas Schwartz (see Kavka, 1982). Chapter 16 in Derek Parfit (1984) is normally considered the original source text. The point presented here has been given a more thorough treatment in another article (Ariansen, 1994).
6. That time is something which can be measured with clocks, and so on, is also a reality that is maintained by a tacit acknowledgement of the rules of the game. But this game does not have moral content.

6 The Limits of Nature

Nils Chr. Stenseth

In the past, people lived (…) according to Nature's conditions so that mankind would survive. Today, mankind must live according to Nature's conditions so that Nature will survive.

Arne Semb-Johansson, 1989

6.1   WITHOUT NATURE, CIVILISATION VANISHES

Nature provides us with our food and all the raw materials we make use of in both more traditional and modern societies. Even those living in fashionable apartments in the middle of New York are dependent on the raw materials nature provides. Even though they themselves have never lived in 'free nature', their lives would deteriorate dramatically if some species were to disappear. It is easy for city-dwellers to forget that they – like everyone else on Earth – are totally dependent on natural resources.

The conservation of natural resources is, therefore, by extension the conservation of human life. The conservation of nature and culture should, in practice, go hand in hand, not least because numerous cultural forms have their basis in natural conditions and in the way nature is utilised. One only has to think of the fishing communities along the Norwegian coast, the rural communities engaged in agriculture and forestry in Østerdalen, the pastoral communities in Finnmark or the Sahel area in Africa, to realise that a preservation of culture rests on a preservation of nature.

In this chapter, I take up the threats facing nature in this century. I will also draw upon some general perspectives put forward by ecologists which are very relevant to our efforts to protect nature. The focus is on the limits of nature, but I will also use the term in a wider – and in my opinion more correct – sense than that which is usual for natural-resource management in Norway (where the term is primarily used with reference to pollution). (See DN Notes, 1993).[1]

Given the fact that the Earth's biological diversity is also threatened in many more ways than just by pollution, this interpretation, which forms the basis of much of the conservation work within environmental management, is too narrow a definition. This lopsidedness may have unfortunate management consequences in that other threatening factors in addition to pollution may easily be forgotten. It is also with some regret that we observe that there often is just such a one-sided focus on pollution. It is certainly positive that one is concerned about pollution problems, both those caused by local or more distant sources. However, we must not forget that nature is also threatened by several other factors – for example, the direct destruction of a species' habitat through the expropriation of the area for other purposes. In some areas, both locally and in other parts of the world, these 'other' threats often represent a far greater danger to nature as we know it.[2]

It is my hope that environmental management will come to accept a broader interpretation of the term 'the limits of nature' as a basis for management practice. If so, management perspectives on natural resources would come more in line with ecological understanding – an understanding which has been reached through considerable research in the area, both basic and applied. This understanding has clearly taught us that there are greater threats against nature than just pollution and over-exploitation.

Finally, I will try to put the ecological discussion in the context of the book's major theme – sustainable development. Sustainable development is first and foremost connected with social-political problems (as earlier emphasised in Stenseth and Hertzberg, 1992). However, one main condition for attaining sustainable development is that the Earth's biological diversity is not emaciated, leading to several of the central ecological problems. An introduction to the relevant specialised ecological approaches to the problem is, therefore, important.

6.2   THE EARTH'S BIOLOGICAL DIVERSITY

From a biological – or 'biogeographical' – standpoint, the world is often divided into those different regions where plant and animal life have several common features, not least in their development. These are called biogeographical regions. We have six such regions in total: the palearctic (including the Nordic countries); the nearctic (encompassing North America); the neotropic (South and Central America); the afrotropic (the African continent, except for the northern parts of Africa, which very much resemble the palearctic region and thus are classified as the same region); the oriental (encompassing the Far East); and the australasiatic (mainly Australia, New Zealand and some of the surrounding islands). These regions are different both with respect to the types and the number of species they sustain.

One thing is indisputable: most of the Earth's biological diversity is found in the Third World. For example, Kloppenburg (1988) estimates that three-quarters of all species are found in the Third World. If we are to conserve the Earth's biological diversity, then the greatest effect would be gained by the implementation of conservation measures in areas where the biological diversity is greatest. Nevertheless, one should remember that it is important to conserve the individual region's local species, not least because these have adapted to local conditions. In many respects, these are the species that actually contribute towards the Earth's biological diversity. These are the species that have a more restricted geographical distribution and as such are most vulnerable to extinction. Species that are found in several areas are often less vulnerable because of their wide distribution.

Table 6.1 gives an overview of the biological diversity in various parts of the world. Specifically, it indicates where the greatest biological diversity within certain large groups of organisms is found. As we can see, it is first and foremost the oriental and afrotropic as well as neotropic regions that are the most species-rich.

Today, biological diversity has almost become a part of daily language but there are more people who use this expression than actually know in detail what it stands for. The term 'biological diversity' (also called biodiversity) refers both to genes and species. Genetic diversity refers to the inheritable variation within and between stocks of organisms. Species diversity, sometimes interpreted as biological diversity in a narrower sense, refers to the number of species in an area and how the number of individual species are distributed among the species found in the same area. There are presently several introductory articles on this topic, among them World Conservation Monitoring Centre (1992). Good summaries are also provided by Wilson (1988 and 1992).

There are particular gradients both with respect to the composition of and abundance of species. Travelling from south to north (in the Northern Hemisphere), the system changes from tropical to more arctic. Furthermore, there are fewer and fewer species as we move towards the poles. The changes we encounter when we travel from the equator to the poles correspond in other respects with the changes we encounter when we travel from the lowlands to the mountains (see Rahbek, 1995). High on the mountains and far to the north is the least abundance of species. (A Norwegian summary of these gradients is found in Stenseth, 1991.)

Species in the arctic areas and in mountainous regions are of course specially adapted to the unproductive and harsh environment. They are possibly species that are extremely vulnerable to the type of changes in temperature we may expect as a result of the global climate change caused by pollution and so on. Species in the more tropical and humid areas are often more well-adjusted to conditions of severe competition (that is to say, living under conditions in which there is a great abundance of species and severe competition among those species for the area's resources). If we are to conserve as many species as possible for the future, we will have to focus on these species-rich regions. However, if we are to conserve species which have adapted to more or less extreme living conditions, we will have to focus on the species-poor areas – which are found in both the species-rich regions and the harsher regions.

Table 6.1 Categorisation of different geographical areas according to biological diversity

Seedlings	Beetles	Amphibians	Reptiles	Mammals
Kampuchea (O)	N. Borneo (O)	Texas (Na)	Oaxaca (Nt)	N. Madagascar (Af)
South Yunan (O)	C. Borneo (O)	C. Colombia (Nt)	Nicaragua (Nt)	S.W. Ethiopia (Af)
Oaxaca (Nt)	N. Baja California (Na)	Tennessee (Na)	S. Colombia (Nt)	Lake Victoria (Af)
Nicaragua (Nt)	S. California (Na)	Florida (Na)	C. Venezuela (Nt)	N. Cameroun (Af)
Nicobar Island (O)	N. Japan (P)	C. Venezuela (Nt)	C. Colombia (Nt)	Ogadan (Af)
N. Peninsula Malaysia (O)	S. Japan (P)	N. Guinea (Nt)	Guatemala (Nt)	S.W. Somalia (Af)
S. Peninsula Malaysia (O)	S. Peninsula Malaysia (O)	S. Colombia (Nt)	Talamanca (Nt)	Dana River (Af)
Laos (O)	S. Borneo (O)	S. Guyana (Nt)	Ecuador (Nt)	Aldabra Islands (O)
Andaman Islands (O)	Texas (Na)	Ecuador (Nt)	Ogadan (Af)	C. Tanzania (Af)
C. Columbia (O)	Tennessee (Na)	The Amazons (Nt)	Uganda (Af)	Malawi (Af)
	The Carpathians (P)			Uganda (Af)
	The Balkans (P)			N. Zaire (Af)
	The Adriatics (P)			S. Cameroun (Af)
				Gabon (Af)
				Bioko (Af)
				E.C. African Republic (Af)

Notes

The table indicates the areas that are richest in the various groups such as seedlings, beetles, amphibians, reptiles and mammals. For each of the groups, the areas are ranked according to a decreasing order of biodiversity; areas with the same order of biodiversity are placed at the same level. The biogeographical regions of the given areas are enclosed in parentheses (P=Palearctic, Na=Nearctic, Nt=Neotropic, Af=Afrotropic, O=Oriental).

Source: Gaston *et al.* (1995)

6.3 THE EARTH'S BIOLOGICAL DIVERSITY IS MAN'S MOST IMPORTANT COMMON RESOURCE

A resource is said to be a common resource if at least two individuals (or groupings) have the permanent right to utilise it freely and retain the benefit themselves (see Stenseth *et al.*, 1993). It is not a condition that the right of use can be traded or disposed of in other ways. The utilisation of a common resource is unregulated if the individual user can determine the extent of his own enterprise. Defined as such, most of our living natural resources would be regarded as common resources. In general, the management of such resources is discussed extensively in social studies literature. This is literature where ecological conditions are not always given adequate place or are outlined in a mistaken way. That is the problem I address in this chapter.

Hardin (1968) has dealt with this theme in general under the title 'The Tragedy of the Commons'. In his discussion, he focuses on unregulated commons. Unfortunately, many of those involved in subsequent discussions have overlooked this fact. Hardin should, in my opinion, have named his topic 'the tragedy of the unregulated commons' (see Stenseth, 1991 and Stenseth *et al.*, 1995:233). For it is the unregulated commons from which we continually take as much as we can – whether it be directly or indirectly. And in a world with increasingly more people, where new technology makes it increasingly easier to influence nature to an increasingly greater extent (be it through pollution, manipulation of the whole ecosystem and landscape, or harvesting of resources), the use of these biological common resources becomes increasingly more unregulated. All things considered, the Earth's growth in population (see Norderhaug, 1994), and (unrestrained) technological development are the main threats against the Earth's biological diversity (see Hardin 1993).[3]

However, we must never forget that as long as there are possibilities of harvesting increasingly more of the Earth's biological diversity and manipulating our ecological systems, and as long as we who use nature increase steadily in number whilst the Earth's resources remain finite and only manipulable to a minor extent (see Stenseth, 1991), then sooner or later we will reach or even exceed several critical boundaries.

We cannot say where these limits lie but we can say that, sooner or later, we will exceed them if we do not change the management of our biological common resources with regard to the crucial issues. Trying to define these boundaries is in my opinion a discussion which is first and foremost of purely academic interest. The knowledge that such boundaries actually exist must, however, be acknowledged – a 'look before you leap' policy would be the best way of doing this (Stenseth, 1992b).

We should remember here that none of the parties involved wants a tragedy. The tragedy is that the individual parties act independently of each other and that they all have a short perspective. The so-called 'Prisoner's Dilemma' is a relevant example here (see Elster, 1977a, 1977b; Hovi, 1992; see also Hovi and Rasch, 1993). For example, we may regard the users of nature as players in a game-theory situation.[4] Each of them can choose between two alternative strategies, which, in this connection, we may regard as 'high' and 'moderate' resource utilisation respectively. Furthermore, for each individual it is best to choose a high utilisation level, irrespective of what the rest choose: if others choose the moderate level, one can take a free-ride on others' exertions. On the other hand, if they choose a high utilisation level, it does not much matter what one does. The conclusion therefore is that all will choose a high utilisation level, which leads to the resource base being depleted, and hence all will be worse off than if all had chosen the moderate alternative.

Adding to this is the fact that we always seem to value most that which we know. We can extract from nature today much more than what we assume we can take out of nature some time in the future. This has to do with how we view – or rather, value – the future as opposed to our present situation. There is a lot of literature on this and I have summarised some of it in Norwegian in a previous article (Stenseth, 1991).[5]

If we are to avoid the kind of tragedy that Hardin discussed nearly 30 years ago, we must introduce restrictions both on who can take which approaches and the extent of these approaches. Unfortunately, it seems that it is increasingly more difficult to gain acceptance for such restrictions – restrictions which have been accepted to a much greater extent in the past and in cultures with more direct links to nature's resources. Without these kinds of restrictions, we will not be able to attain sustainable development. Nature's resources are finite, (see Stenseth, 1991) while our demands seem infinite.

Which restrictions are necessary is a matter for natural science, and particularly for the ecological disciplines. How natural science is going to gain acceptance for and implement these restrictions is a social-political matter of which ecologists and other scientists have a limited knowledge. The rest of this chapter is, therefore, mainly dedicated to the ecological acceptance of the topic.

6.4 CONSERVATION OF BIOLOGICAL DIVERSITY

The conservation of species and groupings of species (and whole ecosystems) is important for many reasons. From an ecological point of view, it is important to prevent human activity from threatening the future existence of other species. If one species becomes extinct, this could easily lead to a torrent of ecologically destructive incidents. We should be aware from the start, however, that species are steadily dying out naturally. It would even be right to say that this natural form of species-extinction has been one of the driving forces behind the evolution that has resulted in the animal and plant life that presently exists on Earth.

The present discussion on conservation is about trying to prevent the accelerated extent of extinction caused by human activity and the resultant devastation of nature. Within modern nature conservation, we are attempting to prevent a drastic reduction of biological diversity being caused by human activity (that often leads to the destruction of the species' habitat and extinction of the species).

Throughout the whole world, species are threatened by various conditions (see below). We say that tolerance limits have been exceeded. It is important to be clear in this connection that preserving individual species, and preserving the environment, are two sides of the same coin. Owing to the ecological interaction which binds the various species together in a very complicated network, we cannot preserve the species without protecting the whole system. On the other hand, the ecosystem is constituted by individual species which interact closely. In other words, we must preserve nature as a whole – and nature's limits of tolerance must not be exceeded.

6.5   THREATS AGAINST STOCKS THAT ARE TOO SMALL

Within ecology, stock is the functional unit. In the literature, stock is defined as the unit within which most of reproduction occurs; some individuals always leave the stock in search of other places to settle (and to reproduce), while individuals from other stocks in other places come into the given local stock. We are talking about the viability of such stocks. A viable stock is a stock where individuals reproduce and survive in such a way that the stock as a whole has a greater likelihood of survival. If the number of individuals within this stock becomes too little, chance may well come to play a critical role, and uncertainty surrounding the survival of the whole stock increases greatly: due to incidental reasons, the size of the stock may easily decrease or just as easily increase.[6]

In ecology, a rule of thumb is that stocks of several thousand individuals or less may be in danger of extinction. The smaller the stock, the greater is the risk that its future existence may be in danger. A good discussion on this is provided by, among others, Mace and Lande (1991).

Some species such as sparrows are widespread over large areas. Such species are not faced with any immediate threat of extinction. However, other species are much less widespread. In certain cases, it involves species where the total global distribution is localised within a comparatively small part of the world: as in the case of, for example, the dwarf goose. Or a species may have a comparatively extensive distribution globally, while the same species may be under threat locally within an area which has traditionally had viable stocks: as in the case of, for example, wolves in Norway where there are so few individual animals left that we have a barely viable Norwegian wolf stock.

An overriding goal for the long-term management of nature is that the various species stocks do not become too small. If they do, there will be a great likelihood that the species will become extinct, either locally or globally. If the species disappear globally, the process is irreversible. If the species disappear locally, we may be able to re-introduce individuals from another area. However, such a re-introduction is not an easy task, not least because the species may have adapted itself to different environmental conditions in different parts of its total distribution area.

6.6   THE EVIL QUARTET

Jared Diamond introduced in 1984 the concept of the evil quartet in connection with the discussion on causes of loss in biological diversity. The quartet contains the four main causes of species extinction:

1.   Destruction and fragmentation (that is to say, segmentation) of the living area (or ecosystem), pollution and other kinds of deterioration of the ecosystem.
2.   Human over-exploitation of plants and animals.
3.   Introduction (incidental or planned) of foreign plants and animals, and hence, competition from these.
4.   Indirect effects of extinction, where the extinction of a species causes the extinction of another species, and so on.

I shall comment further on these four threats below.

Right from the start, it is important to remember that the 'limits of nature' should always be seen in relation to these threats – both individually and as a whole. Unfortunately, the hazards caused by the last two threats are often forgotten when we discuss the limits of nature – and all too often we think only of the threats caused by pollution and exploitation. These are serious threats in themselves – but unfortunately there are much more complex and serious threats to the Earth's biological diversity (see comments in the introduction to this chapter). Of these, the first two are probably the most important causes, even if the last is the most unpredictable and the one that requires the deepest ecological insight if it is to be avoided in a predictable way.

6.6.1   Destruction and Fragmentation of Species Habitat

First of all, many species need relatively large areas with more or less connected habitat of a certain type. If the total possible living area is reduced and/or divided up too much, the species within a large area will be easily divided up into several smaller, relatively isolated local stocks that will be relatively small – so small that their future existence will be threatened. Roughly speaking, living areas may be destroyed in two different ways: either through an area being used by humans in a way that is different from its previous use, or through pollution caused by local or distant sources.

This applies to many of the species that have adapted to our northern coniferous forests. The total area of this type of forest is being reduced mainly by modern practice in forestry. Logging areas are becoming increasingly larger, and old forests are becoming more and more isolated into small areas. Pollution, both local and foreign, also affects our forest areas to a certain extent.

These approaches to the problem are being studied within the ecological disciplines of landscape ecology and ecotoxicology. Landscape ecology has become particularly important in our efforts to conserve the Earth's biological diversity. Ecologists have come to recognise that a stock cannot be considered in isolation, but must be considered in relation to where other stocks of the same species are to be found and in relation to the extent to which there is an exchange of individuals between the different stocks. Where a stock is isolated, it faces a much higher risk of extinction than if it is connected in some way to other stocks of the same species – whether this be through a habitat type that may be crossed by species, or through a network of corridors for the movement of species.

More recent ecological research has produced a lot of relevant knowledge on how the landscape should be shaped in order to best conserve the greatest number of species. For example, it has been shown that the number of species within an area increases with the area's size. This is particularly important if the area to begin with is not large in relation to movement of the actual species. If the total area of a certain type is reduced (for example, old forest), the number of species linked to this ecosystem type will be reduced.

6.6.2   Over-exploitation

All things considered, our activities (including our cultural activities), are dependent on nature's resources – so we must harvest nature's biological diversity. It is unclear to what extent humans, regardless of place, are ever in balance with nature's own self-production. However, it is clear that if there is an increasing number of human beings harvesting nature's finite resources, and if they who do so develop steadily more effective methods of harvesting, sooner or later we will come to over-exploit nature's resources – if there are no restrictions. In many ways, this is the core of Hardin's (1968) 'Tragedy of the Commons' discussed above and in Stenseth (1991).

Over-exploitation has thus become one of the biggest threats to the Earth's biological diversity. If we shoot the last rhinoceros, future generations will only be able to see rhinoceroses in pictures and on film.

To certain extent, this threat is linked to biological research knowledge. For example, biologists are able to indicate the consequences to the stock of a given level of harvest. It is crucial whether we harvest from a large stock or many more or less isolated small stocks. Further, knowledge on what represents a stock is important biological knowledge. Knowledge on the reproduction and survival of species and stock is also fundamental in this connection.

Arriving at a sustainable harvest is, however, just as much a social scientific and economic problem. Considerable insights in this connection may be obtained from game theory. (See, for example, Stenseth *et al.* (1993); good discussions relevant to this topic are also provided by Schulz (1995) and Skonhoft (1995).)

6.6.3   Introduction or Immigration of Foreign Species

The ecological network can often be disturbed in such a way that individual species are forced out and replaced by intruders that either arrive naturally or are introduced with the aid of human beings. Further, species that have been introduced can easily put the indigenous species' future existence in danger. Both may lead to great ecological changes in the ecosystem. Often, species which are introduced also become pest organisms in the new ecosystem, despite the fact that they were not pests or weeds in the area they came from. This is connected to the co-evolution which has occurred in the given ecological system.

Geologically, this was the result of the joining of North America and South America (Diamond, 1984). Today, such exchanges of species between continents usually occur via human activity – either by deliberate introduction or through carelessness.

6.6.4   Indirect Effects of Extinction Caused by One of the Three Previous Conditions

The changes that occur when a species becomes extinct due to any of the above reasons, may easily lead to a cascade of dynamic ecological changes that may then result in additional species being faced with extinction.

The possibility of this type of dynamic cascade-effect occurring is, moreover, one of the main reasons that we should guard against the loss of every species that may be lost. In addition to the fact that each species may be regarded as having its own value (and consequently should be guarded against extinction), the loss of one species can easily lead to the additional loss of other species – including much more visible and economically important species than the species that was lost in the first place. Of course, some species – in purely economic terms – are more important than others. These are the so-called key species; that is to say species that hold key positions in the ecological network in the sense that if they disappear, it will lead to great changes in the rest of the ecosystem.

This is a theme that has concerned ecologists, but which in many ways has not influenced the debate on conservation to any great extent. Naturally, it has something to do with the fact that this is very difficult, and that ecologists do not have – all things considered – the required knowledge. But ecologists know that great potential hazards exist which in turn constitute the main arguments for making a 'look before you leap' policy the basis of resource management.

6.7 CONCLUSION

What then are the limits of nature? They are undoubtedly numerous, and clearly dependent on what we view them in relation to. Limits with respect to pollution? Or, limits with respect to habitat fragmentation, or harvesting?

Ecologists can only to a small extent provide answers as to what are nature's limits, unless the question is defined precisely in a very particular direction – whereby the answer often becomes uninteresting. However, ecologists can provide general insights with respect to which questions one should ask before continuing the accelerated effect on nature. Further, ecologists can provide answers as to possible interactions which may easily lead to seemingly surprising side-effects. And it is insight that is of very great relevance to our efforts to create a society characterised by sustainable development, and whose policy is based on the 'look before you leap' principle.

Therefore, instead of focusing on a detailed quantification of nature's limits (as often attempted in Norway today), the authorities should rather contribute resources for a general building up of expertise within the type of biological/ecological research I have discussed in this chapter.[7] Defining the four different threats against nature's biological diversity is important, not least because we have to relate to them in different ways. Further, our ability to implement counter measures against these threats varies greatly. In many ways, it is the threat of over-exploitation that is the simplest to handle – even though it is also very difficult, not least because of the socio-political conditions that are linked to the harvesting of the Earth's biological resources. This, however, is the simplest factor to counter because we can focus on saving a specific species or a few species from the threat of extinction. As far as the destruction of the species' habitat is concerned, it is much more difficult, not least because we must set up a much more general management profile. Threats caused by the introduction of foreign species may be easy to counter in the sense that it is a matter of the introduction of species due to direct actions. Many species are introduced to new habitats as 'stowaways', which is very difficult to prevent, particularly in a world with extensive travel. However, the indirect dynamic ecological threats are the most difficult to handle, not least because if we are to avoid damaging effects, we must have a range of ecological approaches – often much wider than those available today. Therefore, a cautious precautionary strategy is important: if we are uncertain, we should be very restrictive in allowing intervention in nature.[8]

In conclusion, allow me to briefly link my ecological and interdisciplinary-based discussion to the concept of 'sustainable development'.[9] This is a concept that can be defined (see Stenseth, 1991, 1992a, 1992b; see also Stenseth *et al.*,

1993) as a society where the management of resources is such that future generations may make use of said resources – if they wish to do so – on (at least) the same level as their ancestors. If we overconsume (or in other ways, destroy) the resources now, such that they disappear totally or partially (something which has happened to, for example, the blue whale), future generations will be deprived of the possibility of harvesting these resources. To prevent this, we must ensure that the capability to regenerate resources is secured. Such sustainable management presupposes a solid knowledge of the ecology of the resources.

It should be up to future generations to decide whether they wish to use the resources we use today. However, we should not have the right to deprive future generations of their options, which we would do if we act in such a way that one or more species become extinct. We who live in the present have the ability to influence nature in such a way that a great number of species that are threatened today do not become extinct. We can do this by applying the ecological perspectives I have summarised briefly in this chapter. If we – in spite of such ecological insights – do not stop our destructive influence on nature, we are contributing directly towards not being able to have a sustainable society in the future.[10]

Finally: the theme throughout this book is global equity and distribution – so what can thus be said with respect to this specific theme based on the aspects I have touched on in this chapter?

1. Biological diversity is unevenly distributed in different parts of the Earth (see Table 6.1). Despite the fact that all parts of the Earth clearly have biological diversity worthy of protection, there is no doubt that the greatest biological diversity is found in the poorer Third World. Based on a platform of biological knowledge, it is thus clear that what we today refer to as the poorer world is the one that in terms of sustainability may be the richer part. It is in the Third World that tomorrow's greatest resources lie: it is the Third World that has tomorrow's 'gold'.

2. There is every reason to assume that the Third World, with its enormous biological resources and its weak economy and infrastructure, will continue to be very vulnerable to a further draining of resources. First, part of the Third World were drained of their people (slaves), then their mineral resources. In the future, there is every reason to fear that this part of the world will be drained of its biological resources – this part of the world may even be deprived (whether more or less voluntarily or forcibly) of the rights to decide over its own area's biological resources. The convention on biological diversity (see, for example, Rosendal, 1995) will naturally be of some help; but since biological resources are being evaluated as increasingly more important for all types of industry at the same time as biological diversity is being threatened by vigorous depletion, there is every reason to anticipate a breach in the convention. In this conflict, it is the Third World that loses in the short run, while it is humanity that will be left holding the bag in

the long run. The Earth's biological resources and, in particular, the Third World's enormous wealth of biological resources may easily become a 'tragedy of the commons'. There is no one who wishes to have such a tragedy, but the end result will none the less be just such a tragedy if all parties involved act independently of each other and in a selfish and short-sighted way.

3. Based on the interdisciplinary knowledge I have gained through the UNESCO programme 'Man and the Biosphere' (MAB) among others, it is clear that in spite of the Third World having a larger proportion of biological resources, the high growth in population in this part of the world cannot continue as it has. It is clear that what we usually refer to as the rich part of the world cannot continue to wallow freely in the Third World's natural resources. We in the North must reduce our consumption, while the people in the South must reduce their population growth.

NOTES

1. DN – *Direktoratet for naturforvaltning* (The Norwegian Directorate for the Management of Natural Resources).
2. Unfortunately, it is not only public environmental management that has such a lopsided focus on pollution. Economists have also traditionally placed a biased focus on the problem. (See Førsund and Strøm, 1980). The so-called 'bioeconomy' (Clark, 1976, 1985) is, first of all, relatively undeveloped, but it is also not developed enough for ecological systems other than the marine. This, among other things, is discussed by both Skonhoft (1995) and Schulz (1995).
3. Let me mention briefly that in addition to population growth and a steadily more nature-hostile technology, the distribution of resources – and access to them – is also a problem (see Stenseth, 1992b).
4. For an introduction to game theory, see, for example, Elster, 1977b.
5. Here lies a great interdisciplinary challenge, namely the integration of economic and ecological dynamics, as well as the introduction of ecological dynamics into the game-theory way of consideration already outlined. Hovi (1992) and Stenseth *et al.* (1993) indicate how this can be approached. Moreover, a very important argument is put forward in this connection by Hardin (1985, 1993).
6. It is like tossing a coin: if we toss it many times, we will get more or less about half heads and half tails. But if we only toss it a few times (10 times for example), we will probably end up with a lot more heads or tails.
7. In this regard, it is worth remembering that during the rise in algae growth along the Norwegian coastal areas in the spring of 1988, it was the general – and apparently useless – research by the Biological Institute at the University of Oslo that made the authorities capable of determining the species of algae. And it was this insight that had practical consequences for further work.

8. A theme discussed in Stenseth (1992a, 1992b) and Stenseth *et al.* (1993) among others.
9. Or to be more precise, the concept of 'sustainable management of our resources'.
10. Unfortunately, there are many examples of such neglect of existing know-how – and of the fact that many projects have been implemented that one knew would have unfortunate consequences. Focusing on Africa, I have given examples elsewhere (Stenseth and Semb-Johansson, 1986 and Stenseth *et al.*, 1995).

7 Nature, Market and Ignorance: Can Development Be Managed?

Oluf Langhelle

The next few decades are crucial. The time has come to break out of past patterns. Attempts to maintain social and ecological stability through old approaches to development and environmental protection will increase instability. Security must be sought through change.

Our Common Future, 1987.

Is it possible to steer development towards a more sustainable path? There seems to be widespread agreement that present development is not sustainable. At the same time, it appears to be very difficult to change the course of development, and there appears to be widespread scepticism towards the possibilities for social management (Sejersted, 1988, 1989).

The idea of sustainable development, together with other ideologies of progress, builds on the belief that humans are responsible for their own destiny and that this forms their present and future existence (Eriksen, 1992). Sustainable development defines both a developmental path and the scope or limits within which this development should occur. In other words, it is not just any development, but a desired development which fulfils certain conditions of sustainability.

Furthermore, *Our Common Future* believes that such a development is possible: 'Humanity has the ability to make development sustainable ... technology and social organisation can be both managed and improved ... widespread poverty is no longer inevitable' (WCED, 1987:8). In other words, sustainable development can be attained. It also seems that it is political will rather than ability which is the critical factor: 'in the final analysis, sustainable development must rest on political will' (WCED, 1987:9). As such, *Our Common Future* is an optimistic report, even though the description of the global ecological and social crisis may be depressing. It is characterised by a positive view on change and an altogether optimistic trust in the ability of policy and technology to steer the future on to a path that will serve humanity (Eriksen, 1992:140).[1]

111

In this chapter, I raise the issue of the Brundtland Report's management optimism by looking more closely into the arguments of those who have been most sceptical and critical about the possibilities for management and planned change. In light of the development goals in the concept of sustainable development – which can be linked to both society (social equity in time and space), nature (nature's carrying capacity) and the relationship between the two – there are two very different groupings that stand out in this connection; neoliberals, and the schools of environmental philosophy which are based on ecology. Even though these groupings are usually politically antagonistic to each other, there are several similarities in their views on, first, the possibilities for management and planned change,[2] and second, in the fact that they both prescribe non-intervention in spontaneous orders. Moreover, these groups are among the strongest critics of the concept of sustainable development and the development path it defines. Even if it were possible to steer development on the path advocated by the World Commission, one should not (in their eyes) do so.

While neoliberals have criticised what they call 'social engineering', representatives of environmental philosophy have criticised what they call 'technological optimism' (Eckersley, 1992:51), or 'technocentrism' (O'Riordan, 1981:11). Even though the criticisms directed against social engineering and technological optimism/technocentrism seem, to begin with, quite different, this is more due to the fact that the criticisms are directed against two different systems, rather than that the arguments themselves are different.

Neoliberals are sceptical about the possibilities of social management, in general, while schools of environmental eco-philosophy are sceptical about the possibilities of managing nature. Their conclusions seem to diverge, however, when it comes to deciding what it is possible and desirable to manage. While neoliberals are critical about social engineering, they maintain that it is possible to manage nature. Likewise, while parts of environmental philosophy are critical about ecological engineering they believe it is both possible and desirable to steer society in a certain direction. This may be illustrated as in Figure 7.1.

For both neoliberals and environmental philosophers, the scepticism about management and planned change is accompanied by normative criteria which challenge the ideas of sustainable development advocated by *Our Common Future*. Neoliberals reject the whole idea of 'social justice', and parts of environmental philosophy reject the anthropocentric bias in *Our Common Future*. In the following I shall contrast these normative criteria with the developmental goals defined by the concept of sustainable development.

I take my point of departure from perhaps the most foremost exponent of neoliberalism, Friedrich A. Hayek; and from the two main strands of environmentalism which, according to the environmental philosopher, Robyn Eckersley (1992), are most 'informed' by an ecological perspective; 'human welfare ecology' and 'ecocentrism'. These strands differ from each other in the sense that human welfare ecology (HWE) is based on an anthropocentric ethic, where only humans are ascribed intrinsic value. Ecocentrism is based on a non-anthropocentric ethic, where also non-humans are ascribed intrinsic value. Næss' (1973) differentiation between 'deep' and 'shallow' ecology is often used in this sense, where deep ecologists are linked to a non-anthropocentric ethic, and shallow ecologists to an anthropocentric ethic. This division constitutes, according to Eckersley (1992), the fundamental division from an eco-philosophical point of view.

Figure 7.1   Alternative views on steering of nature and society

	Steering	
	Yes	**No**
Nature	Neoliberalism	Ecology-based Environmentalism
Society	Ecology-based Environmentalism	Neoliberalism

System (row label on the left, between Nature and Society)

Eckersley (1992) makes no explicit references to *Our Common Future*, but it appears as though she identifies sustainable development as part of the HWE approach.[3] This seems to be a reasonable interpretation of *Our Common Future*, although there are non-anthropocentric passages to be found in it. In the following, however, I question the importance Eckersley attributes to the division between the anthropocentric and non-anthropocentric perspectives. Since both strands are 'informed' by an ecological perspective, it should, in principle, be possible to trace the differences back to the anthropocentric/non-anthropocentric cleavage. As will be evident, it is by no means clear that this can be done.

7.1   INSTRUMENTAL RATIONALITY

Human welfare ecologists and ecocentrists mainly direct their criticism towards the relationship between humans and nature, and the way that humans and the modern industrial society have intervened in nature. The criticism of neoliberals is directed against the relationship between humans and society, and the way humans have intervened in spontaneous orders through constructs like the welfare state. The neoliberal critique of 'social engineering' has been linked to what they see as attempts to realise one or another kind of distribution of goods in society in accordance with a given interpretation of social equity. Social justice (both intra- and intergenerational) constitutes an inherent part of the concept of sustainable development (see Chapter 1), and it also forms a part of the ecocentric approach. In the ecocentric approach the market is subordinate to ecological and social justice considerations (Eckersley, 1992:30).

The so-called crisis of the welfare state has spawned a debate on social management in the broadest sense, and the question has been raised as to whether instrumental rationality – understood as setting up goals and then finding adequate means to reach the goals – is suitable at all as a method for social management (Sejersted, 1988). Kukathas (1989) describes Hayek's project as an attempt to show that the nature of mind and the limited powers of human reason form institutions which aim at organising society to achieve some desired end, or reconstructing it in accordance with some preferred pattern of distribution, largely unworkable. This scepticism towards planned change is also captured by Elster (1984): 'If one considers planned change as a process where one seeks the best available means to realise a given goal, the probability of failure is high' (Elster, 1984:27).

According to Sejersted (1989), the scepticism towards instrumentalist social planning is usually founded on three 'problems'. The first he calls 'systemic constraint', as it implies that we have no freedom of choice: 'We live within a given system that constrains our choices.' The second he calls 'ignorance', as it implies that we are unable to predict the consequences of our actions, and may therefore, achieve the opposite of what we intended in the first place. The third he calls 'indifference', as it implies that we actually don't even know what we want. That is, there is often a conflict between what we want in the short term and what we want in the long term (Sejersted, 1989:3).

Even though all these problems are central to both the neoliberals' criticism of the welfare state and to the HWE/ecocentrists' criticism of technological optimism, I will here focus on the second, that of ignorance. As stressed by Andersen and Sørensen (1992), these problems are of great significance, and they provide a solid basis for criticising 'management-optimistic social-planning visions' (Andersen and Sørensen, 1992) – and thereby *Our Common Future*. There is little doubt that *Our Common Future* contains such a management-optimistic social-planning vision. And given the assumption that present social development is not sustainable, what does the criticism of instrumental rationality imply for the possibilities of realising sustainable development?

7.2 ECOLOGY, 'NATURE'S LAWS', AND THE PROBLEM OF IGNORANCE

Environmental philosophy can probably be best understood as a new scientific paradigm, a set of values or a political ideology (Paehlke, 1989). It is a set of values that has been developed by integrating the findings of environmental science and environmental convictions. The main idea in environmental philosophy is, according to Paehlke (1989), that human society must embrace an ecological perspective more completely. This implies that we must realise that human societies are bound in significant ways by the physical and biological realities of our world. We should not seek to overcome these natural limitations but understand how best to live within them. Man can neither control nor dictate nature, and the only possible solution is to live within the limits of nature (Paehlke, 1989:20).

The limits of nature are also present in *Our Common Future*. Even though it is stated that growth has no set limits in terms of population and resource use, there are ultimate limits: 'ultimate limits there are, and sustainability requires that long before these are reached, the world must ensure equitable access to the constrained resource and reorient technological efforts to relieve the pressure' (WCED, 1987:45). These limits are seen as different for the use of energy, materials, water and land. At a minimum, however, sustainable development requires that the natural systems that support life are not endangered (WCED, 1987:45).

In the ecological perspective which, according to Eckersley (1992), has informed both HWE and ecocentrism, the natural systems that support life are not easily delimited. This perspective is captured by Commoner's (1972) four laws of ecology:

- Everything is connected to everything else.
- Everything must go somewhere.
- Nature knows best (that is, any major human intervention in a natural system is likely to be detrimental to that system).
- There is no such thing as a free lunch.

The fourth law is, according to Commoner, meant to be a reminder that every gain is won at some expense. This law embodies the three previous laws: 'Because the global ecosystem is a connected whole, in which nothing can be gained or lost and which is not subject to overall improvement, anything extracted from it by human effort must be replaced. Payment of this price cannot be avoided, it can only be delayed' (Commoner, 1972:46).

Ecocentrism is, in its own eyes, an informed philosophy of internal relatedness (Eckersley, 1992). It is a picture of reality in which all organisms are interrelated (everything is connected to everything else), and at the same time constituted by these relationships. The world is seen as an intrinsically dynamic, interconnected web of relations in which there are no absolute discrete entities and no absolute dividing lines between the living and the non-living (Eckersley, 1992:49).

Even though Commoner's 'laws of ecology' have inspired both HWE and ecocentrism, they are taken further by the ecocentrists: 'An ecocentric perspective ... recognises that nature is not only more complex than we presently know, but also quite possibly more complex, in principle, than we can know' (Eckersley, 1992:52; see also p. 157). Devall and Sessions are of the same opinion: 'We need to take seriously the ecologist's principle that Nature is more complex than we now know and more complex than we possibly can know' (Devall and Sessions, 1985:145, see also Sessions, 1995:365). In other words, nature is so complex that it is not possible to know how complex it actually is.

This picture of reality has, in the ecocentrists' view, wide-ranging implications for both social and political thought. This world-view, it is argued, stands in sharp contrast to the most pervasive characteristic of the mechanistic and materialistic world-view – that of technological optimism. Progress, efficiency, rationality and control constitute the ideological foundation of technocentrism (O'Riordan, 1981:11). It is a secular religion of faith and hope – a faith in never-ending technological progress and a hope that what they do will work (Devall and Sessions, 1985:135). Technological optimism is defined as the confident belief that with further scientific research we can rationally manage (that is, predict, manipulate and control) all the negative unintended consequences of large-scale human intervention in nature (Eckersley, 1992:51).

In the ecocentric perspective, nature's laws and complexity thus seem to make it impossible to predict, manipulate and control all the negative unintended consequences. Technological optimism is hence replaced by technological pessimism, where humans are seen to have limited abilities to manage nature through science and technology. The best management, according to Devall and Sessions, is, in principle, the least management (Devall and Sessions, 1985:152). This management strategy is also referred to as 'not do', and 'hands off' (Devall and Sessions, 1985:145:147).

Eckersley is less explicit on the issue of control and management of nature. She stresses the need where possible, for developing a more dynamic and symbiotic approach to land management. Such management will acknowledge that humans can live side by side with nature (Eckersley, 1992:40–1). She also stresses that harmonising our relationship with nature, first of all involves identifying oneself with nature in a way that acknowledges the uniqueness and relative autonomy of other life-forms (Eckersley, 1992:90). It is unclear, however, what this actually implies for human actions.

The two issues that, according to Eckersley, highlight the practical differences between an anthropocentric and non-anthropocentric ethic are their differing views on human population growth and wilderness preservation. These are the two 'litmus-test ecological issues'. Ecocentrists are said to be more willing to advocate long-term reduction in human population, and advocate the setting aside of large tracts of wilderness, regardless of how useful this is to humankind (Eckersley, 1992:29).

These responses seem to follow both from ecocentric values and the complexity of nature. It reflects a concern with letting all beings, human or non-human, unfold in their own way, that is, 'letting things be' (Eckersley, 1992:156). The environmental crisis is seen as a result of both an inflated sense of human self-importance and a misguided trust in our capacity to understand biospheric processes completely (Eckersley, 1992:156). By 'letting things be', the problem of ignorance seems to be solved. It is better to keep our hands off and to let things be, rather than to intervene in nature. And if one has to intervene, it must be done with care and humility. If nature is so complex that it is not possible to know how complex it actually is, this may also be seen as a rational way to relate to nature. But it is, as I shall return to later, highly uncertain whether the complexity of nature can support a conclusion of 'letting things be' or 'hands off'.

7.3 HUMAN WELFARE ECOLOGY AND ECOLOGICAL RATIONALITY

Dryzek (1987) offers a HWE-approach to environmental philosophy.[4] Dryzek is probably the person who has most systematically tried to answer the question of whether it is possible to manage nature rationally. Dryzek's focus is on the capacity of different 'social choice mechanisms' to handle environmental problems.[5]

Environmental problems concern discrepancies between ideal and actual environmental conditions stemming from interaction between human and natural systems. The character of the natural systems, and the way they interact with human systems, create special demands for human problem-solving. This is because a great deal is special about natural systems. Ecosystems as entities thus have some distinctive features which have implications for the nature of environmental problems.

First of all, ecosystems exhibit a high degree of interpenetration. This means that ecosystems are always open. Every ecosystem exchanges both energy and materials with other ecosystems, so that it is difficult to define the boundaries of specific ecosystems. In other words, everything is connected to everything else.

Secondly, ecosystems feature 'the ubiquitous presence of emergent or non-reducible properties'. An emergent property is defined as 'any characteristic of a system which is not predictable from a knowledge of the elements of that system'. One cannot predict the properties of carbon dioxide based on the knowledge of the properties of carbon and oxygen. This means that the extent of the life-support capacity (or the earth's carrying capacity) of the ecosphere could not be predicted on a basis of a knowledge of its component ecosystems, precisely because of the global ecosystem's emergent and non-reducible properties (Dryzek, 1987:27).

One emergent property is so important that it warrants being classified as a third distinctive feature – an ecosystem's 'self-regulating quality'. This self-regulation is 'non-teleological': 'no central controller sets goals, monitors feedback, and acts in response' (Dryzek, 1987:27). The following illustrates this mechanism: if a species threatens to explode demographically, the number of predators will probably increase in response and thus 'regulate' the system (Dryzek, 1987:27).

The fourth and final feature is closely connected to the self-regulating quality of ecological systems. Dryzek labels this 'dynamism'. It manifests itself in three qualities: homeostasis, adaptiveness and succession. The homeostatic quality of self-regulation enables ecosystems to maintain their essential structure and functions in the face of exogenous shocks, and they to some extent remain intact when confronted with human-induced stress. The second quality – adaptiveness – implies that ecosystems can adapt to permanently changed conditions through natural selection. The evolution of physiological characteristics and behavioural traits is achieved through natural selection. The third quality – succession – is defined as a spontaneous developmental process involving changes in species composition over time. During succession, the physical environment itself can be modified; for example, a sand dune can be converted into rich soil (Dryzek, 1987:27–8).

Given these ecosystem characteristics, the nature or circumstances of environmental problems can be captured as follows:

- The first and most striking feature of environmental problems is complexity: this feature is 'potentially devastating to some of our familiar conceptions of problem-solving'.
- The second feature is that environmental problems often will be non-reducible: therefore, they cannot always be solved through the resolution of its parts.
- The third feature is 'temporal and spatial variability': temporal variability means that the ecological context of any problem will not remain fixed. Spatial variability arises because ecosystems, their components, and human systems can combine in diverse ways in different environments. Thus, oil pollution in the Arctic Ocean is a very different matter from oil pollution in temperate waters.
- The fourth feature is 'uncertainty': this concerns both the nature of present or future conditions, and the consequences of human actions.
- The final feature is that environmental problems often are 'collective': that is, large numbers of actors have a stake in them (Dryzek, 1987:28–31).

Even so, there is a bright spot: The property of ecosystems that Dryzek calls 'spontaneity'. An ecosystem's spontaneity is its capacity to handle problems without human interference (Dryzek, 1987:33). Spontaneity is a direct consequence of ecosystems' homeostasis and adaptiveness. That ecosystems have been surprisingly invulnerable to, for example, oil spills, may be interpreted as a reflection of this property.

Given these characteristics, the central question Dryzek tries to answer is what a rational interaction with ecosystems would involve. And Dryzek's view corresponds with the minimum requirement for sustainable development in *Our Common Future*: 'Maintenance of the capability of human and natural systems in conjunction to cope with actual or potential shortfall in life support' (Dryzek, 1987:53). This is labelled 'ecological rationality' by Dryzek, and is viewed as both a principle and a form of functional rationality.

This principle implies that non-intervention in natural systems is untenable: 'Ecological systems perform productive, protective and waste-assimilative functions. While the protective and waste-assimilative aspects of anthropocentric ecological rationality may be best served by leaving nature well alone, the productive aspects will not' (Dryzek, 1987:45). This is also in accordance with *Our Common Future*: 'Every ecosystem everywhere cannot be preserved intact' (WCED, 1987:45). Ecological rationality thus requires a degree of intervention in natural systems, even though, according to Dryzek, this 'falls far short of extreme ecological engineering' (Dryzek, 1987:46).

The anthropocentric foundation and the opening for some intervention in natural systems lead to what seems to be a somewhat different view on human interaction with natural systems. Human intervention in natural systems need not be synonymous with ecological destruction, and one should, according to Dryzek, be wary of arguing that ecological rationality implies the same thing as minimising interaction with natural systems.

In accordance with the symbiotic relationship advocated by the ecocentrists, however, an ecologically rational human–nature system will also, in this perspective, be a system where the human and natural components are in a symbiotic relationship. Ecologically rational practice involves 'intelligence with, rather than control over' (Dryzek, 1987:195).

But what is intelligence with? What is a symbiotic relationship with nature? Dryzek's evaluation of different existing social-choice mechanisms such as the market and democracy, is rather discouraging for the possibilities of ecological rationality: 'none of the more prominent social choice mechanisms in today's world can stake even a moderately good claim to ecological rationality' (Dryzek, 1987:179). Given the complexity, non-reducibility, temporal and spatial variability, uncertainty, and collectivity that form the circumstances of environmental problems, how, then, is it possible to steer society according to the principle of ecological rationality?

7.4 SOCIETY, SPONTANEOUS ORDERS AND THE LAWS OF THE MARKET

While the ecocentrists want to minimise interaction with natural systems, and human welfare ecologists want to reduce the present interaction with natural systems, neoliberals want to minimise state intervention in society. For neoliberals, it is not nature – but the good society – which is presumed to lie outside of human control. Friedrich A. Hayek is the social scientist in modern times who has most enthusiastically supported the thesis that attempts to plan and control society lead to negative consequences (Lundström, 1992).

According to Hayek, 'progress by its very nature cannot be planned' (Hayek, 1960:41). As with the ecological engineer, the social engineer commits the same mistakes by thinking that it is possible to construct – not nature – but human society. 'Constructivist rationalism' assumes 'that all social institutions are, and ought to be, the product of deliberate design' (Hayek, 1973:5).

Society is, as Bailey (1988) points out, viewed not as a constructed order, but as a natural order in the neoliberal approach: 'Basically society is seen as a natural order in which satisfactory social institutions arise unintentionally. Interference, conscious design via planning and "politicisation" of social provision are all seen as dangerous disruptions of a spontaneous social order' (quoted in Bauman, 1994:15). If the homology of ecosystems and social systems are taken to heart, the search for ecological rationality in human affairs would consist of an identification in social systems of ecological constructs such as interpenetration, emergent or non-reducible properties, self-regulating properties, homeostasis, succession, adaptiveness and mutuality – the factors which maintain the 'rationality' of biological ecosystems (Dryzek, 1987:41). In many ways this is just what Hayek is doing.[6]

Constructivist rationalism, according to Hayek, derives its basic ideas from the Enlightenment, most notably from René Descartes. By defining reason as logical deduction from explicit premises, rational action by Descartes came to mean only action determined by known and demonstrable truth. From this view it is a short and almost inevitable step to the conclusion that 'only what is true in this sense can lead to successful action', and that only institutions and practices which have been designed by human beings are worthy of our appraisal (Hayek, 1973:10).

This intellectual tradition, however, is false both in its factual and normative conclusions, because existing institutions are not all the product of design, nor is it possible to make the social order wholly dependent on design. This erroneous view of rational constructivism is closely connected with the equally false conception of the human mind as an entity standing outside the cosmos of nature and society, rather than being itself the product of the same process of evolution to which the institutions of society are due (Hayek, 1973:5).

It is, according to Hayek, impossible for any individual to acquire the knowledge necessary to master social processes. The 'hubris of reason' thus manifests itself 'in those who believe that they can dispense with abstractions and achieve a full mastery of the concrete and thus positively master the social process' (Hayek, 1973:33). The acknowledgement of ignorance and limited knowledge is what is lacking in the rational constructivist tradition. The argument thus parallels the ecocentrists' critique of technological optimism, but is directed towards the management of society – not nature. 'Social engineering' – 'the notion that man can consciously choose where he wants to go' – is 'a delusion' (Hayek, 1989:51).

The acknowledgement of ignorance thus leads to an anti-constructivist position. Just as Eckersley argues that 'the wisest course of action from an ecocentric perspective is not to presume that we know the thrust of evolution' (Eckersley, 1992:157), Hayek maintains that society's laws and institutions should not be subsumed under instrumental rationality. Instead, society should be allowed to evolve spontaneously.

Many of the institutions of society are, in Hayek's view, the result of customs, habits or practices, and not of deliberate planning. These are neither invented nor observed with a clear purpose in mind – they are characterised by tacit knowledge:

> Man is as much a rule-following animal as a purpose-seeking one. And he is successful not because he knows why he ought to observe the rules which he does observe, nor is he even capable of stating all these rules in words, but because his thinking and acting are governed by rules which have by a process of selection been evolved in the society in which he lives, and which are thus the product of the experience of generations (Hayek, 1973:11)

Rules have – just as with the evolution taking place in ecosystems through natural selection – gone through the same process of natural selection, or what Hayek calls 'adaptive evolution' (Hayek, 1960:59).[7] In *The Constitution of Liberty* (1960), Hayek gives the following definition of a spontaneous order: 'When order is achieved among human beings by allowing them to interact with each other on their own initiative – subject only to the laws which uniformly apply to all of them – we have a system of spontaneous order in society' (Hayek, 1960:160).[8]

Spontaneous orders are not, however, limited to the functioning of the market. Spontaneous orders operate at all levels of human activity – physiological, psychological, social, political and moral. As Lundström (1992) points out, rules have the same optimising effect at all these levels. Civilisation, according to Hayek, 'rests on the fact that we all benefit from knowledge which we do not possess' (Hayek, 1973:15).

A spontaneous order is a 'self-generating or endogenous' order. Hayek calls this *kosmos* (grown order) in contrast to *taxis* (made order). Kosmos is governed by Nomos, universal rules independent from individual intentions, while taxis is dominated by Thesis, constructed rules which aim at reaching specific goals. The rules that regulate how society functions and ensure its survival are, for Hayek as well as for Hume, 'rules of justice' (Hayek, 1976:16). To be identified as 'rules of justice', these rules must embody three qualities:

1. they must be general and abstract;
2. they must be known and secure;
3. they must respect individual equality before the law (Hayek, 1960:207–9).

An order that is regulated according to such rules is a spontaneous order. 'Rules of justice' maximise the individual's freedom and create the conditions for social evolution or progress. These laws serve the permanent preservation of an abstract order, what Hayek describes as a 'timeless purpose which will continue to assist individuals in the pursuit of their temporary and still unknown aims' (Hayek, 1976:17).

For Hayek, progress is both material progress and a formation and modification of the human intellect. It is a process where adaptation and learning create opportunities that were not known before. Progress is thus the succession of the social system. The price we have to pay for progress (or succession), is the exclusion of goal-oriented rationality at the political level. In the same way as the self-regulating properties of ecosystems are non-teleological, society should also be so arranged. Hayek himself points to the resemblance with biology:

> Biology has from its beginning been concerned with that special kind of spontaneous order which we call an organism. Only recently has there arisen within the physical sciences under the name of cybernetics a special discipline which is also concerned with what are called self-organising or self-generating systems (Hayek, 1973:37).

This resemblance makes its appearance in Hayek's account of the distinguishing properties of the market as a spontaneous order. The two most important features of the market in Hayek's account are, first, that it is a 'corrective mechanism' (similar to the self-regulating mechanisms of ecosystems) in the sense that it adjusts or co-ordinates individual action by informing people when their actions are incompatible with the intentions or purposes of others or with their own. Second, it is a dynamic social process (similar to the dynamism of ecosystems) which loses its co-ordinating effect when attempts are made to arrest it (Kukathas, 1989:95).

The market is thus a discovery procedure, 'which allows us to test our knowledge of the preferences of others, of our own future preferences, and of the compatibility of the various plans of action' (Kukathas, 1989:96). The guidelines in this process are the information generated in the market through prices, volume, advertising and so forth. Most important, however, is the knowledge generated through failure:

> co-ordinating individual actions will secure a high degree of coincidence of expectations and an effective utilisation of the knowledge and skills of the several members only at the price of a constant disappointment of some expectations (Hayek, 1976:107)

Just as adaptiveness constitutes a part of the dynamism of ecosystems, failure serves the same function in the market. Some, therefore, must suffer unmerited disappointment (Hayek, 1976:71). Activities which serve no demands or needs are eliminated in a process of adaptation. If nature is brutal in the constant struggle for survival, the market should be the same. The price of progress is, as with nature, that some must be sacrificed.

Hayek (1989) differentiates between two distinct types of evolutionary process: biological and cultural evolution. Both are perfectly natural processes. But even though they are analogous in important ways, they are not identical and possess important differences. All cultural development rests on inheritance, but in contrast to biological evolution, this is inheritance of acquired characteristics, 'in the form of rules guiding the mutual relations among individuals which are not innate but learnt' (Hayek, 1989:25).

Cultural evolution is thus brought about through transmission of habits, customs, practice and information, 'not merely from the individual's physical parents, but from an indefinite number of "ancestors"' (Hayek, 1989:25). The process furthering the transmission and spreading of cultural properties by learning, makes cultural evolution comparatively faster than biological evolution (Hayek, 1989:23–5). Finally, cultural evolution operates largely through group selection (Hayek, 1989:25). Rules are observed because in fact they give the group in which they are practised 'superior strength', and not because this effect is known to those who are guided by them (Hayek, 1973:19).

Hayek's anti-constructivism is directed towards culturally transmitted rules. They should not be the object of rational calculation. The rationalist who wants to subject everything to human reason is faced with a real dilemma, according to Hayek: 'The use of reason aims at control and predictability. But the process of the advance of reason rests on freedom and the unpredictability of human action' (Hayek, 1960:38). In the same way that controlling the evolution of nature will lead to unintended negative consequences, control over the evolution of society will result in the same.

All of the problems claimed by ecocentrists and human welfare ecologists to be special for environmental problems, thus also appear in this perspective. Not only are spontaneous orders seen as highly interpenetrated, they have emergent properties, self-regulating qualities, and – like ecosystems – are dynamic with homeostasis, adaptiveness and succession. Any attempt to tamper with spontaneous orders to achieve a specific goal (such as social equity or sustainable development), faces the same circumstances that characterise ecological problems such as complexity, non-reducibility, temporal variability (both in space and time), uncertainty and collectivity.

There is an important difference, however, and that is the claimed vulnerability or lack of homeostasis in spontaneous orders: 'Attempts to "correct" the order of the market will lead to its destruction' (Hayek, 1976:142). Directing individuals towards common visible purposes (like sustainable development) must in Hayek's view produce a totalitarian society (Hayek, 1976:147).[9] Hence, spontaneous orders seem to be far more vulnerable than ecosystems, and this vulnerability makes it dangerous and undesirable to attempt to construct or plan a society according to given objectives.

Instead, the role of the state is to secure the conditions for the functioning of spontaneous orders. Two mechanisms of change are given: natural selection and the invisible hand. This is the only way to avoid the problem of ignorance. But the consequences of refraining from attempts to control society are overwhelming:

> Since a spontaneous order results from the individual elements adapting themselves to circumstances which directly affect only some of them, and which in their totality need not be known to anyone, it may extend to circumstances so complex that no mind can comprehend them all (Hayek, 1973:41).

The best management strategy is therefore the same as for nature: The best management is the least management. 'Not do' and 'hands off'. Not nature – but the market and society. *Laissez-faire*: letting things be and flowing with the market rather than forcing the market. Intelligence with; rather than control over. These are the conclusions drawn in the neoliberal perspective. But just as with the complexity of nature, it is not obvious why the two mechanisms of change – natural selection and the invisible hand – necessarily should lead to a preferred state of being. The claim that 'the market knows best' seems no more convincing than the claim that 'nature knows best'.

7.5   WHO DOES KNOW BEST?

There is no doubt a striking similarity between the ecocentric/human welfare ecology view of nature and the neoliberal view of spontaneous orders. In the one perspective, the market knows best; in the other, nature knows best. These two positions seem impossible to reconcile. But what implications can be drawn from the problem of ignorance? To what extent can ignorance support a conclusion of letting things be or keeping hands off nature or society? To what extent is it reasonable to expect that a minimising of intervention in nature or spontaneous orders will lead to a preferred state of being or sustainable development?

As Dryzek points out, the thesis that nature knows best, at the extreme, implies that the spontaneity of ecosystems is best left alone. Accepting that nature knows best implies that nature is superior in system design and maintenance. Any such argument, according to Dryzek, can provide the basis for a total respect for nature and all its work (Dryzek, 1987:44).

It is when human interests and needs are drawn into the picture that 'nature knows best' becomes problematic. Nature will do very well without humans, while humans are dependent on nature's life-support systems to survive. Humans thus have to intervene in nature to be able to meet human needs. At the extreme, 'nature knows best' seems to resolve the antagonistic relationship between humans and nature, but at human expense.

The claim that 'nature knows best' is, as Commoner also pointed out, a rather extreme claim. But the claim that any man-made change in a natural system is likely to be detrimental to that system, has merit if understood only in a properly defined context. Since the structure of a present living thing or the organisation of a current natural ecosystem has gone through years of natural selection and evolution, nature is probably 'best' in the following sense: the artificial introduction of an organic compound that does not occur in nature, but is man-made, is very likely to be harmful (Commoner, 1972).

Hence, 'nature knows best' has a very specific, but limited, meaning. The idea does not say that any man-made organic compound that does not occur in nature will be harmful. It says that *risks* will *probably* be lower if one utilises already existing organic compounds in nature. It does not exclude the possibilities of scientific research and empirical testing of such man-made compounds. This is, therefore, not an 'absolute law', but a rule of prudence. Whether a man-made organic compound is harmful or not is an empirical question and not a metaphysical one.

What further implications can one draw from the problem of ignorance? Lundström's (1992) analysis of Hayek's anti-rationalism is highly instructive in answering this question. Anti-rationalism represents a deeper form of wisdom, according to Hayek, because it recognises the limits of human rationality (Hayek, 1973:29). Attempts to realise specific collective goals (like sustainable development or social equity) will only lead to the opposite of what is intended. If progress is to be secured, society must be maintained as a spontaneous order. This requires the abstention from the use of political means to realise specific goals, even though these may seem necessary (Hayek, 1973:61). Society should not, and cannot, be managed rationally according to specific goals, but must be allowed to evolve spontaneously. This is the core of Hayek's anti-rational evolutionism.

But what conclusions can be drawn from a claim about the limits of human rationality? As Hayek himself argues:

We know little of the particular facts to which the whole of social activity continuously adjusts itself in order to provide what we have learned to expect. We know even less of the forces which bring about this adjustment by appropriately co-ordinating individual activity (Hayek, 1960:25).

It is as Lundström points out, the thesis of tacit knowledge that leads to an anti-rationalist stance toward political and social institutions. Anti-rationalism, however, faces a basic paradox according to Lundström:

> We cannot know how we can reach a goal. But if we admit our lack of knowledge, we will reach it. This paradox leads to a fundamental theoretical dilemma in Hayek's entire political philosophy: if it has practical implications, it is basically rationalistic and constructivistic. If it doesn't have practical implications, it is metaphysical and fatalistic (Lundström, 1992:9).

This paradox can also be expressed the following way: how can something which is tacit be known? What reason does one have for believing that tacit knowledge can lead to optimal behaviour? Hayek and other neoliberals have no problem with formulating concrete policy recommendations. This, however, is an expression of a goal-oriented rationality. It contradicts, *prima facie*, Hayek's anti-rationalism, and points towards the conclusion that Hayek himself is a constructivist.

Further, it is difficult, according to Lundström, to see how Hayek's own thesis can stand above the evolutionary relativism he claims characterises all human knowledge. Hayek ends up, therefore, in the paradox of self-reference. The empirical judgements that Hayek makes on the limits of human rationality must be restricted by the same relativity and incompleteness as all empirical judgements. To avoid being self-defeating,

> it needs to imply a statement of facts – a statement that optimal actions cannot be chosen through conscious, rational calculation, but rather they are reached through blindly following cultural rules. The content of the thesis of tacit knowledge then is not tacit, but rather articulated and conscious. (Lundström, 1992:19)

Statements about the possibility of rationally controlling social processes are, according to Lundström, empirical and not epistemological:

> A declaration that certain measures cause certain effects are either true or false....If one argues that there are limits for human rationality, this can be interpreted either epistemologically or empirically. But an epistemological limitation does not imply an empirical limitation. It is one thing not to be able to see *Das Ding an Sich* and quite another not to be able

to predict the effects of a particular economic policy (Lundström, 1992:13–14).

The fact that there will always be phenomena that one will never understand does not lead to any practical conclusions as long as one cannot set limits for the unknown (Lundström, 1992:16). The view expressed in the ecocentric perspectives of Eckersley, Devall and Sessions – that nature is quite possibly more complex, in principle, than we *can* know – can be approached in the same way. If nature is more complex than we can know, this does not lead to any practical consequences, as long as the limits for the unknown are not set. Nor does the fact that there is a *Ding an Sich* imply that one should refrain from trying to extend conscious empirical knowledge of both market processes and nature. 'Nature knows best' can either be interpreted epistemologically – thus being metaphysical and fatalistic without practical implications – or it can be interpreted empirically, thus being rationalistic and constructivistic with practical implications. But then again, it will contain the same relativity and incompleteness that all empirical judgements do, and the law that nature knows best can at 'best' only be a rule of prudence. Both of the above perspectives in their most extreme positions – implying total respect for either market or nature – seem to offer little guidance for how to realise a path towards sustainable development.

7.6 THE ETHICAL INJUNCTIONS OF SUSTAINABLE DEVELOPMENT

Appealing to the authority of nature (as known by ecology), or to spontaneous human orders, is no substitute for ethical argument. Ecological science cannot perform the task of normative justification (Eckersley, 1992:59), and neither can theories of spontaneous orders. Sustainable development as advocated in *Our Common Future* undoubtedly has an anthropocentric bias. The satisfaction of human needs and aspirations are the major objectives of sustainable development (WCED, 1987:43). But even though this is seen as the primary goal, the report does not claim that it is the *only* goal. It should instead be seen as the point of departure, or initial understanding of sustainable development.

The Brundtland Report explicitly argues that the conservation of nature does not rest solely on an anthropocentric ethics: 'It is part of our moral obligation to other living beings and future generations' (WCED, 1987:57).[10] Does this mean that these obligations are internal to the concept of sustainable development? *Our Common Future* does not elaborate further on this, and it is unclear as to how this is to be understood. But the above passage can be seen as an extension of the meaning of sustainable development.

As pointed out in Chapter 1, *Our Common Future* argues that loss of plant and animal species can limit the options of future generations. Conservation of nature is, therefore, justified within an anthropocentric perspective as an 'equal opportunity principle' between generations. This constitutes an inherent part of the concept.

The non-anthropocentric extension seems, however, more difficult to encompass in the above framework. Non-anthropocentric ethics directly challenge the human-centred approach, and it is not at all clear if this is a possible extension at all. One could argue that these two perspectives are mutually exclusive (Dobson, 1996).

This need not be the case, however. It is in fact possible to argue that even non-anthropocentric ethics, like deep ecology and ecocentrism, are biased towards human beings, and thus compatible with the major objective of development – the satisfaction of human needs and aspirations (Luke, 1988; Grey, 1993; Wells, 1993; Seippel and Langhelle, 1993). As the founder of deep ecology, Næss (1984) argues that human needs, goals and desires are sometimes to be taken as privileged and overriding – but no precise, general answer can be given for *when* human interests are to override non-human interests (Næss, 1984:267).

It is thus unclear to what degree and in what direction an inclusion of non-anthropocentric ethics changes the actual content of sustainable development and its policy implications. It is questionable if the division between anthropocentric and non-anthropocentric ethics amounts to anything else than giving different arguments for the same things. As Eckersley (1992) also argues, the philosophical differences between ecocentric and green anthropocentric theorists should not obscure the commonalities between the two.

This is, however, what Eckersley's 'litmus test' for ecopolitical issues seems to do (Eckersley, 1992:29). It is by no means clear why similar conclusions on issues of human population growth and wilderness preservation cannot be justified in both perspectives (Wells, 1993). As Norton (1986) argues, the distinction between anthropocentric and non-anthropocentric motives loses importance as emphasis is placed on long-term values to protect biological diversity. Both a long-term reduction in the number of people on earth and the preservation of large tracts of wilderness can be justified within a pure anthropocentric perspective.

Our Common Future argues that species conservation is not only justifiable in economic terms: 'Aesthetic, ethical, cultural, and scientific considerations provide ample grounds for conservation. But for those who demand an accounting, the economic values inherent in the genetic materials of species are alone enough to justify species preservation' (WCED, 1987:155). The problem, according to Eckersley, is that if we restrict our perspective to an anthropocentric ethic, we can provide no protection to those species that are of no present or potential use or interest to humankind (Eckersley, 1992:38). Ecocentrism, with its recognition of the interrelatedness of all phenomena and *prima facie* orientation of inclusiveness of all beings, is, therefore, far more protective of the Earth's life-support system (Eckersley, 1992:52).

But protecting the Earth's life-support system is seen as the minimum requirement for sustainable development in the human-welfare approach of *Our Common Future*. Furthermore, the interrelatedness of all phenomena is also part of the ecological understanding of human welfare ecology. It is therefore highly problematic to decide which species are of present or potential use or interest to humankind, since species can play important roles in the functioning of ecosystems, regardless of their direct present or potential use or even interest to humankind. 'All species are therefore important and deserve some degree of attention' (WCED, 1987:165). The goal advocated by *Our Common Future* is to preserve a representative sample of the Earth's ecosystems, which, in practice, can mean that the total expanse of protected areas should be at least tripled (WCED, 1987:166).

In addition, an ecocentric perspective allows 'all entities (including humans) the freedom to unfold their own way unhindered by the various forms of human domination' (Eckersley, 1992:53). But how are we to do this in practice? 'Nature', in many cases, is not something untouched by humans, but partly 'man-made'. One example is the cultural landscape along the coast of Europe facing the Atlantic Ocean. At one point in time, this stretched from Portugal in the south to Lofoten in the North Norway. The cultural landscape was created by coastal farmers who removed forest and vegetation through scorching and turning pasture over to domestic animals.

This form of livelihood is over 4000 years old. Today, these areas are on the verge of disappearing because this form of livelihood is displaced by modern farming methods. According to Kaland and Brekke (1994), this, together with air pollution, has led to there being almost no moors south of Denmark. This is because cultural landscapes, like ecosystems, 'break down completely when the form of livelihood is discontinued, with its consequences for plant and animal life' (Kaland and Brekke 1994:17–18).

Even an ecocentric approach then, cannot avoid the choices as to which type of 'nature' or ecosystem one wants to preserve. If everything is allowed to evolve in its own way, moors will, in time, transform to forests, and disappear. As such, 'letting things be' or 'hands off' provides few guidelines for making such a choice. In light of Eckersley's conclusion that the ecological crisis can be solved, at least temporarily, without the cultivation of an ecocentric culture (Eckersley, 1992:185), the differences between anthropocentric and non-anthropocentric ethics seem exaggerated.

If this is so, the incorporation of non-anthropocentric ethics within the framework of sustainable development seems plausible. As Skirbekk (1994) points out, the practical difference is, in many cases, not between a comprehensive ethical anthropocentrism and ethical gradualism (as proposed by Skirbekk, 1994, and Wetlesen, 1991), but between an ecologically uninformed, short-term and local anthropocentrism on the one hand, and an ecologically well-informed, long-term and global anthropocentrism on the other (Skirbekk, 1994:116; Seippel, 1995; Seippel and Lafferty, 1996). As Wells (1993) argues, even if we accept an anthropocentric analysis, this does not imply that the approach must be short-sighted or uninformed. The case for preservation of the environment does not, therefore, depend on a particularly pure view of ethical obligations to the natural world (Wells, 1993:526).

7.7 NEOLIBERALISM AS ECOLOGICALLY UNINFORMED ANTHROPOCENTRISM?

Does neo-liberalism thus constitute an ecologically uninformed, short-term and local anthropocentrism? According to Eckersley (1993), free-market environmentalism has four principal characteristics: (1) it is sceptical towards the idea of limits to growth; (2) it is an unrestrained development philosophy; (3) it is characterised by a scientific and technological optimism, and a general belief that human ingenuity will solve any ecological problems; (4) it emphasises material values (Eckersley, 1993:9).

Our Common Future is often claimed to be biased towards economic growth (Reid, 1995). There is a difference, however, between free-market environmentalism and the approach of the World Commission. In *Our Common Future*, the ultimate limits to global development are determined by the availability of energy resources and the biosphere's capacity to absorb the by-products of energy use. These energy limits may be approached far sooner than the limits imposed by other material resources (WCED, 1987:58).

In the neoliberal approach, the belief in human ingenuity is what leads to a different view on the limits to growth and development. Neoliberals must be said to have an incredible faith in the human mind: 'As long as liberal society exists, this resource (the human mind) is inexhaustible and can readily replace or find substitutes for all other 'natural' resources. The incredible ingenuity of the human mind is the solution, not the problem. Rather than shackle it, we must free it to create new miracles' (Smith and Jeffreys, 1993:392).

A 'new miracle' would, according to Smith and Jeffreys, be cold fusion. This could potentially offer mankind limitless, inexpensive and clean energy, a prospect which leads the two authors to the following conclusion: 'It is not much of an exaggeration to say that if human ingenuity were supplied with unlimited energy, anything would be possible' (Smith and Jeffreys, 1993:394). As such, neoliberalism, or free-market environmentalism, differs both from the human welfare ecology approach of *Our Common Future* and from ecocentrism in their views of limits to growth.

If neoliberals are pessimistic with respect to the management of human spontaneous orders, they are extremely optimistic with regard to the management of nature. The belief that we can readily replace or find substitutes for all other 'natural' resources seems, however, hopelessly at odds with the epistemological foundation of the Hayekian perspective. Not only do the limits of human rationality disappear when they go from society to nature, but they have managed to identify what, according to Hayek, is 'impossible' – the operating principles of both human and natural spontaneous orders.

In the view of the neoliberals, environmental problems are not conceived as market failures, but rather as examples of the failure to allow markets to exist (Smith and Jeffreys, 1993:392). Since free markets are naturally self-correcting, the risks to future generations arise not from exposure *to* capitalism but from exclusion *from* it (Smith and Jeffreys, 1993:392). Spontaneity is, as with ecosystems, a property of human orders, and makes it possible to handle problems without deliberate human (state) interference. If all of nature is integrated into the market, the problems will resolve themselves.

The followers of Hayek, to the extent that they acknowledge the existence of environmental problems, prescribe a three-fold strategy for solving them: (1) turning nature into a market by dispensing property rights; (2) the enforcement of property rights; and (3) technological 'fixes'. This strategy is linked to what Hayek calls 'the inseparable trinity', namely law, liberty and property (Hayek, 1973:107, DiLorenzo, 1993).[11]

If sustainable development was shorn of all its redistributive implications, this strategy could be interpreted as an neo-Hayekian accommodation to the concept. The state would maintain a framework of universal rules within which individuals could pursue their goals, and where the framework would include rules to prevent environmental damage that threatened global life-support systems (Meadowcroft, 1997). But as John Gray (1993) points out, 'there are areas where the extension of property rights is enviable or merely too costly to be reasonably envisaged' (Gray, 1993:133, Eckersley 1996). Who, we might ask, are going to own the oceans or the atmosphere?

As long as problems of species extinction, energy limits and climate change are not acknowledged, however, the neoliberal strategy hardly qualifies – in the view of *Our Common Future* – as a sustainable development strategy. It seems that it is the belief in the self-correcting forces of human spontaneous orders, and the 'impossibility' of market institutions being self-defeating, which colours the scepticism found in much neoliberal literature towards the existence of environmental problems. This is especially true for climate change. It is thus not scepticism towards science *per se*, but the rationality of (free) markets that seems to be at stake. If the market creates life-threatening environmental problems, or in any other way is self-defeating, this is devastating to the thesis of the rationality of spontaneous orders. The scientific findings of IPCC (1995), and the growing scientific consensus that species are disappearing at rates never before witnessed on our planet (WCED, 1987:148), fit badly with the rationality of human spontaneous orders in the neoliberal view.

Even more problematic, however, is the fact that there is no 'system' in the neoliberal perspective which would be able to correct the market in a proper way. The scepticism towards state interference is so deep that one could wonder how the state could manage the task of distributing property rights at all. If spontaneous orders fail, humanity is doomed in the neoliberal perspective. Hence, capitalism 'must come first' (Smith and Jeffreys, 1993:398).

7.8   SCIENCE – FRIEND OR FOE?

Greens are, however, also ambivalent about science. Much Green environmental thinking has been highly critical to science and technology. This stems partly from the role they have played in bringing about ecological problems. Humans (or scientists) invented CFCs, nuclear power, pesticides and so forth, and scientists may be viewed as active collaborators in our society's ecological destruction (Yearley, 1992:514).

Despite this, the environmental movement has become more and more dependent upon the information and knowledge produced by science, both in the identification and description of environmental problems, as well as the prescription of solutions (Beck, 1992). As Yearley (1992) points out, the ozone layer is only available as an object of knowledge because of our scientific culture. It is, therefore, misleading to claim (as Eckersley does), that the environmental crisis is the result of a misguided trust in our capacity to understand biospheric processes completely (Eckersley, 1992:156). It could just as well be the contrary. Because we have not understood biospheric processes and the possible impacts of anthropogenic emissions, these problems have been allowed to escalate.

Modern western science is further accused of being anthropocentric, instrumental, atomistic, technocentric and containing 'scientism' – the conviction that empirical-analytic science is the only valid way of knowing (Eckersley, 1992:51). Science itself, however, is rooted in uncertainty. Theories and empirical findings can always be questioned, criticised and in the end abandoned. Both theories and empirical judgements contain relativity and incompleteness. Science hardly offers certainty. In Anthony Giddens' (1994) perspective, science can offer a sense of security only when risk is seen as external risk. It is different, however, with what Giddens refers to as manufactured uncertainty:

> Manufactured uncertainty...has quite different connotations – for science, technology and industry are at the very origins of it. Some may start to mistrust science and retreat from modern industry. Yet science and technology are the only means of bringing their own damage into view. Ecological

thinkers develop their critiques only by presuming an apparatus of science and the whole social infrastructure which goes with it. Many look to the very forms of science and technology which in other contexts they attack to define for them what 'nature' is (Giddens, 1994:208).

Giddens' conclusion is thus clear: 'We cannot escape from scientific-technological civilisation, no matter what "green nostalgias" it tends to provoke. Living in an era of manufactured risks, means confronting the fact that the "side-effects" of technical innovations are side-effects no longer' (Giddens, 1994:212). Science is thus indispensable in modern society. It does not, however, imply that the role of science should not be criticised or questioned, or that science is the only solution to environmental problems. They cannot be solved just through the introduction of even more science and technology (Giddens, 1994:223).

But there is another possible problem with the increase of scientific knowledge which Hayek points to; that is, that the range of acknowledged ignorance will grow – not decline – with the advance of science. This because the more men know, the smaller the share of knowledge that can possibly be absorbed by one single mind. More knowledge thus creates new obstacles to the management of nature: 'While the growth of our knowledge of nature constantly discloses new realms of ignorance, the increasing complexity of the civilisation which this knowledge enables us to build presents new obstacles to the intellectual comprehension of the world around us' (Hayek, 1960:26).

The more we know about nature, the more difficult a sound management of nature could turn out to be. Even more knowledge could thus have its unwarranted effects. But science and technology are part of a solution to environmental problems, even though science cannot tell us what we want with our lives and what kind of society we want to live in. Appealing to the authority of nature (as known by ecology), or spontaneous human orders, cannot substitute ethical argument and political deliberation. Neither can it perform the task of normative justification.

7.9   CONCLUDING REMARKS

The problem of ignorance, the possibilities of rationally controlling social and natural processes, and unwarranted effects of human intervention in both society and nature, constitute, in one sense, problems without a solution. Understood epistemologically, these problems are simply something we will have to live with. Risks and uncertainty are inherent to modern society. They cannot be escaped. What we know for certain is that we don't know what the future will bring. But leaving development to nature or the market (or to spontaneous orders more generally) does not solve the problem of ignorance. Do we have any reason to believe that non-interference automatically will lead to a sustainable development path? What about possible unwarranted effects of non-intervention?

There is no doubt that sustainable development will require intervention in both human and natural systems. To do so, science is an indispensable tool, and the unwarranted effects of technical innovations, anthropogenic emissions, economic policies, social policies, and so forth, are being both identified and brought into the public arena. These empirical findings constitute the foundation of future politics and the policies of sustainable development. One should, therefore, not refrain from trying to extend conscious empirical knowledge of both market processes and nature. The problem of ignorance, approached empirically, is what makes planning for sustainable development possible. We know a great deal about what is necessary for solving environment and development problems. The problem of climate change, species extinction, global poverty and so forth, are not problems which we face blindfolded and in total ignorance.

The empirical foundation, however, constitutes only one, although a crucial, part of sustainable development. Sustainable development is also an ethical system which partly defines what the goal of future development should be: meeting the needs of the present without compromising the ability of future generations to meet their own needs. As such, sustainable development is a guiding principle for human interaction with both natural and human systems. By prescribing society as a natural system, or a socially purposeless order, neo-liberals conceal the fact that market institutions, except in their most rudimentary forms, are not natural phenomena – the spontaneous results of human actions – but artefacts of law and creatures of government (Gray, 1993:135). Government is 'the superintendence of market institutions', with the aim of ensuring that market institutions are not self-defeating (Johnston, 1989).

Just as 'nature knows best' implies, in its extreme, total respect for nature in all its work, 'market knows best' undermines possible and necessary goal-oriented collective action. Integrating environmental and developmental concerns raises new challenges for planning and management. And although both natural and human systems are complex, this does not necessarily imply that problems are insoluble. Planning and management are not contingent on superhumans, but on humans who are capable of acknowledging problems, seeking new solutions and acting collectively. This is what the realisation of sustainable development is all about.

NOTES

1. If it had not been like this, it would, according to Eriksen, have been unthinkable that a social-democratic head of state like Gro Harlem Brundtland could be 'one of the idea's foremost champions' (Eriksen, 1992:140).

2. The antagonism between these two groupings is clearly expressed in the following: 'Greens have been some of the most vociferous critics of such neoconservative ideologies as American Reaganism, British Thatcherism, and their respective successors. Not surprisingly, emancipatory theorists have passed over conservatism (traditional and neo-) as a source of political enlightenment' (Eckersley, 1992:22).

3. Eckersley seems to prefer the expression 'socially just and ecologically sustainable society' (Eckersley, 1992:30). This is, however, in accordance with the concept of sustainable development in *Our Common Future*. (See introduction.)

4. In recent years, Dryzek has shifted towards an ecocentric direction. See Dryzek, 'Strategies of Ecological Democratisation', in Lafferty and Meadowcroft (1996).

5. A 'social choice mechanism' is defined as 'a means through which society – whether local, national, supranational, or global – determines collective outcomes (i.e. outcomes which can apply to all its members) in a given domain' (Dryzek, 1987:7). Dryzek evaluates seven different existing social choice mechanisms. These are: market, administered system, law, moral persuasion, polyarchy, bargaining, armed conflict. Radical decentralisation and practical reason are two social choice mechanisms advocated by Dryzek. These are not existing social choice mechanisms, but social choice mechanisms which could be designed (see Dryzek, 1987:179–84).

6. In Dryzek's view, human social systems are not exactly like ecosystems. If nothing else, human social systems contain only one species. This argument, however, does not necessarily make social systems less complex than ecosystems. But as Dryzek also notes: 'Social systems and ecosystems may have their parallels, but so do social systems and electrical systems' (Dryzek, 1987:41).

7. Hayek stresses that this is not borrowed from biology, but in fact the other way round: 'Since the emphasis we shall have to place on the role that selection plays in this process of social evolution today is likely to create the impression that we are borrowing the idea from biology, it is worth stressing that it was, in fact, the other way round: there can be little doubt that it was from the theories of social evolution that Darwin and his contemporaries derived the suggestions for their theories' (Hayek, 1960:59). In *The Fatal Conceit* (1989), Hayek makes the following point: 'recent examinations of Charles Darwin's notebooks ... suggest that his reading of Adam Smith in the crucial year 1838 led Darwin to his decisive breakthrough' (1989:24, 146). The editor, though, W.W. Bartley III, has added the following: 'There does not appear to be any evidence that Darwin read *The Wealth of Nations*. - Ed.' (p. 24n1).

8. In *Rules and Order* (1973:36) Hayek gives the following definition of an order: 'a state of affairs in which a multiplicity of elements of various kinds are so related to each other that we may learn from our acquaintance with some spatial or temporal part of the whole to form correct expectations concerning the rest, or at least expectations which have a good chance of proving correct'.

9. It is doubtful whether spontaneous orders are as vulnerable as Hayek has claimed. The mixed economy and welfare state of Norway cannot in any meaningful sense of the word be said to have led to a totalitarian society.
10. That there are other reasons for conservation is also stated in the following: 'there are also moral, ethical, cultural, aesthetic, and purely scientific reasons for conserving wild beings' (WCED 1987:13).
11. As Thomas DiLorenzo states in the article, 'The Mirage of Sustainable Development' (*The Futurist*, Sept./Oct. 1993): 'Private property, free markets and sound liability laws...are essential for a clean environment, and for economic growth.'

8 Sustainable Development: Caught between National Sovereignty and International Challenges

Jon Birger Skjærseth

8.1 INTRODUCTION

The Brundtland Commission's Report *Our Common Future* and the follow-up *Agenda 21* place their main emphasis on defining the content of sustainable development. (The concept of sustainable development will not be discussed in this chapter. The main focus will be on how goals related to the environment and development may be achieved through international co-operation, independent of the concrete content of these goals.) How common objectives may be achieved in practice through international co-operation has been given lower priority. The main problem with the institutional reforms that are actually proposed is that they do not take seriously the principle of the right to national self-determination as a fundamental limitation in international environmental co-operation. This principle holds important implications for what is realistic to aim for in the international arena. *Agenda 21* advocates more binding international co-operation. Ironically, it is not binding within the framework of international law. The main issue in this chapter is what limitations are set by the principle of national sovereignty on realising the international institutional reforms proposed in *Agenda 21* and *Our Common Future*.[1]

I shall first look closer into the consequences of the right to national self-determination for international co-operation in environmental conservation. Briefly, the main problem is that international environmental agreements that aim to solve common problems must conform to the individual country's own interests – often to countries that are the least enthusiastic. After which, I shall go into the Brundtland Commission's proposal on the following institutional reforms:

- integration of environmental concerns in all affected sectors;
- improvement of links between science and politics;

- an increase in effective international co-operation;
- an increase in binding international co-operation.

The proposals here are organised so that they correspond to different phases in a typical international environmental co-operation: lack of integration of environmental concerns are an important cause of the problems; science is necessary to diagnose the problems; effective international co-operation is important for arriving at common decisions on solutions; while the extent of obligation has consequences on whether resolutions are implemented and international agreements are complied with. These proposals will be taken up in Section 8.3. In the conclusion, I shall briefly discuss the principle of national sovereignty and some possible short-cuts around this principle.

8.2   TRANSNATIONAL ENVIRONMENTAL PROBLEMS AND THE RIGHT TO NATIONAL SELF-DETERMINATION

There are over one hundred and fifty international environmental agreements based on the principle of the right to national self-determination. Even though some have functioned relatively well, there are few, if any that have been adequate to solve the problems that they have been established for. Even though no country will gain from an ecological breakdown in the long term, it is often the material self-interest that weighs the most when concrete alternative solutions are proposed. Experience from international environmental negotiations clearly shows that material interests are important. During the 1987 Montreal Protocol negotiations on the fight against ozone-depleting substances, it went so far that UNEP's (United Nations Environment Programme) General Secretary, Mustafa Tolba, declared that 'everything is about who will get an advantage in relation to whom: whether Du Pont will gain, relative to European companies' (*New Scientist*, 1988:25). Great Britain has been given the appellation 'The Dirty Man of Europe'. Among other things, this is because it has been a 'laggard' in Northeast Atlantic co-operation. In the North Sea, the ocean currents flow anti-clockwise. Effluent from Great Britain and the continent is transported from the southern part of the North Sea up towards Skagerrak and the Norwegian coast. Thus, Great Britain is very little affected by its own actions, and is less interested in stricter regulations. On the other hand, Norway, is lying downstream and involuntarily imports pollution through both sea and air. Therefore, Norway has clear material interests in influencing other countries to reduce their effluents.

But it is not only different material interests that create disagreement in international environmental co-operation. Different traditions, norms and political ideologies are also important. Even if we moved the Norwegian state and society to the British Isles, it would be quite unlikely that Norway would have initiated a 'British' environmental policy, despite having the same interests.

The significance of political ideologies are, for example, an important explanation why the EU has not succeeded in introducing a common carbon and energy tax. Great Britain has time and again put its foot down, not because it will be a big loser in the economic sense, but because it is an opponent in principle of (environmental) taxes in the EU.

Against this, one may hold up *Agenda 21*, which is the result of negotiations among 171 countries, as an example that it is actually possible for sovereign states to agree on a comprehensive set of common international guidelines.[2] On one hand, there is little doubt that *Agenda 21* contains several sensible objectives that, through the UNCED (United Nations Conference on Environment and Development) process, has been given both weight and legitimacy. On the other hand, the fact that it is not binding has meant that many countries have not been willing to commit to implementing measures for 'sustainable' development. Moreover, both the initiatives and objectives in *Agenda 21* are very generally formulated. A combination of the lack of both concreteness and bindingness makes this a 'tame' set of principles that allow the countries themselves to define the follow-up.

For example, few countries will disagree with an environmental convention whose goal is to hinder a type of pollution. The problem is, however, that different countries often have totally different interpretations of what it is to hinder pollution in practice. As a rule, different interpretations correspond to different interests. In the co-operation on North-eastern Atlantic Ocean pollution, for example, some countries were of the opinion that to prevent pollution was the same as to reduce the effluent of potential polluting substances. Others were of the opinion that one had to have empirical proof that each single one of these substances had a damaging effect before they would discuss pollution. This conflict handicapped the co-operation for almost ten years. Common agreement on general non-binding principles is often a necessary first step, but one should not have illusions that harmony will prevail when principles are turned into concrete measures.

If one accepts that self-interest becomes more important when words are transformed to action, then this may also explain to a certain extent why some transnational environmental problems are 'solved' more effectively than others. This can be illustrated by the fact that the world community has agreed to phase out the most ozone-damaging substances, while it was not possible to attain more than a stabilisation of emission in the new Climate Convention of 1992, even though researchers had arrived at the conclusion that CO_2 emissions had to be reduced by 60 per cent to stabilise the level of greenhouse gases in the atmosphere.[3]

The emission of ozone-depleting gases is a problem that affects all countries. No country will gain from increased ultraviolet radiation, and a population with a weakened immune defence system will have a higher frequency of skin cancer. Moreover, it has been relatively easy and cheap to find substitute substances for the most important ozone-depleting gases. Furthermore, these gases have no critical significance to the economy of the OECD countries, and there were only 17 chemical companies in 16 countries that produced chlorofluorocarbon (CFC). Therefore, it is no coincidence that the 58 countries that were responsible for 99 per cent of the world's CFC production in 1990 agreed to phase out all CFC within the year 2000. These goals have since been intensified and emissions have been reduced drastically.[4] But it is impossible to say whether this will solve the problem. The atmosphere needs a long time to get rid of ozone-depleting gases. Even if all emissions are halted today, the depletion of the ozone layer will continue for almost another one hundred years.

The greenhouse effect however, is a more difficult problem. The effects of global warming are very uncertain. Moreover, there is speculation that some countries will 'gain' from a warmer climate, while others will 'lose'. For example, small island states in the Pacific fear that they will disappear into the sea, while other countries expect a larger harvest. In other words, the effects of climate change are assumed to be quite different for different countries. Just as problematic is the fact that the solutions to such problems require comprehensive energy-political measures that affect the very core of modern economies. The climate problem is hence a more difficult political problem than ozone depletion. Another important factor is related to the level of know-how and degree of uncertainty. The identification of transnational environmental problems and the formulation of initiatives are closely related to science and the generation of expertise. Researchers know a great deal about the causes and effects of some problems, while there is great uncertainty surrounding other problems. Besides, the extent of disagreement among researchers varies from country to country regarding different problems. Therefore, we may conclude that some 'common' problems are politically and scientifically more 'malign' than others. This is an important explanation of why some problems are 'solved' more effectively than others. But there is also reason to believe that different types of co-operation vary in effectiveness. In other words, some institutional settings are more effective than others. It is in the area of ambiguity between the right to national self-determination, national preferences and various institutional settings, that we should evaluate the institutional reforms proposed in the Brundtland Report and made concrete to some extent in *Agenda 21*.

8.3   PROPOSALS FOR INSTITUTIONAL REFORMS

Chapter 12 of *Our Common Future* is dedicated to proposals for institutional and legal reforms for realising common actions. The evaluation of existing institutional settings is very critical:

Attempts to maintain social and ecological stability through old approaches to development and environmental protection will increase instability. Security must be sought through change (WCED, 1987:308).

With this as a premise, the report ascertains that the time is ripe to break with earlier patterns. The main idea is that new institutions should be aimed at the causes of problems, and not just symptoms. The most important proposal is that sustainable development should be an integrated part of the mandate to central departments, international organisations and large private organisations. Even though the main emphasis is placed on integrating environmental concerns at the national level, the integration of environmental and development policies should also be a main objective in existing international institutions (*Agenda 21*, Chapters 38 and 39).

Secondly, it is also proposed that international environmental policy to a great extent should be based on science. The main idea here is that one should make informed choices – that is to say, political prioritisation should be based on the best available knowledge (WCED, 1987:326–7 and *Agenda 21*, Chapter 35).

The third point may be consolidated under the designation, 'more effective international co-operation on environmental protection'. The economic capacity connected with international bodies should be increased to transfer more resources, technology and know-how, particularly to developing countries. This is a critical condition for getting these countries to join in implementing common objectives when they themselves have no resources for follow-up (WCED, 1987 and *Agenda 21*, Chapter 37). Increasing the scope of participation in international co-operation is also proposed. Both voluntary organisations and industry should be included in order to play important roles. This is also a recurring point in *Agenda 21*. The fourth proposal is based on the fact that it is not desirable to 'maintain an international system that cannot prevent one or several states from damaging the ecological basis for development' (WCED, 1987: 313). The prescription here is that 'The international legal framework must also be significantly strengthened in support of sustainable development' (WCED, 1987:312). How this is to be done concretely is elaborated on. *Agenda 21* advocates binding resolutions that take all countries' special needs and interests into consideration. Furthermore, it proposes a strengthening of international conflict-solving mechanisms where appropriate, and which all countries agree on (*Agenda 21*, Chapter 39). This clearly shows that *Agenda 21* is based on the principle of national sovereignty and the veto rights of all countries.

8.4 HOW TO TACKLE THE CAUSES – INTEGRATION OF DIFFERENT SECTORS INTERNATIONALLY

Most environmental problems are caused by legitimate activities within various social sectors in each individual country. For example, agricultural and transport policies have consequences for the emission of greenhouse gases. Therefore, the solutions to such problems are dependent on all affected sectors being included such that environmental concerns are made the basis at the early phase of the decision-making process. The same argument is also relevant at the international level where other types of international co-operation have consequences for the environment. It is not necessarily the international environmental institutions that have the greatest potential to influence transnational environmental problems. Institutions that attempt to regulate world economy and trade are at least equally important. Even though the advantage of integrating environmental concerns in such institutions is evident, it appears that it is very difficult to put into practice due to at least two reasons. Firstly, many countries see environmental requirements that are linked to trade and economic co-operation as unacceptable meddling in national prioritisation. Secondly, purely organisational conditions create barriers that make effective co-ordination difficult. In practice, we may conclude that 'development sectors' continue to overrule 'sustainable' sectors and concerns.

Both the Brundtland Commission and *Agenda 21* place the main emphasis on reforms within the UN system. This is understandable, since the UNCED process sprang from the UN system. Even though the UN is the only global organisation of co-operation with universal membership, it is not the UN's agricultural policy through FAO (Food and Agriculture Organisation), or industrial policy through UNIDO (United Nations Industrial Development Organisation), that are the main causes of the problems internationally. These are the responsible global institutions focusing mainly on the economy and trade, like the World Trade Organisation (WTO, previously GATT), the World Bank, the International Monetary Fund (IMF), as well as the regional institutions: OECD, NAFTA, and the EU. To follow the Brundtland Commission's own logic, it is first and foremost here – at the source – that it is important to integrate environmental policy in other sectors.[5]

Agenda 21 (Chapter 2) emphasises that environmental and trade policies should mutually strengthen each other in working towards sustainable development, even though there is disagreement on the extent to which trade is a direct cause of environmental problems. Even though trade and the environment were on the agenda when the Uruguay round was started in 1986, an inactive work group from 1972 was revived in 1991. The group was particularly involved with production processes, environmental labelling and packaging stipulations. The final resolution from the Uruguay round mentioned the environment, but it did not succeed in including concrete environmental concerns. However, work on this will be pursued through the World Trade Organisation (WTO). An important reason for not including concrete environmental concerns is the scepticism of developing countries towards linking trade and the environment. Developing countries have accused OECD countries of 'eco-imperialism'; that is to say, they fear that environmental concerns will be used as a handy argument for implementing protectionist measures for their own industries (Esty, 1994: 185). In addition, developing countries do not want to be told which environmental problems are most important. They want to have the right to define their own problems themselves, and prioritise scarce resources in a way that will provide direct benefits (Esty, 1994:185 and 197). This is a clear example of how different national interests hinder the integration of environmental concerns.

An EU-appointed Task Force determined in 1989 that the internal market would lead to several negative environmental effects – particularly in the transport sector – and stressed that a more intensive integration of environmental concerns was an important measure. In the Single European Act that came into force in 1987, it is stipulated that environmental concerns should comprise a part of other areas of the EU's policies. This formulation was further strengthened in the Maastricht Treaty, which stipulates that environmental concerns should be integrated both by definition and implementation in the Union's policies. The reason for the new formulation was that environmental concerns had been included to a very small extent in practice. Lack of follow-up is connected with lack of real political prioritisation, as well as organisational conditions. The EU Commission defines proposals for legislation, and hence is the most important organ for the integration of environmental concerns at an early phase.

As far back as 1979, the so-called Spirenburg Report asserted that the EU Commission's deep sector-segmentation was the most serious deficiency in its administrative structure. Among other reasons, this is due to a lack of a feeling of common identity between the leaders of the 23 directorates. This is a problem in all large bureaucracies, particularly at the international level. The consequence of this is that even though there is political will for integration and co-ordination, there is no guarantee that it is actually done.

The EU's climate policy is a good example of both the potential and drawback with sector-integrated international institutions. The fact that the EU covers most issue-areas made it possible to formulate a common climate policy for 12 countries where all affected sectors were involved. Eight of the Commission's 23 directorates were involved, where the co-operation between the Directorate of Energy and Directorate of the Environment was a critical condition for moving the process forward. But they did not succeed in including the Directorate of Transport, which had responsibility for a sector that accounted for about a quarter of the union's total CO_2 emission. While seven directorates worked on formulating initiatives for limiting carbon-dioxide emission, the Directorate of Transport worked on initiatives for the liberalisation of the transport market.

Hence, we may conclude that both national and organisational conditions make it difficult to integrate environmental concerns in practice in large international institutions. Moreover, the convergence of political will and actual ability to integrate is not a given.

8.5   INFORMED CHOICES? FROM SCIENCE TO POLITICS

Lack of will and ability to integrate environmental concerns in other sectors at all levels bring to light the reasons why the 1980s was the decade when the consequences of both regional and global environmental problems became evident. Forest degeneration in Germany and the death of fish in Scandinavia at the beginning of the 1980s, the detection of the hole in the ozone layer over the Antarctic in 1985, Chernobyl in 1986, the algae 'invasion' in the North Sea in 1988, and the *Exxon Valdez* accident in Alaska in 1989, were the most visible symptoms of lack of 'sustainability'.

Science plays an important role in the understanding of the effects, and how such problems can be solved. *Agenda 21* (Chapter 35) emphasises that the scientific understanding of environmental problems should improve so that politicians are provided with the best possible basis for decision-making. The main initiatives proposed are increase in research capacity and focus on long-term effects. These are of course important, but there are also many barriers in this area. Firstly, international co-operation requires international consensus on what the problems are. This is extremely problematic because knowledge must be perceived as legitimate. Secondly, there is not necessarily a connection between low uncertainty, high consensus and political will for action. Thirdly, paradoxically, more research may lead to greater uncertainty. High uncertainty is always welcome ammunition for those who do not wish to do anything.

Lack of legitimacy and consensus are directly linked to the coupling between political interests and the production of knowledge. Briefly, the point is that all countries will base their environmental policy on science as long as it backs up national preferences.

When it doesn't do this, politicians may then try to control the knowledge production in international scientific co-operation. This leads to low legitimacy, which makes it understandable that developing countries do not automatically 'buy' the OECD countries' perception of global environmental problems. For example, the politicisation of scientific councils is a well-known phenomenon in the co-operation on North-eastern Atlantic Ocean pollution (Skjærseth, 1994:6).

Problems with great uncertainty, lack of consensus and legitimacy were the main reasons why the UN in 1988 brought together seven hundred of the world's leading researchers in an international climate panel to study global warming. The agreement on a 60 per cent reduction in CO_2 to stabilise the level of greenhouse gases in the atmosphere is being described as very 'robust' (Lunde, 1991:128). On the other hand, developing countries perceived the process as less legitimate than the OECD countries did, because they were poorly represented on the climate panel. In spite of this, it was the USA that got most of the blame for not achieving more than the stabilisation of emissions by the year 2000 at the climate convention of 1992. An important reason why the

USA put its foot down was that drastic reductions would be too expensive, both politically and economically.[6]

An example of how more knowledge can increase uncertainty may be found in the connection between ozone-depleting gases and global warming. Until 1992, researchers reckoned that ozone-depleting gases accounted for about 15 to 20 per cent of climate effects. This expertise gave the work of reducing such substances extra political weight because one could kill two birds with one stone. In 1992, the UN's climate panel launched the thesis that this effect could be offset by the actual depletion in the ozone layer (WMO/UNEP, 1992). Hence, the bonus disappeared, and countries that had no interest in doing anything could argue that such profound changes in expert knowledge in the short term indicates that we know too little to act. However, this paradox cannot be resolved, and is no argument against it being sensible to know what one does and why. Such concerns must, however, be weighed against the 'precautionary principle'. The most concrete element in this principle is that it switches the burden of proof so that it is those who are involved in potentially environmentally-damaging activities who must prove that such activities are safe. Beyond this, the precautionary principle is extremely difficult to put into operation.

8.6   EFFECTIVE INTERNATIONAL COOPERATION – FROM POLITICS TO COMMON ACTION

The USA could stand firm during the climate negotiations because international environmental co-operation in general, and *Agenda 21* in particular, are based on voluntariness and unanimity. The problem is that it is often the ones who consume the most resources, or pollute most, who have the least interest in strict regulations, when they themselves are not directly affected by environmental problems. The possibility of employing majority procedures may therefore be the only means to include those who have the least interest in realising common objectives in practice. More effectiveness in decision-making in international environmental protection co-operation is also closely connected with the integration of environmental concerns in other sectors.

Problems with the unanimity principle are the reason why the 1989 Hague Declaration on New Principles for International Environmental Protection Co-operation advocated establishing a new international authority that could make decisions on majority resolutions. As with *Agenda 21*, this declaration is not binding. However, the introduction of majority resolutions comes into conflict with the principle of national sovereignty, and it runs into problems of the scope of co-operation.[7] Given that voluntariness is the basis, it is quite unrealistic to believe that environmental 'laggards' will go along with a supranational issue-defined environmental protection co-operation where they know beforehand that they will be out-played. That is to say, they will be forced to do something they would otherwise not have done. The conditions for such co-operation are probably:

(a) that there are good chances of belonging to the majority at the next cross-roads;
(b) that 'laggards' may get compensation in other issue-areas.

If we assume that different countries are 'laggards' in relation to various environmental problems, this may be solved by establishing environmental co-operation that covers several environmental problems. This is quite a problem, given that today's international co-operation structure comprises 150 issue-specific agreements. In the case of consistent 'laggards' in relation to various environmental problems, the only solution may be to link international environmental protection co-operation to other issue-areas like trade and the economy. This may provide the necessary room for 'package solutions' where countries may be compensated for other areas. This may also mean that one condition for transferring national sovereignty in order to solve a transnational environmental problem may be that one also should transfer sovereignty in relation to other environmental problems, or in other issue-areas, as in the EU.

But it will not help very much to impose environmental initiatives on other countries that do not have the resources to implement them. This is the reason for *Agenda 21*'s focus on the transfer of money, technology and know-how. Very few of the traditional regional environmental agreements have provisions that make it possible to transfer resources to those who cannot afford to implement the initiatives. An important reason is that most countries are reluctant to allow other countries to have influence over their own resources. Moreover, it may be against the 'polluter pays' principle. But if the polluter cannot pay, there is no other alternative.

The problem of resources is most precarious in co-operation that involves developing countries. This problem has been high on the agenda in global cooperation on climate, biodiversity and the ozone layer. It has been evident that even though new multilateral environmental funds have been established to solve global environmental problems, it has been difficult to put these funds to use because, among other reasons, the OECD countries will not allow other developing countries to control the money. In ozone co-operation in 1990, they succeeded in establishing a multilateral fund of $240 million, even though it has been shown that it was a problem to collect the money. It was also emphasised in the text of the agreement that this fund was an exception, and that it should not be a precedent. Problems with the introduction of a new practice are also clearly seen in the tussle concerning the Global Environment Facility (GEF). The GEF is a multilateral financial institution – linked to the World Bank and the UN – which has responsibility for allocating resources to developing countries concerning global environmental problems. One problem is that the OECD countries do not like the idea that the developing countries should have too much influence on how resources should be allocated, fearing that resources would be used for purposes that they were not meant for. However, opinions vary as to what is a reasonable use of resources, because there is disagreement on whether the problems are local, regional, national or global. This is fairly straightforward with respect to problems with ozone. It is much harder to decide whether biological diversity is a national or global problem. Who has the right to what in the rational use of resources is hence not always clear.

Increased participation in international co-operation from voluntary organisations is difficult to bring about in practice where resolutions with 'teeth' are made, because many countries do not wish to show their cards. Moreover, it is a double-edged sword with respect to the possibilities of bringing about effective environmental solutions. The Bergen Conference in 1990, which was a follow-up to the Brundtland Commission's report, introduced a whole new practice in participation. At the preliminary conference, six equal parties were defined that should negotiate towards a common action programme: government, industry, trade unions, environmental organisations, youth groups and researchers. However, environmental organisations were generally given access where no binding resolutions were made. The big environmental conferences mainly adopt proposals which reflect declarations of political will, and not judicial obligations. Voluntary organisations have had problems with gaining access to regional co-operation that makes binding resolutions with significant economic consequences for member countries. But here also, there has been progress since the mid-1980s; for example, in the North-eastern Atlantic co-operation on ocean pollution. From being totally excluded, the representatives of the voluntary organisations were first allowed to hold an opening presentation before the commission meeting. Some years later, they were allowed to have representatives with observer status at the commission meetings.[8]

However, increased participation is problematic in three ways. Firstly, the environmental organisations' perception does not necessarily amount to good solutions. An example of this is the dumping of waste in the sea. Even though such dumping is a small problem in comparison with 'invisible' land-based emissions, both environmental organisations and politicians have given it great attention. In the North Sea, the result is that dumping is on the verge of becoming history, but pollution has nevertheless not diminished, because land-based emissions have received too little attention (Oslo and Paris Commissions, 1993). However, it is not right to lay the blame on pressure from environmental organisations alone. There was much to indicate that politicians and environmental organisations have had common interests. Politicians have shown that they are capable of acting without it costing too much, while environmental organisations have gained more members and more money.

Secondly, it is hardly the case that environmental organisations always win out. Powerful industrial interests that are the cause of the problem, but are often not affected by it themselves and that in the end must foot the bill, represent a strong opposition. An example of this is the intense lobbying around the EU's climate policy – particularly attempts to introduce a common energy and carbon tax that was supposed to be resolved before the Rio Conference. The tax became the object of an extremely intensive lobby action in Brussels. Industry, represented by the European Employers Association (UNICE), stood together against higher tax and in the end achieved their goal that the EU should not introduce taxes before the rest of the OECD countries had done the same. The international environmental organisations in Brussels did not manage to cooperate on a common strategy and were outmanoeuvred by industrial interests (Skjærseth, 1993).[9]

Thirdly, participation from voluntary organisations during international environmental negotiations may lead to diplomats and politicians concentrating mainly on popular causes that may garner political gains on home ground, rather than looking for reasonable solutions – a phenomenon that is well-known from the UN's general assembly meetings.

Even though there is no natural connection between broad participation and effective international co-operation, there are many examples to indicate that such participation has been a critical condition for succeeding. In ozone co-operation, it was of critical significance that the major chemical companies participated because in the end they are given responsibility for developing new technology. And even if broad participation may lead to 'weaker' resolutions because several special interest groups are involved, there is every indication that implementation of initiatives in practice becomes easier when all parties involved have had their say.

8.7   BINDING INTERNATIONAL CO-OPERATION – FROM ACTION TO COMPLIANCE

When common resolutions on initiatives are made, the signatory states should implement international agreements. As it is clearly not a matter of course that all countries do this, both the Brundtland Report and *Agenda 21* advocate a more binding international co-operation. From the perspective of the nation-state, the principle of national sovereignty lays down certain obstacles for an effective international judicial system. An important issue that should be resolved is how binding international resolutions are. It depends both on the precision and judicial status of the resolutions. Here, there is often a conflict of interests. The most ambitious resolutions, where countries have bound themselves to percentage reduction of emissions, are often not binding within the framework of international law. As a rule, the more general text of the agreement is binding. The extent to which resolutions are binding has therefore less significance than one would think, because the binding formulations are often so general that it is extremely difficult to trace breaches in an agreement.

Secondly, one is dependent on a system that can monitor the agreement and find out who has breached what. However, such a system presupposes that states give up their sovereignty and submit to an independent monitoring organ. There are very few countries that are willing to report on their own breaches of international agreements. This is probably one of the main reasons that the lack of reporting from countries that participate in international environmental co-operation is quite common. Generally speaking, the monitoring of international environmental agreements is very poor, because most countries do not want others to see their cards. The debate surrounding the organisation and mandate of the EU's environmental bureau is indicative of the fact that the antagonism between the need for independence and desire for national control arises even in a tightly integrated co-operation between relatively homogeneous countries. The European Parliament's Environmental Committee emphasised that the bureau should have a high degree of autonomy in relation to member countries, to ensure independent inspection and impartial information. While the goal concerning information was upheld in the final proposal, the one concerning independent inspection was rejected. Moreover, it was resolved that the bureau should be organised under a committee where the representatives of member countries could control the information flow.

Thirdly, what happens if it is determined that a country has breached an international obligation? In 1989, the Oslo Commission, with the consent of Great Britain, resolved to ban the dumping of industrial waste in the North Sea by 1990. In the same year, the British government permitted the dumping of 50 000 tons of chemical waste into the North Sea. This led to fierce protests from the other countries, but there was little they could do to prevent the dumping because there is no judicial system that can intervene quickly and effectively. As a rule, the International Tribunal in the Hague requires that all involved parties must agree that the court shall try the case. If this is not required, the court cannot enforce its verdict. The reason for this is that there is no proper parallel to a national government at the global level. Sanction mechanisms are closely connected with the decision-making process. If majority procedures are used, it is highly probable that countries that are out-voted will not be interested to keep their obligations. The use of majority procedures will hence increase the need for effective monitoring and sanctions. The alternative, which is probably more effective, is the use of majority procedures and compensation of antagonistic countries.

The EU is probably as close as we have come to an international co-operation that is based on member countries subsuming their national sovereignty over specific issue-areas, like the environment. Increased use of majority procedures, and linking issues and political pressure directed against laggards, have resulted in about three hundred environmental directives and other legal texts in the area of environment. However, the problem has been that incomplete follow-up of the directives has increased in proportion to higher efficiency in decision-making. The EU Court then has the authority to intervene. For example, in 1992, Great Britain was sentenced for not fulfilling the EU's drinking-water directive. Nevertheless, if Great Britain fails to fulfil a directive, there is little that the EU Court can do. The Maastricht Treaty certainly allows the court to impose fines. If such fines are not paid, one can withhold subsidies from the EU's structure fund until the fines are paid.[10] However, the use of such initiatives can be quite time- and resource-consuming, and it remains to be seen whether they will have any practical significance.

8.8   THE WAY FORWARD: SOVEREIGNTY AND POSSIBLE SHORT-CUTS

To point out the problems of overcoming transnational challenges is a relatively thankless task. It is worse still to identify the solutions. In conclusion, I shall therefore briefly look at three possible strategies. The first is based on the problems surrounding the principle of national sovereignty. The second looks more concretely at the possible ways around this principle. The third is based on decentralised solutions.

It is important to differentiate between formal sovereignty and real independence. The formal definition of a state in the Montevideo Convention of 1933 has as its basis the concept of a state as a political unit with a permanent population, a demarcated territory, and a government that is independent enough to uphold international obligations. These criteria are still applied in international law, and they were written into the UN pact of 1945. This pact should protect the sovereignty and integrity of established states (Østerud, 1994).[11] However, in real terms, states have always been interdependent. For example, 80 to 90 per cent of sulphur and nitrogen fallout in Norway comes from production in Great Britain, Russia and Central Europe. Even though Norway is formally a sovereign state, the country cannot solve this problem alone. The UN pact's focus on the formal sovereignty of all states means that in practice, it supports Great Britain and Russia's formal right to decide themselves whether they will continue to discharge nitrogen and sulphur. However, their formal self-determination affects Norway's real self-determination. The common transfer of formal political sovereignty, that is, the decision-making authority of an international organ, could in this case increase Norway's real independence and self-determination over its own territory. An increasing recognition that in the area of environment there may be antagonism between formal sovereignty and real independence may eventually lead to international environmental institutions achieving greater authority.

Given the present international system, which to a great extent is based on voluntariness and veto rights for all countries, one may consider various international institutional reforms that can increase the possibility of attaining 'sustainable development'. As we have seen, the most important challenge lies in the integration of environmental concerns in all sectors to tackle the causes of the problems. At the international level, an important barrier lies in bringing about a common understanding of what the most important problems are. The basis of both the Brundtland Commission and the UNCED process seems to be the idea that 'we are all in the same boat'. To a certain extent, it is right as regards global challenges, but it is just as important to acknowledge that some have cabins on the sun-deck while others have to be content with a place under the car-deck. In other words, it is important to acknowledge that different groups of countries often have very different interests. This implies that developing countries' scepticism against linking trade and the environment, as well as disagreement on the function of the multilateral funding institutions, is not necessarily a pedagogic problem which can be solved by the transfer of expertise and information. The consequence is that international institutions should reflect different interests and perceptions of what the problems are, through a combined economic and technological commitment as to what are perceived by developing countries as local and national problems, and what are perceived by OECD countries as global problems.

As regards organisational barriers that hinder the integration of environmental concerns in practice, this problem seems unsolvable in the sense that the splitting of spheres of responsibility in various sectors will always create coordination problems when the problems that are to be solved cross over spheres of responsibility. One possible step in the right direction here may be to allocate less responsibility for co-ordination to environmental sectors – whether it is environmental departments at the national level or the environmental directorate in the EU – and more environmental responsibilities to sectors that are causes of problems, like industry, agriculture, transport and energy. This is related to the fact that 'old' departments that are the cause have more power than relatively 'young' environmental departments, which makes effective coordination difficult to implement in practice.

Production of knowledge that is regarded as legitimate by all parties can be improved by emphasising broader geographical participation. When the world's leading climate researchers are convened based on scientific criteria, the result is a very uneven representation between the North and the South. Bob Watson of the American space organisation (NASA), who had a key responsibility for cooperative scientific work on the ozone problem, put it like this:

Let's go ahead and have a person from a certain country, even if that person has nothing to contribute. We might be able to get something started there,

or at the very least that person might be able to take the message home
(Liftin, 1991:6).

An alternative to introducing majority procedures that are binding for the
minority may be to establish co-operation that increases possibilities for adopting 'package solutions'. Possibilities for some 'give and take' for all will increase
when several issue-areas are seen in context. Countries that fare poorly in one
area may get compensation in another, which may lead to solutions that otherwise would not have been possible. Given the present structure of international
co-operation with 150 environmental agreements, there should be room for the
merging of agreements that verge on each other. This may also reduce problems of co-ordination, overlapping and work-duplication between the various
international organs. For example, one may question whether it is necessary to
have a separate protocol that regulates air-transported sea pollution within the
scope of the Paris Convention – which regulates land-based emissions into the
North-eastern Atlantic – when there is a separate convention on long-range
transboundary air pollution (ECE Convention of 1979) in which almost the
same states participate. However, the advantages gained from merging agreements should be weighed against the drawback of negotiations becoming more
complex and unclear.

The issue of who should participate in international environmental co-operation is as important as it is difficult. As we have seen, there are good arguments
both for and against broad participation. Just as important, however, is the
issue of when they should participate and at which level. One problem in international environmental protection co-operation seems to be that non-gov-
ernmental participants, for example industrial companies that will be affected
by the resolutions and who eventually have the responsibility for implementation, are often brought into the proceedings at a late stage. The consequence
of this may be that national positions in international negotiations are being
formulated without giving particular thought to the fact that resolutions are to
be implemented, and that the excluded target-groups have other priorities and
approach strategies. It can lead to the active opposition of international goals
by target-groups who feel they were not able to put forward their interests when
the premises were made. For example, one may imagine a model whereby non-
governmental parties participate in the formulation of national positions and
implementation, but not necessarily in international negotiations. This will
satisfy the principle that all affected parties are being heard, at the same time
that the international negotiations probably become more effective.[12]

The possibilities of establishing effective international systems for sanctions
are small. The challenge here, probably lies in making agreements as 'transpar-
ent' and clear as possible. At least, it will increase the possibilities of tracing
breaches of agreements and exposing those who do so to international condem-
nation.[13]

A third strategy – which is closely linked to participation – is to focus on decentralised solutions rather than supranational ones. This is a major debate that can only be touched on briefly here. Firstly, the argument that is often used to support this perspective is that decentralisation of authority will weaken the international economic competition that intensifies the exploitation of natural resources and deterioration of the environment. Secondly, local authorities have a greater understanding of ecosystems that are the basis of their existence. Thirdly, smaller communities have historical experience in creating sustainable and local forms of economic development (Hurrell and Kingsbury, 1992). Against this, one may object that there is no correspondence between rational environmental management and local government. For example, it is doubtful whether the great predators in Norway should have their fate decided by each individual municipality. Besides, there is no guarantee that a decentralised system will not lead to problems that require regional and global co-ordination. As we know, each municipality does not have its own ozone layer. Such solutions will be even more complicated to put into practice, because the number of participants will increase significantly. Nevertheless, this perspective rests on an important principle which says that decisions should be made at the lowest possible level in relation to the potential solution of the problem. It will both stimulate broad participation and influence, and prevent unnecessary bureaucratisation.

8.9 CONCLUSION

The idea of a decentralised world system seems to be just as politically remote as that of a global world government. Moreover, it is doubtful whether any of these models will promote the attainment of sustainable development. The three strategies that are discussed here, however, include all the elements that do not necessarily stand in opposition to each other, and which together can contribute towards the tackling of causes and the effecting of solutions.

Firstly, there is a need to invest international environmental institutions with greater authority to make the decision-making process more effective, and to ensure compliance in relation to transnational problems. An increasing realisation that in the area of environment there may be a conflict between formal sovereignty and real independence may in time bring this about.

Secondly, there exist several 'short-cuts' within today's state sovereignty system that can contribute towards tackling the causes more effectively, stimulating the possibility of making informed choices, making international environmental protection co-operation more efficient, and stimulating compliance.

Thirdly, all co-ordination and co-operation should be adapted to the level at which the problem lies.

NOTES

1. It must be emphasised that many institutional reforms that are proposed in *Agenda 21* and *Our Common Future* are linked to national institutions. However, in this chapter, the main focus is on international institutions.
2. *Agenda 21* was adopted during the Rio Conference in 1992. This 'action programme' runs to 700 pages, divided into 40 chapters without any form of prioritisation among the different chapters.
3. The Climate Convention does not contain any quantitative emission obligations beyond stabilisation at a level which would prevent harmful changes in the climate systems, and that all countries adopting national climate strategies and implementing measures in accordance with these should limit their emissions.
4. The world consumption of CFCs was reduced by 50 per cent by 1992. The manufacturers of halon in Europe stopped production and phased out CFC production by 1995 (SFT, 1994).
5. It must be stressed that the idea of integrating environmental concerns has gained acceptance in these institutions, which in itself is positive (see, for example, World Bank, 1994). Instead of discussing the gap between rhetoric and practice in all these institutions, I shall use as examples the two most important general problems with respect to the WTO and the EU.
6. The lack of correspondence between scientific advice and political decisions is also evident in the International Whaling Commission (IWC). The IWC's scientific committee adjusted its management procedures and unanimously agreed in 1992 that the North-eastern Atlantic minke whale stock was around 86 700. Despite this, the IWC refused to implement the new procedure (Skåre 1994).
7. It must be emphasised however, that even though majority procedures are a more effective instrument than unanimity when it concerns making decisions, it does not necessarily mean that they will lead to more effective environmental solutions. It will depend from time to time on what the majority wants, and whether the laggards implement the decisions. Moreover, such procedures may be very complicated because there is often antagonism between decision efficiency and requirements for democracy.
8. However, environmental organisations are not allowed to participate in the meetings of the permanent working groups. It is often here that the premises are laid for decisions in the Commission, which in practice, means that environmental organisations have little chance of influencing the decision.
9. The UNCED process also showed clearly that environmental organisations do not necessarily agree on goals and means.
10. The structure funds in the EU are mainly aimed at the poorest EU countries – Portugal, Spain, Greece and Ireland – and hence will not be an effective instrument with regard to Great Britain.
11. The UN's decolonisation doctrine, however, led to a practice other than empirical 'efficiency criteria', though state systems are still based on a political concept of nation (Østerud 1994).
12. Another problem is that most of the permanent international environmental co-operation occurs at a low political level, which often gives the co-operation more of an administrative/bureaucratic character than of real negotiations.

Such co-operation is often enhanced by occasional ministerial-level meetings, and experience shows that it is often then that breakthroughs occur. An increased use of serious negotiations at a high political level, combined with permanent administrative co-operation, will often lead to greater progress.

13.   British diplomats and politicians were not unaffected by the fact that they represented 'The Dirty Man of Europe' during the 1980s. Great Britain's turn-around in ozone, acid rain, and North Sea co-operation at the end of the 1980s can partly be attributed to the fact that the political costs of being the 'slow coach' in international environmental co-operation eventually became greater than the economic costs of reducing emissions.

9 Economic Analysis of Sustainability

Geir B. Asheim

9.1 INTRODUCTION

In the period since the Brundtland Commission's report (*Our Common Future*), the concept of sustainable development has been interpreted in many different ways. I will here limit myself to discussing what the concept entails with respect to our generation's obligations towards future generations. This does not rule out that it might be fruitful to ascribe to the concept a broader meaning; for example, that sustainable development entails obligations for rich countries to assist people living today under less fortunate conditions in other parts of the world. My limitation is due to the fact that sustainability interpreted as *inter*generational justice – justice *between* the present and future generations – is a wide-ranging topic. It in no way reflects a view that *intra*generational justice – justice *within* the present generation – is of less importance.

Sustainability as intergenerational justice is an important subject because our generation – with present technology – is capable of depleting important natural resources and inflicting serious and long-term damage on important environmental resources. In this connection, three questions arise:

1. What are our generation's obligations towards future generations?
2. How can we judge whether these obligations are fulfilled?
3. How can we ensure that these obligations will be fulfilled?

I shall argue that it is possible to provide a definition of the concept of sustainable development that answers the first question in a concise manner. However, I shall use economic theory to show that it is a far more difficult task to formulate rules that can be used to determine whether our generation's resource management is in accordance with the requirement for sustainable development. I shall also point out problems of implementing sustainable development through collective action, given that the institutions that are capable of generating such action are representatives of our generation only. This pessimism does not undermine the importance of our generation acting in accordance with the requirements for sustainable development; the problem is that it is difficult to determine what these requirements are, and to ensure that they are met.

The analysis will be based on economic theory. Normative economic theory is concerned with how resources should be managed to serve human interests.

Positive economic theory analyses how economic systems manage resources. 'Resources' are here taken to mean both natural and environmental resources, human resources (for example, knowledge) and man-made resources (for example, machines). Economic theory is based on an anthropocentric view: resources should be managed to serve human interests. 'Humans' are here taken to mean both existing and future generations. Because future generations' interests are also included, economic theory does not rule out that biological diversity should be conserved in the interest of posterity. Even though such diversity will not be useful for the existing generation, it may serve the interests of future generations.

Economic theory is not limited to an analysis of the goods and resources that are traded in markets; economic theory is not only concerned with what one may call 'narrow economic interests'. The existence of a market system is nevertheless important: market prices can provide information on which good collective decisions can be made, and a market economy is an economic system that, under given conditions, will manage resources in a good way.

The major advantage of the market system is due to the fact that it makes each participant responsible. If an individual wishes to consume a good, or a firm wishes to use a good as factor input, it is necessary for the individual (or as the case may be, the firm) to buy units of the good in the marketplace. The payment transfers to the seller resources that correspond in value to the units sold. Hence, the buyer becomes responsible for compensating the seller for the value that the traded units represent. Under ideal conditions, this system results in goods being utilised where they have the greatest value.

Even under ideal conditions, a market system has one great weakness: it does not ensure a just distribution of income. Individuals with a higher disposable income also have control over a larger part of the goods. In particular if these differences in income are not due to differences in effort, such inequality may appear unjust and provides a justification for the authorities to redistribute income. In real life, a market system has the additional weakness that many goods are not traded in the market place. Among these are many environmental resources. This means that individuals and firms can reduce the availability of environmental resources through pollution, without being made responsible for this by having to compensate the victims of such pollution. Economists call this the negative external effect. Through environmental policies the authorities try to make individuals and firms responsible for their pollution.

With respect to sustainability, this means that a market economy will not necessarily ensure intergenerational justice, even under ideal conditions.[1] Moreover, one important complicating factor is that the authorities today will necessarily be representatives for our own generation. Therefore, redistribution from our own generation to future generations will be a form of charity. The existence of external effects that reduce the availability of environmental resources is also a significant issue in relation to sustainability. Such environmental damage will often have long-term effects, with consequences that are as serious for future generations as for our own. To what extent the authorities will make polluters responsible for their pollution will in such cases depend on the extent to which our generation wishes (and is able) to transfer income to future generations.

In addition to the anthropocentric view on which economic theory is based, I shall make the following assumptions in this chapter. The concept of sustainable development will be discussed in a global perspective; as an obligation that the present inhabitants of the Earth have towards future generations. I shall also assume that each generation's quality of life is dependent on what it receives in inheritance from previous generations and on what it bequeaths to future generations. For example, a generation with a moderate depletion of natural resources, not much depreciation of environmental resources and an extensive accumulation of human and man-made capital, will have a lower quality of life than if such measures in the interest of future generations were not implemented. The term 'quality of life' is assumed to include more than material consumption: it includes everything that influences the situation in which people live. It is intended to capture the importance of health and culture as well as the amenities provided by having access to environmental resources.

In practice, the generation's quality of life will also depend on how it distributes the available goods. For example, it will be reasonable to assume that a generation that distributes a given amount of goods in an egalitarian manner will have a higher quality of life than a generation that has an uneven distribution of the same amount of goods. Because my point of departure is to discuss intergenerational justice, I shall ignore such dependencies. I shall also ignore problems related to the measurement of quality of life. Neither shall I explicitly take into consideration the fact that the bequest that we leave to future generations will have uncertain consequences; for example, accumulation of environmental hazardous substances and reduction of biological diversity may lead to such uncertainty. Furthermore, I shall not explicitly discuss how population growth threatens to undermine the possibilities for realising sustainable development. To make the analysis easier to understand, I assume that there is zero population growth. Finally, I shall assume that generations follow one another without overlapping. Even under such simplified assumptions, I shall show that sustainable development is clearly a highly problematic goal.

9.2   OBLIGATIONS TOWARDS FUTURE GENERATIONS

The most common definition of sustainable development among economists is the following: *our resource management is sustainable if the quality of life that we ensure ourselves can potentially be shared by all future generations.* If this requirement is also extended to future generations, the definition will have to be reformulated as follows: *our resource management is sustainable if it constitutes the first part of a feasible development with non-decreasing quality of life.*[2] The definition does not entail that the development actually realised will lead to non-decreasing quality of life. The reason is that sustainability does not preclude that a generation can sacrifice itself for future generations to such an extent that it achieves living conditions that are lower than the previous generation, even when all generations act in accordance with sustainability.

As defined above, sustainability appears to entail that our generation is allowed to sacrifice itself to benefit future generations. On the other hand, future generations are not able to sacrifice themselves to benefit us. This asymmetry can be explained by the fact that we can give our consent to sacrifice ourselves for future generations, while a corresponding consent cannot be obtained from future generations. This understanding is weakened if we assume that all generations meet without each individual generation knowing which generation it will actually become.[3] In such a perspective, the direction of time does not preclude that future generations should sacrifice themselves to benefit earlier generations.

My own view (Asheim, 1991) is that this asymmetry is based on a belief that if we sacrifice ourselves, future generations will get more in return than the sacrifice we had to make. In other words: our sacrifice is an investment that gives a positive net return: if our sacrifice leaves us with a lower quality of life compared to the quality of life that future generations can enjoy, this leads to increased inequality. However, simultaneously the 'cake' that is to be shared increases. On the other hand, if we impose a sacrifice upon future generations, their sacrifice will have to be greater than the rise in the quality of life that we can enjoy. If our quality of life is higher than theirs, such a policy from our side will lead to greater inequality, while simultaneously reducing the 'cake' to be shared. In other words, while redistribution from future generations to our generation is believed to have a positive net cost, redistribution from our generation to future generations is believed to have a negative net cost, in the sense that the future gets more in return than we originally sacrificed.

According to this view, a belief that investments have positive net return, provides a normative basis for sustainability. I shall call this a belief that the Earth is productive. In a geological perspective, there are millions of generations that will potentially descend from us. Therefore, we are not making a big mistake if we conceptualise this as if we are the first of an infinite sequence of generations. It is uncontroversial to claim that we – with our highly developed technology – have the capability to destroy the resource base to such an extent that all future generations will have a lower quality of life or have their existence threatened. On the other hand, if we today make decisions that benefit future generations, this could lead to a rise in the quality of life for all future generations. If we believe this to be a valid description, it is not difficult to realise that our generation should not allow itself a quality of life that cannot also be shared by all future generations. Because if our quality of life were higher than that of future generations we would be able to generate an infinitely lasting rise in future generations' quality of life by making a finite sacrifice ourselves, while simultaneously reducing intergenerational inequality.

I have argued above that a belief in a positive net productivity is a normative basis for sustainability. At the same time, it is also such a positive productivity that makes it possible to hope that sustainable development actually can be attained. If distribution between generations was a problem of sharing a finite 'cake' among an infinite number of generations, sustainable development would neither be possible nor desirable. Hence, to argue that the survival of humanity is a concern for our generation is closely linked to a belief that such survival is possible.

The requirement for sustainable development does not imply that we have to sacrifice ourselves until the increase in the quality of life for future generations becomes equal *at the margin* to the reduction in our quality of life. Combined with a belief that humanity can survive, the consequence of such a criterion would be that our generation would have to make great sacrifices and hence, be left with a low quality of life. This does not seem to lead to a just intergenerational distribution. Therefore, sustainability does not rule out a development where our generation is able to make additional sacrifices that will benefit future generations more than they will harm us.

On the contrary, sustainable development that is reasonably egalitarian will be characterised by the possibility for such sacrifices, but without these possibilities being utilised. In economic terminology, this means that a reasonably egalitarian sustainable development will be characterised by a positive interest rate. It also means that sustainable development implies that changes in future generations' quality of life will be discounted at a positive rate. If sustainable development is realised in a perfect market economy, this positive interest rate will manifest itself as the market interest rate. At the same time, the interest rate along a sustainable development path may be lower than the market interest rate that has been observed empirically, because the real world's market economy is imperfect and does not necessarily realise a sustainable development. Furthermore, it may be reasonable to assume that the interest rate along a sustainable development path will have a tendency to decline over time if capital accumulation and resource depletion lead to lower productivity.

Theoretically, one may imagine that each generation generates *utility* from its quality of life in such a way that an increase of the quality of life leads to relatively less increase in utility if the quality of life is high to begin with. Thus, utility as a function of the quality of life can be depicted as a function with the form shown in Figure 9.1.

Figure 9.1   Utility as a possible function of quality of life

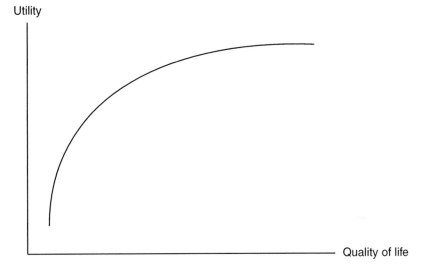

If such a utility function is known, a possible normative starting-point can be to maximise a weighted sum of the generations' utility. This is called a utilitarian welfare function. If an earlier generation is given greater weight than a later generation, we say that this utilitarian welfare function involves positive utility discounting. Alternatively, this positive discount rate is called a positive time preference rate. The natural interpretation of the utility function in a utilitarian welfare function is the following: an increase in utility for one generation is, from a normative viewpoint, equivalent to a corresponding reduction in utility for another generation. This entails that our generation ought to sacrifice itself for future generations until the marginal utility gain for future generations becomes equal to our marginal utility sacrifice. This is achieved by maximising a non-discounted sum of the generations' utility. Therefore, if a utilitarian welfare function is employed as a normative criterion for intergenerational justice, there is no reason to discriminate against future generations by discounting their utility. This is classical utilitarianism, and corresponds in an intertemporal context to the welfare function that Ramsey (1928) used.

With positive productivity, development that maximises a utilitarian welfare function without utility discounting will be characterised by the property that future generations will be better off than us; development will thus be sustainable. Because of the shape of the utility function, such a development will also be characterised by the property that our generation is able to make additional sacrifices that will lead to an increase in the quality of life in the future that is larger than the corresponding reduction in the quality of life at present. This implies a positive interest rate.

The conclusion is thus that with a utilitarian point of departure, there is no reason to discount future generations' utility. However, this does not mean that utilitarianism is an indisputable normative foundation. The foundation can clearly be criticised.

The utilitarian welfare function is based on a utility function that makes one capable of deciding whether a certain rise in the quality of life for one generation is worth more or less than a certain reduction in the quality of life for another generation. For a given utility function, intergenerational inequality in the quality of life will depend on the Earth's productivity. With a high net productivity, the resulting inequality in the quality of life will be large. It is important to realise that utilitarianism requires that the utility function can be determined, based only on normative judgements concerning how to trade-off a change in the quality of life for a poor generation against a change in the quality of life for a rich generation. Hence, the utility function cannot be allowed to reflect the consequences generated when it is employed in the utilitarian welfare function.[4] It is hard to imagine that such a utility function can be given a convincing normative basis.

While the utilitarian welfare function compares *changes in* the quality of life, an alternative is to compare the *level of* the quality of life. The Rawlsian welfare function does this by maximising the quality of life of the generation that has the lowest quality of life. This is often called the 'maxi-min' criterion. Such a welfare function will generally lead to a development where all generations have the same quality of life; the result is totally egalitarian. The level of quality of life that each generation secures along such a development path can be viewed as the maximum sustainable level; that is to say, the maximum level that satisfies the requirement that future generations should be able to share the same quality of life.

Several comments may be tied to the Rawlsian welfare function:

- It will generally be possible to find weights on each generation's utility such that a utilitarian welfare function with these utility weights leads to such an egalitarian path. These weights will be independent of the shape of the utility function. On the other hand, they will depend on production possibilities; with positive productivity, they will assign the greater weight on the earlier generations' utility. This means that future utility will be discounted. Because the result is totally egalitarian, there is, however, no reason to claim that such utility discounting is unjust towards future generations.
- The Rawlsian welfare function may be criticised for the fact that it does not create any development, even though sustainability is ensured (Solow, 1974). If redistribution from the rich to the poor part of the world is not adequate to solve problems of poverty, poverty will be perpetuated. However,

if each generation exhibits altruism for its children – such that the subjective welfare depends on its own quality of life and the subjective welfare of its children – then the maxi-min criterion can create development by maximising the subjective welfare of the generation that is worst off in subjective welfare. It can be shown (Calvo, 1978; Asheim, 1988) that this may result in an increasing quality of life, such that the problem of poverty may be overcome. The point is that the present generation is allowed to save for the benefit of future generations if it considers it to be in its own interest to do so. Intergenerational inequality arises only if it is in the own interest of the first worst-off generation to make transfers to future generations.

- Rawls (1971) himself argues that the maxi-min criterion should be employed as a criterion for *intra*-generational justice, but not for *inter*-generational justice. The argument used (Rawls, 1971:44) to reject the maxi-min criterion in the inter-temporal context, indicates however, that Rawls seems to assume that our generation does not have the ability to increase our immediate quality of life – by depleting natural resources and reducing the long-term quality of environment resources – at the expense of future generations. He writes: 'It is a natural fact that generations are spread out in time and actual exchanges between them take place only in one direction. We can do something for posterior but it can do nothing for us. . . . It is now clear why the [maxi-min criterion] does not apply to the savings problems. There is no way for later generations to improve the situation of the least fortunate first generation' (Rawls, 1972:291). If it is possible for us to improve our own quality of life at the expense of future generations by depleting natural resources and reducing the quality of the environment, the claim 'We can do something for posterior but it can do nothing for us' is incorrect. This seems to undermine Rawls' argument.[5]

- Moreover, Rawls (1971:45) argues against a positive time-preference rate: 'There is no reason for the parties to give weight to mere position in time' (Rawls, 1971:294). However, it is absolutely clear that Rawls does not support the use of classical utilitarianism in the context of intergenerational justice. He writes (Rawls, 1971:s.286–7): 'It seems evident . . . that the classical principle of utility leads in the wrong direction for questions of justice between generations. . . . The utilitarian doctrine may direct us to demand heavy sacrifices of the poor generations for the sake of greater advantages for later ones that are far better off.'

Provided that the assumption of positive productivity holds, both the utilitarian and Rawlsian welfare functions lead to non-decreasing quality of life, and hence, to development that is sustainable. Chichilnisky (1996) has recently put forward a welfare function that is based on what she calls sustainable preferences based on Arrow's (1951) axiomatic approach to social choice. Chichilnisky sets up the following two axioms:

1. The present shall not have dictatorial power.
2. The future shall not have dictatorial power.

She shows that there is a class of welfare functions that satisfies these two axioms. Theoretically, this is an interesting result. However, a welfare function that satisfies the two axioms has the fundamental weakness that there is often no development that maximises the welfare function. The problem is that according to the welfare function, it is desirable to postpone for any finite period of time actions seeking to protect the quality of life of generations living in the distant future, while it is undesirable to postpone such actions indefinitely.

The point of departure here is that the concept of sustainable development does not require that one chooses a particular welfare function as the normative basis. The meaning of sustainable development is not that one particular development is sustainable and therefore better than all other developments. The essence of the concept is that it deems some possible developments – namely those that are not sustainable – as non-acceptable candidates for social choice. In practical policy, this requires that rules for resource management are formulated that provide information on whether the actual development is sustainable or not, and that it is pointed out how collective action can correct the course if development turns out to be non-sustainable. These are themes for the next two sections of the chapter.

9.3   RULES FOR RESOURCE MANAGEMENT

Given the assumption that each generation's quality of life depends on what it inherits from previous generations and what it bequeaths to future generations – and that this relation is known – it may seem an easy task to determine whether our generation's resource management is sustainable. If the inheritance that we receive and the bequest that we will leave behind consist only of one capital good, the rule for sustainability is as follows: let the stock of the capital good that is bequeathed be at least as large as the stock that was inherited.

If sustainable development is considered to be a stationary process, it would seem reasonable to represent the stocks that are bequeathed from one generation to another as one homogeneous capital good, even though in practice, it is made up of many different capital goods. If sustainable development is a static condition, the rule for sustainability would be to leave behind, for every one of the capital goods, at least as much of the stock that was inherited. Such a requirement is often linked to the concept of 'strong sustainability' (see for example, Daly, 1992a). This should not be understood as a definition of the concept of sustainability, but a rule for how sustainability could be attained. It is often presented as a rule that should be followed because the accumulation of one capital good (for example, knowledge) will not compensate for the reduced availability of another capital good (for example, natural and environmental resources). This pessimistic attitude concerning the possibilities for substitution must, however, be linked with the following optimistic view: that it is possible to realise an acceptable quality of life for the world's population by following current paths of development.

'Strong' sustainability entails that no generation will be permitted to exploit non-renewable natural resources even if the resources do not have any value as non-exploited stocks and do not harm the environment when they are exploited. In practice, however, the advocates of 'strong' sustainability allow for the exploitation of such resources as long as this is compensated by the accumulation of stocks of other renewable natural resources, provided that these renewable resources can substitute for the non-renewable resources they replace.

One may argue in this context that sustainable development cannot be a balanced process. Human activity will lead to the depletion of natural resources and the deterioration of environmental resources. For a generation to be able to fulfil its obligations towards future generations, it must therefore compensate such reduced availability of natural capital by accumulating human capital (especially knowledge) and man-made real capital. To be effective, such compensation in the form of knowledge and real capital must have the property that it does not require further depletion of natural resources and deterioration of environmental resources. In other words: knowledge should produce a 'sustainable' technology as the basis for the real capital that is accumulated. As an example, technology for extracting and exploiting non-renewable resources through a process that inflicts long-term damage to environmental resources would be of a non-sustainable kind. On the other hand, technology that harvests renewable resources in a sustainable way without causing pollution could be characterised as sustainable.

The rule that each generation shall compensate for reduced natural capital through the accumulation of human and man-made capital is often called a requirement for 'weak sustainability' (see, for example, Pearce and Atkinson, 1993:104). Again, this is not a definition of sustainability, but a rule for how sustainability could be attained. Supporters of a requirement of 'weak' sustainability can be said to believe in the possibilities that human and man-made capital can substitute for natural capital within certain limits.

If a rule for 'weak' sustainability is to be used, it must be possible to evaluate whether the reduction in the stocks of natural capital is actually compensated by the increase in the stocks of human and man-made capital. To be able to do this, relative prices for the different capital stocks are required. Let us assume that there exist market prices for all capital goods, including natural and environmental resources and human capital. Let us also assume that polluters are made responsible for negative external effects through the environmental policy implemented by the authorities. Under such conditions, it is usual in economic literature (Mäler, 1991:11; Hulten, 1992:17; see also Solow, 1993) to claim the following: a generation's resource management is sustainable if and only if the accumulation of human and man-made capital is at least as large as the depletion of natural capital, when evaluated in market prices. Even under the most ideal conditions, this result is not correct. It is possible that our generation's accumulation of human and man-made capital exceeds the depletion of natural capital when evaluated in market prices, even though we ensure ourselves a quality of life that cannot be shared by all future generations (Asheim, 1994). This result undermines the possibilities for using 'weak' sustainability as an operational rule. This also means that it will be difficult to develop a concept of national income that can serve as a useful indicator of sustainability.

The result that can be established under such ideal conditions, is the following: if development is egalitarian – such that each generation ensures itself the maximum sustainable quality of life – then it follows that for each generation, the accumulation of human and man-made capital is exactly equal to the depletion in natural capital when evaluated in market prices. This is called Hartwick's rule (Hartwick, 1977; Dixit, Hammond and Hoel, 1980). The paragraph above implies that this is not a rule that can determine whether our generation acts in accordance with sustainability; rather, it is a result that characterises a particular sustainable development where the intergenerational distribution is completely egalitarian. Even along such an egalitarian path, the total market value of capital stocks is not constant. This is due to the fact that some capital stocks (in particular, remaining stocks of natural resources) will increase in market value over time. On a global basis, such capital gains reflect reduced productivity, and hence cannot be seen as a source of sustainable income (Asheim, 1996). Hence, a rule requiring that the market value of the total capital stocks be non-decreasing does not – even under ideal conditions – correspond to a requirement for sustainability.

Under less ideal, but more realistic conditions, the possibilities for constructing rules for sustainability are further reduced.

1. Not all capital stocks can be valued given the available market-price information. This applies not only to human capital (knowledge), but also to many forms of environmental resources. Attempts to calculate prices for such stocks for this purpose should be viewed with scepticism.
2. The Earth's population is not constant. With population growth, each generation will have to bequeath more than it inherited. However, it is a complicated issue to determine how large such an accumulation will have to be; it depends, among other things, on the future rate of population growth.
3. A policy for sustainable development will mainly have to be implemented at the national level. Hence, it is important to formulate rules for sustainability which each country can follow.[6] It can be shown (Asheim, 1996) that a

procedure for sustainability for an individual country is not only dependent on the extent to which it compensates the depletion of natural capital by accumulating stocks of human and man-made capital. It will also depend on what capital stocks of natural capital the country has at its disposal. For example, a country that has large stocks of natural capital with a value that increases over time, will have relatively less responsibility for achieving world-wide sustainability than a country without such stocks. In simple models, it can be shown that the needed reinvestment in human and man-made capital stocks as a result of depleted stocks of natural resources should be under-taken by countries that consume resources, not by countries that produce them. For a concept of national income to reflect this, anticipated capital gains must be taken into account. This is usually not done. An empirical analysis of sustainability as presented by Pearce and Atkinson (1993), pro-vides an illustration of this problem. This analysis shows, among other things, that both Japan and Indonesia accumulate man-made capital stocks at a high rate. Japan (with small stocks of natural capital) depletes its stocks of natural capital by a small amount, so that the country is regarded as very sustainable. Indonesia (with large stocks of natural capital) depletes its stocks of natural capital by a large amount, so that the country is regarded as marginally non-sustainable. If sustainability within each country implies that the countries should reinvest natural resources in proportion to resource consumption, greater demands will be put on Japan and less on Indonesia. It may thus be possible that Indonesia is actually more sustain-able than Japan.[7]

What then are the possibilities that remain for employing the concept of sustainable development in practical policy? Such rules will seem to have to involve indicators for the availability of renewable natural and environmental resources that are essential for the production of goods which satisfy basic human needs. Such primary goods comprise food, water and air. Indicators that show the Earth's capability of generating a maintainable production of food and water would therefore be of value.[8] Correspondingly, indicators that show the accumulation of greenhouse gases (and hence, the potential for changes in the global climate) would be important. Pragmatic rules could then be formu-lated based on such indicators.

Because such indicators will have to be based on physical quantities, this approach is reminiscent of the rules for sustainability that advocates of 'strong sustainability' have put forward (see, for example, Daly, 1992a:251). My reason for suggesting similar rules is, however, not a lack of belief that the accumula-tion of human and man-made capital will be able to compensate for depleted stocks of natural capital. From my point of view, the problem is that it appears to be difficult to determine how large such compensating investments will have to be.

9.4   POSSIBILITY FOR COLLECTIVE ACTION

As mentioned in the introduction to this chapter, a market economy, even under ideal conditions, will not necessarily ensure intergenerational justice. The problem is that the bequest that we individually wish to leave to our children is not adequate to ensure for the next generation initial conditions that are as good as those we enjoyed ourselves. Under what assumptions will there be a basis for collective action from authorities that are the democratic representatives of our own generation?

Firstly, a market system often will not make polluters responsible for the damage they inflict on others. Environmental policy is a type of collective action that seeks to force polluters to take into consideration the damage they cause. For global pollution problems, environmental policy will have to be initiated through international co-operation. International agreements concerning the emission of CFC gases and CO_2 are examples of such co-operation that also will have great consequences for intergenerational distribution. Nonetheless, it should be emphasised that environmental policy that makes polluters responsible for the damage they inflict is primarily aimed at preventing wastefulness, so that one may fully exploit the possibilities for improving one generation's quality of life without worsening the situation of another. The fact that a successful environmental policy in this way prevents wastefulness in our management of natural and environmental resources is not alone sufficient to ensure sustainable development. Even without wastefulness, is it possible for the present generation to exploit resources to an extent that undermines future generations' possibilities of meeting their essential needs (see Page, 1977 and Asheim, 1996)? As mentioned in Chapter 1, this is related to the fact that a market system, even under ideal conditions, does not necessarily ensure a just distribution of income.

Hence, the question is whether there is a democratic basis for the authorities of our generation to implement collective action for the purpose of redistributing income from current to future generations. Again, the rationale seems to lie in the existence of external effects, but of a different type than the ones discussed above. It is imaginable that in one generation, there exist two different motives for transferring income to the next generation. The first one is the altruistic concern that we have for our children, which results in a bequest motive within each family. The other is linked to the value we place on providing future generations with an acceptable quality of life. However, to fulfill this latter objective of an acceptable quality of life for future generations, it does not matter much who leaves behind a greater bequest. If an individual family leaves behind a greater bequest, the cost for this will have to be borne exclusively by (the older generation within) this family. At the same time, there is a gain in the form of a better quality of life for future generations that has value for everybody in the present generation. This means that there are positive external effects associated with leaving a bequest (Marglin, 1963). This entails that the authorities that are the democratic representatives of our own generation may wish to initiate collective action for the purpose of transferring income from the present generation to future generations.

How can such transfers be realised as a result of collective action initiated by democratic authorities? Given that the basic problem is that families in their bequest decisions do not take into consideration the impact of their bequest for society at large, the most direct instrument will be to raise the bequest motive within each family. Raising the bequest motive will also ensure that those who receive inheritance will pass more on to their own descendants. It is unclear however, how the authorities will be able to contribute towards such a rise in the bequest motive. The authorities have the possibility of increasing their own public savings. However, such a policy may be fully or partly neutralised through corresponding reduced private savings (Barro, 1974).

If we – in our generation – are concerned that future generations will not be able to attain an acceptable quality of life, the following alternatives are also possible:

1. By supporting research and information, the authorities can make our generation aware of the long-term consequences of the present development. If these consequences are serious, such awareness may strengthen the bequest motive, and thereby increase our collective bequest to future generations.
2. The authorities can – preferably in the form of international co-operation – contribute towards the conservation of renewable natural and environmental resources in a productive state. Such a policy can help maintaining the Earth's capacity to produce food, and preventing global climate change. As mentioned in Section 9.3, this coincides with the type of policy that the advocates of 'strong' sustainability recommend.
3. The authorities can encourage a generation of knowledge that leads to the adaptation of a technology that can be characterised as sustainable. This will increase our generation's possibility of compensating future generations for the damage that we have inflicted on the natural capital at our disposal. It can also increase the possibility that each generation can attain an acceptable quality of life without causing great depletion of natural resources and inflicting long-term and serious damage to environmental resources.

Still, even though the authorities possess instruments for transferring income from our generation to future generations, these instruments are far from perfect.

The authorities will often have to decide on projects that have long-term consequences for the availability of natural and environmental resources. Consider, for example, a project with the following characteristics: implementation of the project will have positive consequences for the present generation, but due to depletion of natural resources and deterioration of the environment, the project will have negative consequences for future generations. Assume also that the effects at each point in time can be evaluated in a meaningful way as a rise or reduction in the relevant generation's quality of life. How should such a project be evaluated by present authorities? To be more concrete: how should future effects of the project be discounted such that the effects at different points in time are comparable? The answer to this question turns out to depend on the extent to which the project will have distributional effects when the private agents' saving behaviour is taken into consideration, and on the instruments that the authorities possess for transferring income between generations.

If private agents neutralise the distributional effects through their saving behaviour, such that compensating investments take place without involvement from the authorities, and such investments provide a return equal to the market interest rate, then the project will benefit all generations if and only if the project has positive net present value when discounted with the market interest rate. Therefore in this case, the market interest rate should be used as the discount rate.

However, it seems more realistic to assume that the project's distributional effects will be neutralised only to a small extent through changes in the private agents' saving behaviour. In addition, it may be doubtful whether the compensating investments that are financed by increased private savings will be based on sustainable technology. Hence, these investments may not be in the interest of all future generations. This means that the project, even after possible changes in the saving behaviour of private agents, will have distributional effects that are unfavourable to some future generations. What discount rate the authorities will have to use in this case will depend on the ability of redistribution of income between generations. Let us introduce the following terminology: if the authorities can realise compensating investments with a return that is equal to the market rate, then they have at their disposal perfect instruments for redistribution. On the other hand, if the authorities can only realise compensating investments with a return that is less than the market rate, then the instruments for redistribution are imperfect.

If the authorities have perfect instruments for redistribution, the future effects of the project should be discounted with the market interest rate. As mentioned previously, a reasonably egalitarian sustainable development in a market system will be characterised by a positive market rate that need not be constant over time. Why should this market interest rate be used to discount future effects of the project being evaluated? With perfect instruments for redistribution, the authorities can undertake alternative investments with a return that is equal to the market interest rate. These investments will be able to compensate for the future negative effects of the project. Hence, if the project has positive net present value when its effects are discounted with the market interest rate, then it will be possible to attain a situation where all generations are better off through such compensating investments. Given the anthropocentric point of departure, the project would then be implemented.

The situation is radically different if we make a more realistic assumption, namely that the authorities lack perfect instruments for redistribution between generations. Then the authorities will not be able to make compensating investments with a return equal to the market interest rate. Therefore, it may well be that the best way of transferring income to future generations is to refrain from implementing the project. This may apply even though the project has positive net present value when future effects are discounted with the market interest rate.

I have discussed above how democratic authorities will want to determine whether a project with long-term negative environmental effects should be implemented or not. The same kind of reasoning could be applied to the evaluation of instruments for the purpose of making polluters responsible for their pollution when such pollution has long-term negative consequences for future generations. In their design of instruments, the authorities must weigh the short-term benefits that polluters have from being able to discharge waste products against the long-term consequences of these discharges. The issue of discounting explicitly or implicitly must enter into this trade-off.

I have previously concluded that it may be a political goal for democratic authorities to increase transfers to future generations, while the available instruments for such redistribution are likely to be far from perfect. This implies that when evaluating a project with long-term negative consequences for future generations, it may be appropriate to discount such effects with a rate that is lower than the market interest rate. To what extent future effects of such a project should be discounted, will depend in such cases on the desirability of redistribution to future generations and the return on alternative compensating investments that the authorities are capable of initiating.[9] Because the extent of discounting depends on democratic authorities' desire and capacity for intergenerational transfers, the discount rate used in such project evaluation cannot be directly derived from principles of intergenerational justice. However, such principles of justice may have indirect significance by influencing the public debate that determines the authorities' desire for transfers in favour of future generations.

NOTES

1. See Page (1977) for a convincing argumentation.
2. The idea of defining sustainability in this way dates at least back to Tietenberg (1984), and seems to have been fairly widely accepted; see, for example, Repetto (1986), Pezzey (1989), Mäler (1989), and NAVF (1990). A critical evaluation of this interpretation of sustainability is given by Pearce *et al.* (1989:32 and 49). Hammond (1994) provides an interesting review of references relating to the concept of sustainable development.
3. That is to say, the generations meet behind a 'veil of ignorance' or in 'the original position' (Harsanyi, 1953; Rawls, 1971).
4. Opposed to this is the view that the principles of intergenerational justice cannot be evaluated independently of the consequences in specific situations, but must be evaluated in light of them. This view appears to be supported by Koopmans (1967), Mishan (1977), Dasgupta and Heal (1979:308–11) and Rawls (1971:20).
5. This discussion of Rawls (1971:44) is based on Torrissen (1994).
6. If some countries are richer than others to begin with, following rules for sustainability in each individual country will not necessarily lead to less inequality between different countries. See Wetlesen's chapter in this book for a discussion of a global sustainable ethic.
7. I thank John Hartwick for calling my attention to this interpretation of these results from the work of Pearce and Atkinson (1993).
8. One problem in this regard is that, in practice, food is not only produced using renewable resources. Energy, fertilisers and pesticides are used in food production and contribute towards reducing the availability of natural and environmental resources.
9. This discussion of the discounting of effects that affect several generations is parallel to the debate on the treatment of distribution effects in benefit – cost analysis.

10 Economic Initiatives and Sustainable Development: an Assessment of Possibilities and Limitations

Stein Hansen

10.1 THE GREAT DILEMMA[1]

The sustainable development advocated by the Brundtland Commission's report *Our Common Future* (1987), presupposes global economic growth (see Chapter 1) and a distribution of assets and income where developing countries are given the opportunity to attain a significant increase in disposable income per capita, as the basis for redressing poverty. Development policies with such a goal will inevitably mean a strategy consisting of raising the poor to the level of the rich (or in any case, in the direction of this level) and creating conducive conditions in the poor part of the world for investments and consumption according to the pattern of present industrial countries.

Such a policy is obviously based on the idea that there are not, and will not be in future society either, serious barriers to material growth. Various production factors – natural resources (including various absorptive capacities), man-made capital, labour supply and an efficient social structure – are assumed to be substitutable for each other, such that the scarcity of one of them causes no significant barriers to the productivity of the others.

At the same time, the Brundtland Commission expresses concern for the global consequences of human production and consumption in the form of pollution, depletion of resources, and the general risk that a deteriorated environment poses for future generations. Such concerns seem to reflect the idea that there are – and will increasingly be – serious limitations for growth; in other words, that some of the key factors in production are complementary and not substitutable.

10.2   POPULATION GROWTH AND THE UNEVEN DISTRIBUTION OF RESOURCE USE

The Brundtland Commission's report makes particular use of a concept of sustainability that covers development both in time and space. The Commission expresses concern over future generations' inheritance, while it cannot accept that the great and increasing gap in prosperity between the rich and the poor countries is compatible with sustainable development.

This issue of distribution is just as complicated for the distribution between existing and unborn generations. Among other things, this is due to political disagreement as to how much and how various kinds of resources are to be transferred from rich to poor countries. Furthermore, attitudes towards this touch on existing domestic distribution of income, wealth and power. Hence, the distributive–political possibilities also depend on such domestic–internal conditions. However, the necessary political, social and economic reforms take a rather long time. Consequently, the aspect of time plays an important role in this case.

We speak glowingly of closing the steadily increasing prosperity gap between the rich and poor countries. At the same time, concern increases for how much environmental burden the Earth can bear before life becomes threatened. Is it at all possible to improve our own living standards, at the same time as the fast-rising population in developing countries also improve theirs? Is there any reasonable relation between the technological advances that are required and the global, natural limitations we must submit to?

While population growth has recently stagnated in the industrialised countries, it is still extremely high in the developing countries of the South. While three-quarters of the world's population lived in the South in 1980, the proportion is expected to increase to around 85 per cent in 2025. At the same time, the world's population is expected to rise to 8.5 billion and increase to 10 billion around the year 2050. More than 90 per cent of the population growth hereafter is expected to be found in the South.

Nevertheless, we should be careful about drawing hasty conclusions on where the global environmental threats lie. The distribution of resource consumption between the North and the South is diametrically opposite. The OECD countries have 85 per cent of global income and have contributed about 80 per cent of the CO_2 emissions since 1950. The energy consumption per capita is 15 times higher in the USA than in China. CO_2 emissions are 'only' 11 times higher because China uses relatively more coal. The average energy consumption per capita calculated in oil equivalent per annum is less than 100 kg in Africa south of the Sahara, 200 kg in Southern Asia, 500 kg in Eastern Asia, 1000 kg in Latin America, and over 5000 kg in the OECD countries. Norway is at the top of the OECD list, with about 9000 kg, while Japan, due to high energy efficiency (which again may be because of dependence on energy imports) 'only' uses 3500 kg.

If present consumption patterns and economic policies persist, and if only one out of every ten children in the coming years is born in the North, this child will consume 3 to 4 times as much as the nine children born at the same time in the South. As such, it is misleading to focus the concerns of the environmental sustainability of development singularly on the rise in population in the South. The enormous differences in resource use between the rich North and the poor South require that as much attention be paid to the consumption patterns in the North. The poverty dimension of sustainability is, however, closely related to the rapid population growth in places where new and well-paid jobs grow at a much lower rate. A continuation of present trends will be incompatible with both our concept of equity and with sustainable global development. The estimated income ratio between the Earth's 20 per cent richest and 20 per cent poorest was 30:1 in 1960. It was during this time that the richer countries deliberately began with active development aid to narrow the North–South gap. However, ten years later, the income gap had increased from 30:1 to 32:1. In 1980 it was 45:1, and in 1989 it had almost doubled to 59:1.

In the meantime, the economic growth in populous Asia has become so high that all indications suggest that at least half of the CO_2 emissions in the next decades will originate from the South. Wholly 90 per cent of the Earth's biological diversity is concentrated in the South, in a small number of 'mega-diverse countries' with the existing rain forests. With prevailing policy and market failures, the growth in population and economic activities in these countries presents a serious threat to sustainable management of these global commons.

The magnitude of the task of reversing the trend in the distribution of welfare between North and South can be illustrated by the following comparison: during the last 20 years, inhabitants of Africa have experienced a declining standard of living in most places, and in many of them it has sunk dramatically from levels which, compared to the North, were inconceivably low to begin with.

The Brundtland Report presented a projection which, in this perspective, could appear to be quite optimistic (most people would say even unrealistic); namely that the average income in the next 20 years would increase by 3 per cent per annum. This would obviously require comprehensive alterations of policies both in the North and South, including a sharp increase in the technological and financial transfers from North to South. Even so, such an effort will not reverse present trends with steadily greater absolute differences between North and South. It is a widespread and scientifically based understanding that the rich countries must have corresponding economic growth to create the basis for the transfers that provide such growth to the South. It is easy to deduce that a 3 per cent annual rise in income for the individual Ethiopian will only come to $3.60. With 3 per cent growth in average income in, for example the USA, the rise per capita will be $633; that is to say, a sum that corresponds to decades of income in, for example Ethiopia. If we view this over a ten-year period, the average income in the USA will have risen by $7257, while in Ethiopia, it will have risen by only $41. The North–South gap will thus continue to widen for a long time into the future.

However, the development in East and Southeast Asia in the last 25 years may indicate that it is possible to break this North–South dependency through persistent, strictly disciplined economic and social policies. The oil-importing, and in several cases raw-materials-poor countries (Japan, South Korea and Taiwan), and the emerging raw-materials-rich countries (like Thailand, Malaysia and Indonesia), have managed to establish an unusually high level of real economic growth without being affected by the oil crisis and depression in the rich countries. They seem to have developed their own driving force independently from that of the rich countries.

On the other hand, development in most of Africa and some of Southern Asia is characterised by dependency on an 'engine' with pulling power, where these countries are still regarded as 'engineless trailers' in international economic development.

A key challenge in North–South co-operation must be to install independent economic pulling power in these societies. It does not seem realistic that any form of global income levelling will occur without such an adjustment. The challenge will consist of finding out and recognising the underlying causes of why the above-mentioned resource-poor countries have succeeded in reducing the prosperity gap compared with OECD countries, while some OECD countries have been left more and more behind. The challenge then is to convert this recognition into economic-political and social-political reforms that adjust for less dependence on raw materials and a more lasting and reliable basis for technology transfer and a broader industrial base. This is not an easy task in countries where, over the past decades, elites have exploited both the masses and the resource base, and without more ado, now feel they are entitled to a socially more sustainable policy. Such countries are typically characterised by a persistently high population growth, accompanied by increasing population pressure on, and over-exploitation of, a steadily shrinking natural resource base. Among other factors, this is because the technology level is very low and technology development is slow or stagnant. Savings and investments in such countries are typically very low or totally lacking, in contrast with the situation in the East and Southeast Asian 'tiger nations'. This issue will be dealt with in the next section.

10.3 CAN ECONOMIC GROWTH AND RESOURCE CONSUMPTION BE DECOUPLED?

The connection between GNP and energy consumption has come into focus in recent years, precisely because one wishes to have a better understanding of the macro-economic interplay and balancing that arise when one weighs 'look before you leap'-based strategies against 'business as usual' strategies for economic development. With the aid of computer-based equilibrium models with a long-term time frame, administrative or economic political initiatives are introduced that aim to dampen material consumption. This is done through, for example, reducing energy use and, hence, also reducing various local, regional and global environmental problems, including the strain on the Earth's limited absorptive capacity for climate gases, among other things. The models are used to study the possible economic, social and environmental consequences of various dimensions of such intervention. In particular, there was concern with the extent to which growth in GNP can be maintained, at the same time as production and consumption are altered to the extent that emissions from fossil energy consumption are stabilised or reduced.

The traditional economic school of thought has been that physical investments in agriculture and industry form the basis for economic growth. In the years between the wars, with high unemployment and untapped resources, the British economist Lord Keynes developed the theory that consumption will be the driving force in the economy. As we approach a new millennium, totally new economic schools of thought are about to take over. These are theories that claim that it is new ideas – the development of new ways of thought that lead to technological advances and new inventions – that will be the economic driving force in the future.

The basic notion is that more of what we already have enough of will hardly maintain welfare. Further economic growth will occur if we become cleverer at rationalising how we can exploit steadily scarcer resources or do without them. In such a growth philosophy, the main task for the authorities is to prepare for precisely this process by giving higher priority to education, learning and research. Idea development comprises very much of what we can characterise as common goods or common assets. The free market alone is not capable of mobilising adequate resources for such purposes. Hence, an overriding authority should intervene and remedy such weaknesses of the pure market mechanism.

At the same time, there are not enough general guidelines for policy in this area. It appears that it is what they do in practice that is crucial. In certain cases, patent protection may be the right thing to do, while in many other cases, the best is to ensure the widest possible spread of new ideas – technology transfer and trade opportunities for developing countries.

This theory appears to fit in well with the actual development path in the East and Southeast Asian 'tiger nations' during the last 30 years. These countries have pursued a persistently deliberate policy of strong commitment to education and training at primary, tertiary and professional levels. The authorities have prioritised preventive work on public health to secure the productivity of the labour force. Population growth has declined rapidly, life-expectancy has almost reached the levels in Nordic countries, and infant mortality has sunk to a Western level.

Parallel to this, an economic and industrial-oriented policy has been pursued to adapt to stable and lasting investment conditions for technology transfer and new investments. For resource-poor countries, it will be crucial to be able to compete, based on a well-educated and efficient labour force, together with reliable start-up and operating conditions for processing industries. It is precisely these that the countries have committed themselves to. Not least because of this, they are about to close the prosperity gap between themselves and the OECD countries.

In great contrast to this is the development in countries that have steadily slowed down and been left more and more behind; absolutely in Africa south of the Sahara, and relatively in Southern Asia. In these countries, saving and investment have persistently constituted a very low proportion of GNP. In practice, education and preventive work in public health have had low priority, in spite of fiery political speeches and programmes that should indicate the opposite. Instead, the authorities have 'bled' tight public budgets persistently to subsidise inefficient, capital-intensive, prestigious public (wholly or partly) owned heavy industry enterprises, power plants, and large mechanised farms that are dependent on costly artificial irrigation installations. On the whole, it is the interest groups who support such enterprises who have sufficient power and influence to secure for themselves capital, energy, water, fertilisers and agricultural chemicals at highly subsidised prices, without regard to costs for society, besides, in the form of pollution, resource wasting, uneven distribution of society's goods, and loss of economic growth. Such conditions create scepticism among international as well as local investors, towards the political and financial stability and reliability of the country, and hence they stay away. This impedes both innovation and technology transfer.

Is a drastic increase in aid transfers or debt remission, then, a contribution towards such a reform process in these countries? Experience from the countries that have succeeded does not confirm this directly. More aid will not increase the total investments in productive projects if an institutional capacity and basis for industry is lacking in the said countries. There must be a commitment to establish an institutional and administrative capacity to match aid transfers so that more aid will contribute towards solving the problems. In many of the countries mentioned, there is much to indicate that lack of such capacity is a greater bottleneck than lack of aid transfers. Debt relief will naturally be able to contribute towards dampening the depletion of a country's currency reserves and towards stabilising the currency rate, hence preparing for a more predictable economic policy. At the same time, it is important to point out that debt relief is not an adequate solution for countries with economic problems. It is important that debt relief is used actively as an element in an economic reform process and not as a 'cushion' for the country's authorities and rulers. Moreover, it must be pointed out that debt relief may very well accelerate the depletion of the country's natural resources due to the fact that resource-depleting infrastructure projects that have been set aside because of the debt crisis can now be implemented with better access to currency. For countries that require more aid and debt relief to go over to a more sustainable development path, it is obvious that conditions linked to the use of such aid will constitute an important premise for a successful implementation of an eventual agreement, even though it is politically very sensitive to broach the subject of detailed adaptation requirements to sovereign nations.

10.4   STUDIES ON GLOBAL AND REGIONAL POSSIBILITIES

The OECD carries out global economic impact analysis with the equilibrium model GREEN. In Spring 1992, the OECD rationalised in a global CO_2 stabilisation study that OECD countries would reduce their total emission by 20 per cent within the year 2010, while individual regions outside the OECD would be allowed to increase their emission by 50 per cent. After 2010, it is assumed that all countries should stabilise their emission at the 2010 level. It was estimated that the necessary tax for these adjustments would have to be about 37 USD per ton of CO_2. The GNP was estimated to have to decrease by 1 per cent in the OECD by the year 2050, in comparison with a situation without such a tax where the corresponding decrease in the level for the world totally was estimated to be about 1.5 per cent. These global limits have (along with other factors) constituted a basis for the Norwegian Long-term Programme's estimates of the effects of a global stabilising CO_2 tax for the Norwegian economy (see the discussion below).

In other estimates made with this GREEN model, the OECD raises the question whether emission reduction limited to certain regions (for example, the OECD area) will lead to other regions (not subjected to such limitations) 'taking over' these emissions, so that the global net effect disappears. Firstly, such an effect could occur if energy-intensive industries simply move out from the area where limitations are imposed to regions without such limitations. Secondly, it may happen that the demand for fossil fuels decreases when such limitations are imposed. Consequently, energy prices will be pressed downwards. As long as one keeps the physical emission regulation in one region, it is reasonable to assume that energy demand will rise in regions that are not subjected to physical restrictions, because energy prices will decrease (if no special energy taxes are imposed or raised in the regions that are not affected).

Analysis of such possible courses of development with the GREEN model shows that the geographical distribution of energy-intensive industries is very little affected by such measures. The fear of 'industry migration' to 'pollution heavens' in developing countries appears to be unfounded. Model estimations indicate that a physical limitation of emissions in the OECD will actually have the intended global effect of very little leakage in the form of increased emission from exempted regions in some developing countries.

Common among these models (and most of the others used for such estimations) is the fact that they are based on the modelling of behaviour and possibility of substitution at the expense of a detailed sector and region division, and the modelling of technological advances. In all the models, technological advance is treated relatively briefly in the sense that one assumes a constant improvement of energy efficiency every year. Sensitivity analysis undertaken with the OECD's GREEN model showed, for example, that the CO_2 tax had to be doubled to attain the same reduction in emission when the change in energy efficiency is reduced from 1 per cent per annum (which is the basis for the course of reference above) to 0.5 per cent per annum. Furthermore, the parameter estimates that are used in these models cannot be used as they are, to predict what will happen when energy prices become much higher than the basis on which the parameter values are estimated. For example, it is assumed in the estimates for the OECD and Norway that the real price for petroleum remains unchanged up to 2030 for the baseline projection. However, sensitivity analysis of the effects of a partial physical restriction on the OECD countries' CO_2 emissions indicates that the conclusions from the basic alternative described above are extremely robust (see Naturvårdsverket, 1992).

The other global overview of effects that is referred to here focuses explicitly on the uncertainty surrounding the assumptions and estimates in such model calculations (see Manne and Richels, 1994). A survey is being carried out among experts working with these issues, and based on their experiences and statements, it is assumed that the uncertainty surrounding critical analysis parameters, and the probability distribution for the outcome, are of special interest for decision-makers. The analysis indicates a wide range of possible global stabilisation costs, from an annual cost as low as 0.2 per cent of GNP, to as high as 6.8 per cent. However, the probability distribution is highly skewed, as expected stabilisation costs lie at around 1.5 per cent of global GNP.

The effects of implementing a CO_2 tax in the EU on GNP and emission of CO_2, SO_2 and NOx have recently been analysed with a European energy-sector model (SEEM), where emphasis is placed on allowing substitution between various energy forms. The estimated SO_2 and NOx effects appear when SEEM is linked to IIASA's regional simulation model for the cross-border transport of acid rain (see Alfsen *et al.*, 1993).

This analysis shows that the effectiveness of a common European CO_2 tax affects in a crucial way how the member countries choose to invest in the energy market. Such a tax will reduce CO_2 emissions by 6 to 10 per cent compared with development without such tax, and hence will stabilise CO_2 emissions in the year 2000 at the 1989 level, even though governments choose to invest in thermal power plants as if no such tax had been imposed. However, if one presumes a cost-minimising investment behaviour in this sector, there will be a substitution of coal for natural gas, and the effect of a CO_2 tax will be a 3 per cent higher CO_2 reduction. It is interesting to note that while the tax is aimed at CO_2 emission, it simultaneously contributes towards reducing emissions of local and regional harmful SO_2 and NOx to a significant degree. These are the secondary welfare and productivity gains that may considerably reduce annual possible GNP losses when such a tax is imposed.

The consequences of global CO_2 stabilisation for developing countries can also be inferred from the estimations of the global models, where they focus on the size of the energy tax rise that the developing countries must have to stabilise their CO_2 emissions, or what it will cost these countries in the form of loss in GNP growth to stabilise or limit their fossil-energy consumption. With these models, one can make various assumptions on the distribution of burdens with stabilisation between rich and poor countries, such as was done in the OECD estimations that are referred to above.

The seriousness of the issue is clearly brought to the fore in the model estimations carried out on the global equilibrium model ECON-ENERGY (see Haugland *et al.*, 1990). Two alternative scenarios are analysed. One assumes global stabilisation of fossil energy use and CO_2 emission at the 1987 level. The other assumes regional stabilisation; for example, that all regions in the world individually do as the OECD countries and set as their goal to stabilise their CO_2 emission at the 1987–90 level. Global stabilisation is taken to mean a common initiative in the form of a globally equal CO_2 tax. For this to ensure stabilisation at the 1987 level, the tax (at a fixed price) should rise exponentially over time from $30 per ton of CO_2 in the year 2000, via $70 in the year 2010, and to $360 in the year 2025, as long as it is assumed that there is constant economic growth, population growth and gradual transition to electricity use in populous developing countries. It seems obvious that such taxes alone cannot solve the political problems that will arise if this stabilisation objective is to be attained.

The scenario based on the premise that global stabilisation of CO_2 emission will occur via regional stabilisation within the model's nine regions exclusively with the aid of regional CO_2 taxes shows even more clearly how hard-hit the initially poor countries will be, should this become the solution for the environment-versus-growth dilemma. Table 10.1 shows how such regional CO_2 taxes will have to grow unequally fast over time to attain the stabilisation objective, given that the countries maintain their economic growth rates at the level they would have been without such taxes (a combination that is of course unrealistic). What the estimates show is that the higher the taxes, the more the economic growth the region or country has to pay for, to attain stabilisation.

The large differences reflect large structural disparities between different regions with respect to energy sources and possibilities for substitution/reduced consumption. The fact that a rise in coal taxes at 40 times the present price in China and 90 times the present price in India respectively, with the USA needing only 6 times more, shows very clearly that this is not a politically realistic way to attain the stabilisation objective. More important, however, is the fact that the estimates emphasise how incredibly difficult it is to attain global stabilisation if OECD countries do not drastically reduce their fossil-energy consumption. There is little to indicate that a policy that goes further than a regional stabilisation within the OECD will be on the agenda anytime soon. Decision-makers are much more occupied with stabilising emissions than with stabilising concentrations in the atmosphere.

Table 10.1 CO_2 taxes that are necessary within each region if global CO_2 stabilisation at the 1987 level is to be attained via the stabilisation of emissions within each region (US dollars/ton of CO_2)

Region	Year 2000	Year 2010	Year 2025
USA	23	33	85
EU	40	59	115
Rest of OECD	75	108	225
Former USSR	4	37	231
Former Eastern Europe	12	63	410
China	15	56	363
India	75	242	1268
Brazil	80	272	1354
Rest of the world	55	136	496

Source: Haugland, Olsen and Roland (1990).

Altogether, this discussion shows that while it is not 'wide open' for reducing the use of fossil-energy forms, there is no longer anything which dictates that a certain reduction in the use of fossil fuels will lead to a proportional reduction in the GNP. Rather, different countries – depending on the industrial structure and the country's economic and social-adaptation capacity – will be capable of changing their energy consumption significantly, without having substantial economic consequences. This conclusion appears to be particularly valid for OECD countries, and especially if one explicitly takes into account the gains for the environment and health when other emissions (including TSP, NOx, and SO_2) are also reduced when CO_2 emissions are reduced. Up to now, one has placed little emphasis on this in the model estimations mentioned.

However, there will also be several developing countries which, to begin with, have arranged matters so that – economically, organisationally and technically – they will be able to save significantly on their energy bills without reducing the economic growth potential, perhaps even the opposite. Here, so-called structural and sectoral adjustment programmes with a focus on economic, institutional and organisational reforms in connection with the management of resources like energy, soil and water, will be of crucial significance. Today, several hundred billion Norwegian crowns more are wasted through inefficient price subsidies on energy, fertilisers and artificial irrigation than developing countries together receive in aid (see Hansen, 1993:20). The World Bank has estimated that developing countries together subsidise energy consumption with $150 billion each year, and of this, $100 billion goes towards keeping the price of electricity down. This policy not only undermines the public budgets of developing countries – which are very tight to begin with – it also hampers economic growth by preventing efficient investments. Among other things, such energy policies counteract investors' interest in and incentive to invest in energy-efficient processes and cleaner technology. This applies to both industry in general and power plants in particular. It is estimated that developing countries with such policies consume 20 per cent more electricity than they would consume if the prices had reflected the true long-term marginal costs of power supply.

With the implementation of economic reforms to change development in a more sustainable direction, it is important to ensure that there are transitional arrangements and gradual adaptation, such that the particularly vulnerable groups do not come out losers in the adaptation process. However, the material living standards and energy consumption in developing countries are low enough to begin with, compared with the rich countries. Even with the most efficient price reforms and technology transfers, it appears that the pressure to attain increased consumption of goods and services – and hence, more energy – is enormous, and probably, unavoidable in developing countries.

All newer existing global and regional model estimations conclude that a stabilisation or moderate reduction of fossil-energy consumption and corresponding CO_2 emissions in the rich countries can be attained at a modest cost in the form of moderately reduced growth in these countries. On the other hand, the cost of CO_2 stabilisation for developing countries will be quite high. There is also wide disagreement between the different models as to whether drastic reductions in energy consumption in the rich countries will entail significant direct economic costs in the form of reduced growth and demanding readjustments. If the latter should prove to be necessary (based on warnings from climate experts and ecologists) it may appear that there is no alternative to precisely such reduced fossil-energy consumption in the rich countries, and thus it is fairly meaningless to speak of such scenarios as 'costly'.

10.5   WHAT ABOUT NORWAY?

The Norwegian government's long-term programme for the period 1994 to 1997 also includes estimates as to what a CO_2 tax will imply in the form of reduced GNP and private consumption in the future. Here, it is also based on estimates using the multi-sectoral MSG model that the Ministry of Finance has utilised and developed during the last 30 years for concrete planning tasks. As a point of departure, the Norwegian government uses a so-called 'basic alternative' to project the economy to the year 2030. Simply put, significant energy and environmental conservation measures lie in the assumptions behind this alternative. One ends up with an energy consumption where CO_2 emissions rise by 4 million tons compared to the 1989 level of about 34 million tons – a level which has been politically adopted as a 'ceiling'.

The same set of models has also been used to estimate the marginal cost of reducing CO_2 emissions for Norway. This has been shown to be rising, and this result corresponds with the experience from similar studies in other countries. With given assumptions on, among other things, the price of 'backstop' technology, the estimates of the Norwegian model show that, for example, a CO_2 tax of \$55 (NOK 383) per ton of CO_2, will reduce CO_2 emissions by 21 per cent in the year 2020 in relation to a specific course of reference, with corresponding GNP reduction at 0.55 per cent. Such a tax level corresponds to roughly 1 Norwegian crown (USD 0.14) per litre of oil. Such a reduction in relation to the long-term programme's 'basic reference' is, however, not sufficient to stabilise CO_2 emissions at the 1989 level, which the parliament has set as the goal. Emissions in the year 2020 will actually be almost 13 per cent higher than in 1989 with such a CO_2 tax.

A stabilisation of the CO_2 emissions at the 1989 level in the period up to 2020 requires that the CO_2 tax is at \$215 (NOK 1500) in 2020, or about USD 0.56 per litre of oil. This will imply a GNP reduction of about 1.3 per cent. The stabilisation of CO_2 emissions in rich countries cannot however prevent increased CO_2 concentrations. It is therefore of interest to look at the economic consequences of even higher CO_2 taxes. A CO_2 tax of \$753 (NOK 5270) per ton of CO_2, will halve the CO_2 emissions relative to the government's basic-reference path, and reduce them by 35 per cent compared to the 1989 level. Such a CO_2 tax corresponds to about NOK 14 (USD 2) per litre of oil. If this is implemented, the estimated GNP reduction will be 2.85 per cent in comparison to the reference path (see Figure 10.1).

Figure 10.1 indicates that at the beginning of such a restrictive policy, one achieves relatively large reductions in CO_2 emissions for each tax unit, and the GNP loss is relatively small for each unit reduction in CO_2 emissions. After that, it becomes more and more difficult to reduce CO_2 emissions by using CO_2 taxes alone, and the costs measured in reduction in GNP become gradually higher and higher. With a tax level at about NOK 5000 (USD 704) per ton of CO_2, an extra CO_2 tax-crown entails only 5 per cent of the CO_2 reduction effect, compared to the effect with the first tax-crowns when the tax was low. And correspondingly, an additional reduction in CO_2 emission when one has already reduced this by 40 per cent in proportion to the reference path will entail a marginal loss of GNP that is five times greater than the marginal GNP loss with the initial emission limit (see Bye and Glomsrød, 1994).

Such energy-price increases sketched here are not necessarily to be regarded as dramatic when one considers a time-perspective of 30 years. Besides, energy

Figure 10.1   Projections of reductions in CO_2 emissions for reductions in GNP for the year 2002, Norway. Percentage deviations from the basic reference path as calculated by the MSG-model.

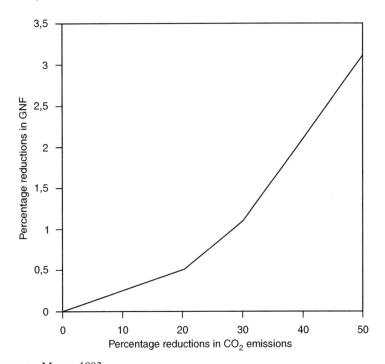

Source: Mysen, 1993

costs constitute a relatively moderate portion of the cost in most of the activities, including transport. That the marginal cost with such a policy is rising, is not surprising either. During the first phase of the restriction, gas-power is replaced by hydro-power, so that only a part of the cost increase from CO_2 taxes has market effect. But gradually, substitution possibilities become steadily more costly, and reducing the scope of the activity will seem to become steadily more attractive in several activities.

In the Sustainable Economy Project, which was a joint project between the Alternative Future Project and Friends of the Earth, Norway, the latter was given political control through an 'environmental parliament'. The NGO set up several requirements for sustainable development, most of them more strict than those on which the government has based its Long-term Programme. A key feature of the project was a protracted dialogue between nature conservationists and economists on the formulation of these requirements so that they could be used in economic long-term planning. This resulted in over fifty specific national environmental requirements from the environmental parliament. About half of these were shown to be too detailed and too geographically limited to be applied in national macro-economic planning models. We tried, therefore, to study the consequences of these requirements by using conventional macro-economic analytical tools, along with sector models for agriculture. The rest of the environmental requirements were transformed into various sustainability indicators which were employed as variables or requirements in model estimates for macro-economic planning and impact analysis models.

In the project, several scenarios were formulated to illustrate possible long-term effects on development in economic and environmental conditions by framing some of the above-mentioned requirements as concrete measures. One of these reflected reduced exploration and extraction activity in Norwegian oil and gas fields. Another scenario was aimed at a gradual increase in CO_2 tax over and above that in the government's long-term programme. A third scenario combined these, showing that the CO_2 tax rise is somewhat less dramatic than when it is the only instrument. A fourth scenario was based on the preceding scenarios, but exempted energy-intensive industries from the CO_2 tax. A fifth scenario reduced job opportunities in the economy, by assuming that people prioritise leisure more.

For each of these scenarios, it was estimated how various indicators for the Norwegian economy and environment would develop in relation to the base-year 1989, and, not least, in relation to the corresponding figures in the government's long-term programme for the period up to the year 2030. In the same way as for previously mentioned analyses of the introduction of CO_2 taxes, the scenarios showed that GNP growth becomes considerably lower in the Sustainable Economy alternative compared to the reference path for the Long-term Programme. However, it is important to note that also in the Sustainable Economy alternative, Norway would experience a drastic rise in GNP and consumption in the course of the 40-year period. It is thus important to assert that even with more powerful instruments for implementing a precautionary strategy, the average material living standard in Norway would continue to rise.

But what about the mix of consumption and production? One is accustomed to hearing from responsible politicians in rich countries that it is not economic growth as such that is the problem, but the growth's content. What makes the use of such macro-economic analytical models particularly interesting from a sustainability perspective is that they contain many assumptions on economic behaviour such as prices, taxes, fees, subsidies and income. These are of a magnitude that can be employed as instruments in the economic policy to come closer to the given goal: for example, on how society wishes to exploit or conserve nature and the environment domestically or internationally. Since the Norwegian macroeconomic MSG model contains a large number of different consumption categories, it is possible to study the effects on the composition of consumption when one uses economic instruments as described in the example.

As an illustration, Table 10.2 shows the results from one of the scenarios in the form of percentage deviation from the composition of consumption in the Long-term Programme for the year 2030. The chosen scenario (number 3) combines reduced extraction of oil and gas with a gradual rise in the CO_2 tax. The estimates show that there will be large changes in the composition of consumption, particularly for private travel and stationary use of oil products, and that was part of the purpose of the measure.

Table 10.2   Percentage change in the various consumption categories in 2030 in scenario no. 3 compared to the Long-term Programme's reference path

Consumption category	Percentage deviation from Long-term Programme 2030
Electricity	1.92
Stationary oil	−35.83
Petrol	−63.24
Automobile buying	−9.83
Public transportation	−9.30
Food	−5.02
Luxury goods	−9.57
Other goods	−9.10
Clothes and shoes	−8.54
Furniture	−10.89
Housing	−13.14
Other services	−7.13
Tourism overseas	−13.54

Source: Estimates from the Project for a Sustainable Economy, carried out by the Research Division of Statistics Norway, Spring 1995.

What about the measurable environmental effects of this alternative economic policy? Detailed emission models have been linked to the MSG model, so that climate changes for several important emission components can be estimated. The development over time in these, compared with the base year 1989, is shown in Figure 10.2, and the emission reductions compared with the Long-term Programme are shown in Figure 10.3.

The results are alarming. On one hand, it is clear that the ideal IPCC 'look before you leap' goal on the stabilisation of CO_2 concentrations will not be attained. For this to be achieved, CO_2 emissions would have to be reduced by sixty per cent in proportion to the base year. Nevertheless, one still comes a good way towards this sustainability goal in that CO_2 emissions will be 35 per cent lower than in the Long-term Programme scenario, and 23 per cent lower than the 1989 base-year. Thus, one still comes well within the Norwegian Parliament's prescribed emission stabilisation goal, and towards a 'look before you leap insurance premium' that is moderately expressed in reduced GNP and consumption compared with the government's scenario.

Figure 10.2   MSG-estimated emissions of selected gases according to the projected reference path of development (Alternative 3: with 1989 = 1)

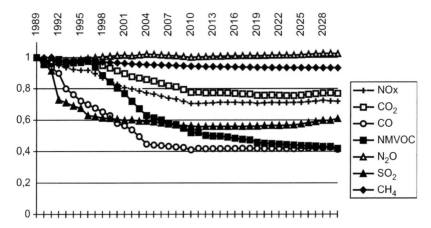

Note: NMVOC = Non-Methene Volatile Organic Compound
Source: Scenarios from the 'Project for a Sustainable Economy', op. cit.

It is equally interesting to note the additional environmental gains with such economic management because these affect health, nature and construction capital in the local community. For most of the environmental emissions large (35 to 40 per cent) reductions are attained compared to the Long-term Programme's results, particularly for VOC, SO_2 and CO, but also close to 20 per cent reduction for NOx and N_2O. Compared to the base-year 1989, reductions are attained for all local environmental emissions, except for N_2O, which is stabilised. Reductions are particularly large (about 60 per cent) for VOC and CO_2, but 40 per cent reduction for SO_2 is also significant. For NOx, the reduction is around 25 per cent.

What then, is the national-accounts value of such environmental improvements? The Central Bureau of Statistics' researchers have attempted to calculate this within the research programme SAMMEN with the same model apparatus (see Bye and Glomsrød 1994:11–15). While in the conventional estimates with MSG and similar models, one assumes that the factor inputs of capital and labour are just as productive as before a drastic reduction in pollution, here one assumes that this productivity is affected negatively by local air pollution. Hence, the costs of such measures are overvalued when they are calculated. Based on damage functions, dose-response relations, valuation of lost working hours and increased depreciation in buildings and roads, the marginal pollution cost per kilo of emission for SO_2, NOx, CO_2 and volatile particles (VOC) has been calculated. Based on this, the various oil products' marginal pollution and traffic-related costs per litre of oil product are estimated.

Figure 10.3   Percentage reduction in various emission components compared to the basic reference path of the Government's Long-term Programme

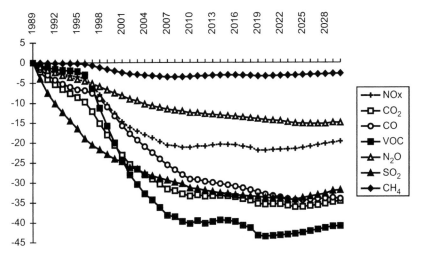

Note: NMVOC = Non-Methene Volatile Organic Compound
Source: Scenorios from the 'Project for a Sustainable Economy', op. cit.

Calculations of the marginal external costs from pollution, wear and tear on roads and traffic accidents show that it is diesel in particular and petrol which appear to involve great negative environmental costs, and which can be internalised to a great extent with the aid of economic instruments in the form of environmental taxes that correspond to the marginal damage that consumption entails. The calculated total environmental and traffic gains with marginal cost-oriented taxes are estimated at around 17 billion crowns in the year 2000. This corresponds approximately to the fall in GNP that was initially calculated for the same year with the introduction of such taxes. There is every indication that when marginal environmental loads are significant to begin with, and price-setting which internalises these drawbacks does not occur, the social-economic gains with optimal environmental taxes would go far in neutralising the loss that apparently arises in the form of reduced GNP as a result of structural adaptations in the various production and consumption sectors.

There also exists another analysis under the auspices of the Sustainable Economy Project which focuses especially on the effects on the welfare level of including the benefit of reducing such harmful emissions of substances that are complementary to CO_2 emissions. The analysis has a ten-year perspective, utilises a somewhat different macroeconomic model than the ones described above, and is based on an economy with a tax system where the relative prices in society are skewed away from cost-oriented prices on marketable goods and services. In this case, a tax reform where the state's income from increased CO_2

taxes is neutralised by a reduction in employer tax contribution will be able to raise the society's welfare level (Håkonsen and Mathiesen, 1994). This so-called 'having your cake and eating it too' (double dividends/gains) result is totally in accordance with economic theory, because one reduces the total inefficiency in the economy by substituting a price-distorted tax on labour with a resource tax that internalises a negative environmental effect. By gradually expanding the content in the model's welfare function and the emissions and environmental effects included in the calculations, the estimated social benefit of a given CO_2 reduction and the level of the optimal CO_2 reduction are increased.

As a point of departure, the analysis assumes that it is only goods consumption that creates benefits and that one introduces a resource tax that distorts the resource price away from the resource's socio-economic cost, and, thereafter, distributes the tax income as a fixed sum to each consumer. In such a society, one may easily conclude that the welfare level will fall as the resource tax rises. However, if benefits are extended to include both consumption and leisure, and at the same time it is open to 'recycling' tax income from the CO_2 tax with a corresponding reduction in the employers' contribution, then there will arise economic efficiency gains in society. This is due to the fact that total price distortions are reduced when the CO_2 tax is raised, and CO_2 emissions and emissions of complementary polluting substances are reduced. Here however, it is important to stress that the result appears to depend on what one assumes about the labour market. In particular, it is important to emphasise that within the scope of general equilibrium analysis, empirical calculations suggest that the choice of structural conditions as to how the labour market functions is more important for the total socio-economic consequences than are the estimates one chooses for the strength of the reaction of labour supply to a rise in wages. The calculations show that welfare increases in relation to the starting-point, even with a 30 per cent reduction in CO_2 emissions. The highest welfare gain in these calculations with neutralised budget effects, was a combination of a CO_2 tax at \$82 per ton of CO_2 that reduces CO_2 emissions by 15 per cent in proportion to the reference path, and a halving of the labour tax for employers.

It is however, important to emphasise that such high welfare gains from reducing CO_2 and complementary emissions are closely connected with the fact that, to start with, the economic policy does not internalise negative environmental and traffic effects. Should the latter be achieved with relevant tax instruments, the efficiency gains from the combination of CO_2 tax and reduced employers' contribution will be much less or be annulled (see Strand, 1994).

10.6   CONCLUSIONS

Nearly everyone is a supporter of sustainable development, and many have clear opinions as to what is not sustainable production and consumption. However, it is much more difficult to determine what sustainable development consists of, and to what extent it is meaningful to formulate national sustainability strategies independently of what other countries do. In particular, the latter concerns the management of global life-support systems such as the atmosphere, the ozone layer, biodiversity, and the capacity to absorb and break down climate gas emissions at a rate that prevents climate change from happening too quickly, and the corresponding ecological imbalances. However, it also applies, to a large extent, to national self-sufficiency strategies, in that it could well be imagined that the total capacity to support a large and growing population on Earth will require efficient trade and co-ordination across politically determined national boundaries that are arbitrary seen from the perspective of resource access and management.

Given a lack of clear guidelines as to what is a sustainable policy, it becomes even more important to determine what kinds of burdens on local and global resource bases for productive activities and for receiving waste and emissions alternative production and consumption patterns will entail.

The present analysis shows that, firstly, one can reasonably assume that it should be possible to maintain and even raise living standards in relation to today's level in the rich countries, with a substantially lower consumption of resources and corresponding polluting emissions. A considerable change in consumption will have to occur, but this is hardly more dramatic for the individual than changes we have had to adapt to since the Second World War. What is new is that the changes which seem necessary to prevent a continued non-sustainable strain on the Earth's resources and ecosystems require considerable intervention and initiatives in the form of political control via prices and taxes or more direct regulation. The cost of such initiatives can be seen as a modest insurance premium to secure living conditions for our children and grandchildren, and the insurance premium in the form of reduced economic growth is far lower than what we have been accustomed to pay for such premiums in case of fire, burglary, theft or accident. There is no doubt that such a development perspective is more sustainable than what we experience at present. What is not easy to asess, however, is how much more we need to do to ensure that development is actually sustainable; how fast should it be implemented; and what these extra initiatives will cost in the form of adaptation costs and reduced conventional growth. It should also be pointed out that if the alternative is long-term degradation then adaptation to a sustainable development could hardly be called an 'expense'. This underlines how important it is to identify alternative development paths, and to use this as a basis for estimating the costs connected with the various alternatives.

For developing countries, the situation may appear to be somewhat different, even though they are – to an even greater extent than the OECD countries – dependent on taking measures against a system that is out of control, because they have so little resistance and so few resources to adapt themselves to a fast changing ecosystem. These countries can be said to have a moral claim to a larger piece of the global 'pie', in particular where it concerns emissions of climate gases and the available absorptive capacity for these. At the same time, some of these countries possess the lion's share of the Earth's biodiversity, despite lack of current gains from preserving them. These two conditions indicate that it should be important to make international conventions on the preservation of biodiversity and climate control effective as soon as possible. The poorer developing countries are the most vulnerable if irreversible climate changes should accelerate, and a loss of biodiversity would be a loss of their most important national asset.

This is the basis for maintaining a global environmental facility (GEF) that will finance differential costs through projects that the Earth will benefit from, but which the developing countries themselves do not see themselves benefiting from. By building up such a fund, it will gradually be possible to make it attractive for developing countries to allow projects with global beneficial effects to be implemented on their own soil. At the same time, the rich countries should (1) contribute considerably more to such a fund, and (2) 'clean up their own mess' to a far greater extent than today.

NOTE

1. The argument in this section is developed more fully in Haavelmo and Hansen (1992).

11 The 'Technology Factor' in Sustainable Development

Ingunn Moser

Increasingly the world is described as – and is becoming – dependent on modern science and technology. Yet, this is not fundamentally new. Science and technology have been central elements in the West's cultural development and self-understanding for several centuries. Science and technology have played an active part in forming industrial society's relationship with nature, other people and cultures. How does this relate to a growing recognition of the close links between global environmental and development crises, and modern Western life forms? What roles do modern science and technology play in the developments which have become critical – in social, cultural and natural environments?

In a time of challenge to the authority and legitimacy of science and technology as sources of reliable knowledge and solutions for the world's distress and suffering, it becomes urgent to understand how science and technology integrate with cultural and political projects. The report of the World Commission on the Environment and Development, *Our Common Future* (1987), also indicates unease at the ambivalence of technological development, and expresses a need for change in research and research policy. The reorientation in science and technology that is put on the agenda in connection with policies for sustainable development will, however, depend on a more complex understanding of research processes and the historical, cultural and social conditions and relations they are tied up in than is given in the report. The purpose of this chapter is to raise the technology question within the debate on sustainable development. I intend to create recognition and understanding of the need to problematise the involvement of science and technology in the increasingly critical developments we experience today. The goal is to offer frameworks of understanding in which to locate and assess debates on technological developments and controversies on the possibilities and limitations of technology.

11.1 TECHNOLOGY IN *OUR COMMON FUTURE*

The World Commission for Environment and Development, and the report *Our Common Future*, initiated discourses whereby the world's political authorities, international bodies, grassroots movements, scientists and industry

193

were brought together to debate the survival of nature and the goals for our development.

The 1992 Earth Summit in Rio de Janeiro was a manifestation of the mobilisation of a colourful community, characterised by political conflicts and cultural antagonisms, differences in power and opportunity of being heard. The debate on sustainable development is still a cacophony (hence: discord) of different voices and dialects that try to make themselves understood and to prevail in the new political arena. Nevertheless, the meeting-places and discourses represent possibilities for participating in the struggle to define the problems and formulate the challenges. *Our Common Future*, as well as international negotiations, discussions and documents that have followed up on the World Commission's input, are manifestations of these struggles for power and the possibility of speaking up and being heard. Many have later asked whose common future we are talking about here, and whether it is not just a new drive on the side of the rich and powerful to shift the focus from modern Western development crises to questions of global ecology and common interests. But the struggles are not decided once and for all; the controversies in the wake of the World Commission's work contribute towards changing the agenda and bringing in new perspectives and challenges. One issue that has emerged in this context is that of the roles and conditions of science and technology in a sustainable common future.

Until recently, the technology question in sustainable developments has not been raised in the forums and discourses with most power to influence global development paths. Modern science and technology have been regarded as unambiguously progressive, necessary and neutral driving forces and means for realising undisputed political goals like growth, progress and development. Science and technology have been treated as the suppliers of solutions, and their personnel as 'helpers' and experts. The relationship between modern science and technology and the problematic developments in social, cultural and natural environments, has not been made an issue. This in spite of the recognition that science and technology are undeniably involved in both acute catastrophes and more chronic environmental and developmental crises. The burdens imposed by technological development on social, political and natural environments have been known from the very first stages of industrialisation, but have been judged as secondary effects or transient phenomena which further advances in science and technology would overcome. In modern Western culture, we have pinned our hopes on and invested our trust in science and technology; in the belief that uncertainty will disappear and that technological solutions will be found to our problems.

In general, this applies to the work of the World Commission for Environment and Development as charted in *Our Common Future* and as followed up in international negotiations, discussions and documents.[1] In these documents, it is suggested that science and technology should to an even greater extent be brought into the making of political decisions and policies on sustainable development.

It is implicitly assumed that sustainable development will become steadily more dependent on modern scientific and technological expertise; an expertise that is assumed to be independent, objective and non-political. Science and technology are assumed to be given practices, they are identified with modern Western institutions for the production of knowledge and are not problematised. Sure enough, scientific knowledge is connected with uncertainty, and risks follow technological encroachments and systems, but science and the management regime of 'sustainable development' must accept responsibility for these inherent uncertainties. The impression which remains is of a fundamental technical optimism, where risk can be overcome with the help of more science and technology, and where more science and technology can watch over, extend and move boundaries for the production and consumption patterns which we know to be critical for sustainable development.

Technology is ascribed an extremely important role in *Our Common Future*. On several occasions, the commission expressed expectations and hope that new technologies such as information technology, space technology, material technology, chemical and energy technologies and modern bio- and gene-technology will make possible a transition to sustainable development. Technology is introduced in one of two key elements on which the Commission bases its visions and strategies for the realisation of sustainable development:

> development that meets the needs of the present without compromising the ability of future generations to meet their own needs (WCED, 1987:43).

The first key concept makes social equity the basis, both as a moral obligation and as a necessary condition. Meeting the essential needs, in particular, of the world's poor should be given first priority. The other key concept is:

> the idea of limitations imposed by the state of technology and social organisation on the environment's ability to meet present and future needs (WCED, 1987:43).

Two other quotes explain and clarify what is meant here:

> The concept of sustainable development does imply limits – not absolute limits but limitations imposed by the present state of technology and social organisation on environmental resources and by the ability of the biosphere to absorb the effects of human activities. But technology and social organisation can be both managed and improved to make way for a new era of economic growth (WCED, 1987:8).

> Growth has no set limits in terms of population or resource use beyond which lies ecological disaster. Different limits hold for the use of energy, materials,

water, and land. Many of these will manifest themselves in the form of rising costs and diminishing returns, rather than in the form of any sudden loss of a resource base. The accumulation of knowledge and the development of technology can enhance the carrying capacity of the resource base. But ultimate limits there are, and sustainability requires that long before these are reached, the world must ensure equitable access to the constrained resource and reorient technological efforts to relieve the pressure (WCED, 1987:45).

The other key concept and quote clarifies the conditions and assumptions that the Commission bases its issue formulation and strategies on – its understanding of technology and its world-view. How we arrange matters, which strategies we choose and the prioritisation we make to attain a desired sustainable development will depend on how we understand the relationship between nature and people: between, on one hand, the 'natural', and on the other hand, technological, social and cultural development.

The World Commission understands technology as 'the key link between humans and nature' (WCED, 1987:60). Technology represents a limitation, but at the same time, a condition that is subsumed in its boundary-breaking character. It expands and shifts the limits for man's intervention in nature. Nature is represented as a resource base, with known and knowable boundaries. However, man's treatment of nature creates 'added value'; and with the aid of technology, natural limits are shifted. In this view, technology and division of labour (social organisation) represent man's progress out of and over nature, that is to say, out of the need, scarcity and struggle for existence we have attributed to nature. Along with social organisation, technology represents the dynamic and productive, the possible and open.

The technological factor is regarded as of primary importance in the sense that it constitutes a mainspring for the economic growth that the report presumes (WCED, 1987:4), and that it

will continue to change the social, cultural, and economic fabric of nations and the world community. With careful management, new and emerging technologies offer enormous opportunities for raising productivity and living standards, for improving health, and for conserving the natural resource base (WCED, 1987:217).

Let me come to grips with the condition, 'with careful management'. For those who read *Our Common Future* closely, the report also suggests alarm, doubt and reservations on the part of science and technology. The picture is not clear and not without cracks and holes.

The direction of technological developments may solve some immediate problems but lead to even greater ones (WCED, 1987:44).

Emerging technologies offer the promise of higher productivity, increased efficiency, and decreased pollution, but many bring risks of new toxic chemicals and wastes and of major accidents of a type and scale beyond present coping mechanisms (WCED, 1987:16).

The technologies of industrial countries are not always suited or easily adaptable to the socio-economic and environmental conditions of developing countries. To compound the problem, the bulk of world research and development addresses few of the pressing issues facing these countries . . . (WCED, 1987:60).

The problem is that this alarm has no outlet for its expression, no form and discourse to be expressed in, no conceptual frame in which to reflect upon this duplicity or antagonism. Hence, one does not stop here; the report elegantly skips over to postulations of the necessity for risk management and a reorientation of technology (WCED, 1987:49). To solve all the tasks that a realisation of sustainable development is dependent on would presume a shift in technology – such that it takes environmental conditions and developing countries' needs more into consideration (WCED, 1987:60). How this research policy or programme is to be implemented in practice, and how it would change modern knowledge-generating institutions, is not taken any further. The report only indicates that public policy must ensure that commercial firms find it worthwhile to take the environment more into consideration in its technological development, and that publicly funded research also needs such guidelines (WCED, 1987:60). Technological development must thus be controlled, or managed, politically. At the same time, such political control is not obvious or unproblematic. Traditionally, scientific inquiry and knowledge have been understood to require freedom and not control; they bless us most when we leave them in peace. The same freedom is required by industry and the market for their technological development. This ambivalence is not resolved, nor made explicit in the Report.

It is probably unrealistic to require that a political document like *Our Common Future* should make an issue of its own understanding of technology. The document will mobilise a community and a discourse for action and change in a field of conflicting interests and great differences in power. It is the result of negotiations where even technology and research represent strong interests in the struggle to define challenges and strategies. Is it perhaps better to understand breaks and inconsistencies in the Commission's view on technology as small victories for other interests than those of industry, research and national authorities, in the struggle for agendas and strategies? The impression one is left with is thus that of a fundamental technological optimism, where risks can be overcome with the aid of more science and technology, and where more science and technology can monitor, extend and shift the limits of production and consumption patterns that we know to be critical for sustainable development. The re-orientation that is suggested in the programme should occur within known boundaries without substantially challenging either our knowledge-generating practices or the cultural and social intercourse with technology. Change can be summed up in a commitment to new, better and bigger technology – with the proviso that risk management is integrated and that it contributes towards reducing the pressure on the natural resource base.

But after more than twenty years of acknowledgement of environmental and development crises within the grassroots movement and in the political arena, as well as within the research community, and after a strong commitment to research into these problems, including a research programme for an 'alternative future', it appears that Norwegian research and research policy on environment and development are characterised by frustration. At a summary conference on Norwegian research strategies on environment and development in 1992,[2] I was struck by the whole attitude of humility and admission of alarm, doubt and defeat. With so many strong wills and so much goodwill, why are we still at a dead-end? What are the terms and conditions for the changes we are all hoping for?

My contention is that such movements for change presume a more complex understanding of research processes and the historical, cultural and social relationships they are bound up in. It is my conviction that one condition for further progress is that we work with science and technology as integral parts of cultural and political projects, through analysing and keeping to our own development model historically and reflexively, and to the role of modern science and technology in this. In a collection of articles, *Technology and Culture*, Francis Sejersted (1991, published in Norwegian) issues the challenge as follows:

> If we are to take control of development, we must know where we are going. And then we must proceed from a discussion on management problems that assumes that the goal is given. We must work with our understanding of technology as culture, and we must deliberately try to form the symbols of new possibilities (Sejersted, 1991:5).
>
> Thus we need a technology policy in the real sense. And with policy, one not only means adequate means to realise the agreed-on goal. It requires that through public discussions, one works with our common understanding, our symbols and our dreams, and that we provide room for expressive action as well as instrumental action (Sejersted, 1991:49).

But to work with technology as problematic political and cultural projects, we need conceptual frames and discourses for our ambivalence and anxiety. Today, these are not only lacking in political and public debate, but also within research itself. Hence, it will be easiest to commit to the ostensibly safe and known: 'free research' and trust that uncertainty and future developments within science and technology will be to our advantage. There are so many problems that have to be solved, time is running out, doubts never set root, and anxieties are never dwelled on.

One example of such desperate technological optimism is the controversy surrounding the potential of biotechnology in connection with sustainable development. Both in *Our Common Future* and in the final documentation from Rio,[3] biotechnology is promoted as an environmentally benign technology that will be necessary for the attainment of sustainable development. Discussions on the ethical and political aspects of this technological development are framed by the same interpretations and strategies; biotechnology is promoted as a morally necessary solution for environmental and development crises – for problems of poverty and pollution, biodiversity and climate change.

As mentioned earlier, promoting technology as the solution to political and ecological problems has a long history and tradition in the evolution of modern industrial society. It reiterates dreams, suppositions, assumptions and patterns of behaviour that we know well. Modern Western science and technology have been perceived as the driving force behind development and as the source of solutions that offer security and abundance where there exist or existed uncertainty and scarcity. These cultural images and dreams seem to be so strong that dearly bought experiences with technology are never reflected on and adapted to. They are rewritten and sink into a kind of collective oblivion. The other, hidden and suppressed, stories of the tale of science and technology in the great development process are never brought forward and used as a basis for a reconstruction of this narrative, for new narratives of the past and future, what we have become and what we can become.

But which are the experiences and stories that are continuously being rewritten? What can we learn from the protest movements and critical traditions that have been mobilised? What lessons and theoretical and political resources do we have at our disposal to tackle technology as part of the problem, and not only as the solution?

11.2 HEIRLOOMS: EXPERIENCES WITH TECHNOLOGY

According to conventional accounts, modern science and technology have their own internal dynamics and logic, and their own internal control systems that drives research 'forward'. They are independent of and transcend their social and cultural contexts. Academic freedom, logic, the experimental method, rational argumentation and a research community that is engaged in attaining a consensus on controversial discoveries are assumed to ensure that only the best arguments win and only humanity's universal interests steer research. Science is supposed to be 'objective' and universal, superior to all other forms of knowledge. In this view, technology is the application of scientific knowledge to meet human needs.

In opposition to such an 'internal' understanding of science and technology, accusations have been raised about involvement in war, in social and racial conflicts, and in ecological destruction. Social – or 'external' – criticisms against science and technology were mobilised by the widespread protest movements against militarism, racism and sexism in the 1960s and 1970s.[4] The enlistment of science and technology in genocide in the Vietnam war, with the development of napalm bombs at the prestigious Harvard University, came as a shock to both researchers and students. Likewise, Rachel Carson's *Silent Spring* (1962) came as a kind of 'bomb' with its attack on the chemical industry's war against nature. These revelations discredited the pretensions of science and technology to distance and independence, with regard to social structures and relations of power, and hence, to objectivity and progress. According to externalistic understandings of science and technology, research consists of social practices and processes, and cannot be understood independently of the society they originate from. Modern science and technology are, as such, political, and are challenged to take responsibility for their participation in social conflicts.

As a consequence of such a practice-oriented understanding of science and technology, the division between these forms of knowledge is dissolved; modern science and technology are regarded as fundamentally entangled and mutually dependent forms of knowledge. Developments within technology render possible developments within science, and vice versa. Since the advent of information technology and gene technology, the division has become meaningless. What is instrumental, intervening knowledge and what is explanation or interpreted reflection are no longer separable. Research is reality-producing practices through interpretation, production of meaning and interventions. None of these elements in the research process occur in an ideal space where social and political forces are suspended.

Previous externalistic criticisms focused narrowly on economic production relations as the determining power structures, both in society and research. In capitalist societies, technology and science would necessarily be the means to create and maintain capitalist power relations in production. The possibility of new and better science and technology had to lie in the transition to another – socialist – society. With the waves of theories on biological determinism and socio-biology in the 1970s, race and sex were also thrown into the discussions on the conditions of science. Natural scientists, science critics and activists in protest movements were mobilised, formed alliances and confronted the biological theories that claimed to prove the genetic basis for intellectual inferiority in ethnic and social groups, as well as for male dominance and patriarchal social structures.[5]

Turning to the critiques of biological determinism, the investigation into the other side of science in society – society in science – became just as urgent.

Science and technology are not just in society in the way that they some times serve illegitimate interests and develop ideology. Society is in science, and it is not just a coincidence. This is a much more disturbing admission, which in its turn radicalised the social critiques. Science and technology are social and cultural projects, formed in power structures and coloured by dominating values in the societies and cultures they originate from. As such, they are constituted by, as well as constitutive of, cultural and social conditions. Science and technology are reality-producing and -reproducing practices.

In the women's movement, a critique of science and technology evolved within a general critique of patriarchy as the determining power structure in society. Patriarchy was understood as a system of power that works through relations in reproduction, and through the division of labour between women and men. Patriarchy was regarded as also constitutive of other power relations and hierarchies; the suppression of women, classes, ethnic groups, deviant gender roles and nature are all linked. The awareness of the close relations between the suppression of women and of nature, of the meanings associated with women as nature – or more natural or closer to nature (versus men as culture and rationality) – and of the role of the sciences with regard to confirming and strengthening these power relations, led feminists to challenge the patriarchal power relations which also permeated science and technology. Here, they could draw on the externalist critics who understood science and technology as tools in the hands of the powerful, introducing new or strengthening old entrenched power structures. In the feminist version, the critique was of science and technology as an expression of patriarchal power and as a means to control women and nature.[6]

In *The Death of Nature: Women, Ecology and the Scientific Revolution*, Carolyn Merchant (1980) deconstructed the texts of the forefathers of modern science and technology with respect to their modern, Western and patriarchal values. Here, she found the rationale for a violent science and technology that aimed to master and control a capricious (feminine) nature; her secrets had to be wrested from her, and she had to be penetrated and mastered through force. The biologists Ruth Hubbard (1990) and Evelyn Fox Keller (1992), have studied how the understanding of genetics, evolutionary processes and human nature within the biological sciences are based on, confirm and reproduce patriarchal views of reality, values and relations. For example, it is often assumed that aggression, violence, egoism and competition lie in our (masculine) genes, and that the struggle for existence and egoism lead us to reproduce ourselves and to produce as many offspring as our (competitive) fitness allows.

Modern science and technology are powerful social constructions, and biology has been shown to be a rewarding object of study of how power and politics work in our generation of knowledge. Nature seems to be an arena of struggles to define who we are and what we can become. As such, Darwinian theories can be said to reflect and project a crude and brutal social order on nature. These biological theories have been used and are steadily being used to legitimise the same individualistic competitive society. During the time of Darwin, industrial-isation and urbanisation won through and left behind a mass of people who had previously belonged to traditional farming communities in a new social order which really had become a struggle for existence. The question is whose 'nature' it is, and whether we are doomed to be what we have become.

A feminist theory of science deconstructs – lays open and criticises – these assumptions. It shows how they work and play themselves out both in the world of research and the society the knowledge is used in. A feminist science aims at developing alternatives that are the basis for other, more benign relationships and conditions.

In a parallel critique of science and technology that takes an ecological stand-point, Vandana Shiva has analysed science and technology as a Western, patri-archal and colonial project that aims to control people and natural resources.[7] Central to this project are the ideas of development and progress as freedom from, and control over nature, and as driven 'forward' by Western science and technology. This critique focuses on the destructive developments in the wake of the transfer of Western science and technology to other cultures and eco-logies. It is no longer controversial to claim that the Green Revolution – the transfer of Western industrial models for agriculture to countries in the South – has been a failure. It not only failed with respect to solving the hunger problem, it was shown to be deeply involved in social and political processes that con-centrated wealth and power in the hands of a few. Ecologically, it introduced foreign, vulnerable mono-cultures at the expense of local diversity, and a resource-intensive industrial agriculture. As a result, poverty and environ-mental crises have grown deeper. Local communities have been deprived of their means of livelihood. Violent conflicts over the control of natural resources are spiralling.

The point here is to show that science and technology can never be separated from social and political relations, cultural projects and ecological relations. During the 1960s and the 1970s, a truth and a slogan were established that science and technology have their political economies, that is, a household that is political. As such, one links the cultural project of modern science and techno-logy to economic, social and political relations. Shiva goes further and radical-ises the basis for this economy; she draws nature into the same political field. Science and technology have thus not only a political – capitalist, patriarchal and colonial – economy, but also a political ecology. Nature is a political categ-ory; 'nature' is a concept whose content we fight over to determine who we are and what we can become. 'Nature' is a cultural construct with which we define the boundaries between ourselves and others (humans and nature). By defining something as nature, we build hierarchies and ascribe various values to various people and natures. In modern times, science and technology have played an important role in these cultural interpretation and construction processes. Until recently, however, modern science and technology have been capable of denying their relationship with nature as a relation, socially and culturally constituted, as more than just a naturalised necessity, and the only one and best form of knowledge. Some of us have avoided confrontation with the political ecology of our science and technology – its account with respect to ecological and social sustainability, use and management of natural resources, and its intercourse with the living nature we ourselves are a part of.

11.3 CHALLENGES: PROBLEMATIC INTEGRATION

In the introduction to the anthology *Global Ecology: A New Arena for Political Conflict*, Sachs (1993) compares the research- and technology-dependent 'management' of the world after the 1992 Earth Summit in Rio to driving a car (development) at high speed along the edge of the abyss, equipped with radar, monitors and highly educated expert personnel who continuously monitor, test and manoeuvre the biophysical limits of tolerances. For over twenty years, we have heard warnings that we are heading straight towards the abyss, but we can still turn around in time. But now have we found a smart solution that does not require us to stop? So far, this represents little new; a political strategy for development that is carried on, and now even risk-controlled and -managed by modern science and technology.

Modern science and technology are becoming steadily more involved and integrated both in political structures and strategies, as well as in our daily life and activities, and in a culture that threatens life on Earth. This challenges science and technology to go beyond being suppliers of solutions, and participants in the research complexes, to go beyond being 'helpers' and experts. The conference 'Humanistic Perspectives on Technology, Development and Environment' in Oslo in 1991 gathered together researchers from many countries to look into the social and cultural bearings of the global environmental and development crises, and focused in particular on the role of science and technology in these processes. The final report states that:

> One of the conclusions to be drawn from the discussions at the conference was that we as participants in the research complex and the technological communities in the North, must seek alternatives and create projects for change in our part of the world – and recognise ourselves also as part of the problem and not only as producers and suppliers of solutions.[8]

As researchers, we not only observe, analyse, understand and solve problems 'out there'; the knowledge we generate is a (re)productive force. Science not only reveals reality, it invents – or constructs – it too. None of us has a privileged position outside worlds in crisis, that guarantees critical distance and innocent knowledge. Knowledge generation is constructive, creative and productive on reality, and it produces and distributes chances of life and death. As Evelyn Keller points out, this is:

> nowhere so dramatically in evidence as in the successes of nuclear physics and molecular biology, that is, in the production of technologies of life and death. (Keller, 1992:9)

Once we admit this as a fundamental condition for all forms of knowledge generation, the challenge is to develop ways to make researchers responsible for their production of knowledge.[9]

The research complex is also regarded as less important within critical environmental and women's movements, even when science and technology are acknowledged to be implicated in gender-specific, racial, ethnocentric, colonial, capitalist projects and practices. So much of our cultural trust is invested in scientific and technological solutions that whenever it becomes problematic and disturbing, we seem to slide back to simpler models and solutions. When it is shown that science and technology are involved in the crises they are meant to resolve, we cry for more freedom and independence for research, rather than to take direct responsibility for the social, cultural and ecological relations our knowledge (re)produces. It has been difficult – despite the obvious political life of science and technology – to see how politics plays itself out in the processes and products of research. When we are confronted with these problematic relationships, we often choose defensive strategies. We do not seem to know how to approach and work to change the world-producing apparatuses that modern science and technology actually are. We lack a grasp of science and technology as culture, and as integrated in modern society.

One problem is that the projects for change, sustainable development and a common future suffer under a constant pressure of time and a need to use modern science and technology as the means to solve problems and relieve suffering in the world. There is never time to work for change in science and technology; the need for knowledge with authority and legitimacy seems to stand in the way. Judging from the accusations that are aimed at postmodern critiques – which raise the question of the legitimacy of modern science as the authoritative discourse of truth – we need, for moral and political reasons, a science so powerful that we cannot afford to question the other consequences of this power. Both women's and environmental movements have based their politics and policies on science being conquered as a tool for other interests. In this perspective, science must be used in all its authority to point out suffering and injustice, to speak for those who do not have a voice, those who have less power and are less privileged.

But it is a question of whether we can afford not to take the issue seriously; not to use the time to suspend authority and to puzzle out the conditions for, and the effects of, our knowledge-generating practices – as well as new strategies. Each day, we live and experience the consequences of a knowledge form which has abstracted itself from realities, relations and meanings it is a part of, to such an extent that it undermines its own basis in life.

Against such a charge, a traditional internalist account will still regard science and technology as an independent enterprise, but maintain that its limits must be continuously upheld and defended against intruders with illegitimate motives and ambitions. Consequently, the issue of science and technology in society is an issue of use or misuse, and the issue of culture and society in science and technology is an issue of excluding (subjective and special interest) values; of keeping the path of science and technology pure. One 'saves' science and technology by reference to the fact that problems do not attach to science and technology 'in themselves', but to external political conditions.

But if we follow the argumentation of the critical traditions I have presented, the issue can no longer be about misuse or biased research, because science and technology are social relations and culture. So what is the issue?

It must be about critical reflection on social and cultural conditions; on how these work in scientific and technological knowledge production; and how we can be (made) responsible for the knowledge that we generate. A premise that lies under the critical tradition is that science and technology 'in itself' or 'as such' is an abstraction, a construct or fiction. The argument is mobilised each time new and promising advances – where biotechnology could be said to represent the latest technological panacea on the market – are shown to lead to exploitation and maldevelopment; when hunger, need and resource-loss rather than the alleviation of suffering are the results of the exertions of sincere, well-meaning researchers and politicians. But science and technology are always realised in concrete social, cultural, historical and ecological contexts. Both the meaning and use of knowledge are always contextual; they never exist outside time and space, social relations and structures, cultural hopes and anxieties. They are social and cultural constructs, and cannot be separated and isolated from the context within which they operate.

When we approach this issue of science and technology from a historical viewpoint, it appears that modern science received the status as the only discourse with authority and legitimacy through social and political struggles in Europe during the seventeenth and eighteenth centuries (see Shapin and Schaffer, 1985). Science was an important element in the strategy that the growing bourgeoisie used to free themselves from the power of the church and nobility. Modern science evolved as an alternative discourse to religion and tradition, and as a new authoritative discourse for secular affairs. The hope was to discipline the citizens and to create peace in areas ravaged by religious and civil war. In this process, scientific knowledge had to be carefully separated from power and politics. Authority and absolute independence were of great significance; knowledge had to be universal and objective. Nature was made an independent court of appeal and asked to speak for itself – and to stand against faith, superstition and political persuasion. From now on, the consensus on facts of natural phenomena, studied in experiments and witnessed by members of the civil public, was to settle disputes of authority in a peaceful way. Neither divine power nor the secular power of the state could deny the existence of a vacuum; the birds in Robert Boyle's air-pump experiment all died to the last one.

The development of modern science and technology was integrated in the development of the modern liberal social order. They developed together and confirmed and strengthened each other. When the bourgeoisie achieved its 'victory' over church and nobility, science had played a part in it. It was ascribed a status as being the only truth-bearer and premise-supplier and, with time, science became integrated in and constitutive of the social order from which it arose – an order that was based on distinct boundaries between nature and culture, science and politics, private and public, subjective and objective, and a polarisation between the genders. (See Harding, 1986; Keller, 1985; Brenna, Moser and Refseth, 1994.)

A more current example involves the controversies on modern bio/gene technology. Biotechnology cannot be abstracted from its context. It cannot be evaluated outside the social, cultural and ecological relations in which it is integrated. As such, biotechnology cannot be discussed separately from the pressing issues of the relationship between biotechnology and biodiversity, the political role of biotechnology within North–South relations, the role of biotechnology in a capitalist world economy, biotechnology's relation to cultural values as nature's intrinsic value and respect for the integrity of all living beings, or biotechnology's conceptions of knowledge and nature, and so on.[10]

One cannot, for example, promote biotechnology as a morally necessary solution for global poverty and environmental crises, without encountering contradictions. The argument assumes that more food means less poverty, and that biotechnological research and development are aimed at the production of food for the poor. This is a prime example of our cultural faith in technological solutions. But technology cannot solve problems that are in their 'nature' political and economic; food is a distribution problem.

In the market-economy system, purchasing power is not distributed according to needs. Any additional production of food as a consequence of biotechnological production methods will not be freely distributed to the needy. Biotechnology is neither a hobby technology for horticulture, nor is it for small farmers who live in and off the forests in India. It is a resource-intensive technology that falls under industrial production methods for agriculture. This type of agriculture requires intensive irrigation, fertilisers and the use of pesticides. Without all these costly and energy-intensive input factors, nature will not become more productive. And we here encounter the other problematic condition: that biotechnological development is aimed at the production of food for the poor. Biotechnological research and development mainly occur in the private domain of large industrial concerns and multinational companies. Even though much biotechnological research and development is still being carried out at universities, it is bought and paid for by private industry. The lag-time that previously – if ever – existed between research and development disappears with the development of biotechnology (Nybom, 1993). The proportion of biotechnological research and development that is aimed at increasing the nutritional value of say, grain, rice or maize, is minimal. Within biotechnology in agriculture, what is pushed is development of resistance to pesticides in industrially produced seeds – so that the industry can sell its seeds and pesticides as an integrated package solution to farmers. Another large industry is what is called 'industrial foods', which is industrially produced substitutes for raw materials that were previously imported from countries in the South to countries in the North. With the aid of advanced biotechnology and the free flow of genetic resources from the South to the North, the farmers and countries in the South will become more dependent on the North, and more vulnerable ecologically, while the countries in the North will become economically independent and at the same time, richer compared to countries in the South.[11]

11.4 TECHNOLOGY AS POLICY AND CULTURE: STRATEGIES FOR CHANGE

This does not mean that other more benign and sustainable scientific and technological developments are not possible – on the contrary: science and technology are neither determined by their internal dynamic or logic, nor by social and cultural power structures. They are social and cultural constructs, and can always be (re)constructed in new ways and in new relations. There are always other possible ways and means, that are more responsible, reflexive and humble. But how do we get there, and what does it mean with respect to which conditions and strategies for change we identify and put our energies into?

In conclusion, I shall say something about the possibilities and conditions for change that I see within the conceptual frames and discourses I have discussed. I shall also link some comments to the importance of opening up to debate this field of different discourses on the role of technology in our common future, of playing out the different understandings and their politics against each other.

A technology-deterministic position involves the assumption that research can neither be controlled nor stopped. For a long time, policies based on theories of an autonomous technology have allowed men in science and technology great latitude, without the possibility of anyone being made responsible for the development. This view of technology functioned well as long as the belief in growth and progress, conditional on the technological development, could be maintained. Today, we have lost this innocence. We cannot bypass this; we must take responsibility for the negative and unforeseen consequences of technological development, in the form of risks, catastrophes, pollution, unemployment, and so on. The question is just how, and which alternatives do we have? A thoroughly modern, but simple and naive view of science and technology that takes present knowledge forms, practices and institutions for granted as the only possible and best in the world, has, as mentioned previously, no grasp on ambivalence and anxiety. Within this framework, one only sees the constant 'conquests' that science and technology make in the service of mankind. Here, there is no room for alternatives other than improvements, in the sense of progress within the same. The future is only a projection of the present, for good or evil, but preferably for good. If one has thus compromised oneself with the form of science and technology we live with, isn't it more than natural that one invests the remainder of one's trust in the fact that continued scientific and technological development will create better solutions?

Within this framework, the answer to the question of the role of science and technology in sustainable development is caught in a fatal, but very tempting either-or; either the optimism or the pessimism of science and technology, either total criticism or an embrace without criticism. As I see it, this simple dichotomy still dominates too much of the critical and constructive thinking and action in projects for alternative and sustainable futures. We cannot afford to stay here for long, and we should move further on. The big question is not whether sustainable development is dependent on science and technology, but what kind of – and how we attain – desired changes in science and technology. A main point in this chapter is that as our world becomes more and more dependent on science and technology, and is drawn deeper into political structures and processes, the modern research complex forms a steadily more important arena of change in the work for sustainable development. Participants in the modern research complex become critical actors in a project for change – not only in relation to other social institutions like economics and politics, but in relation to the institutionalisation and authorisation of historically and socially shaped scientific cultures. I shall return to this later.

The limitations in the view of science and technology as propelled by and conditioned only on its own dynamic and logic are presented and interpreted in my discussion of the World Commission on Environment and Development's view of technology. It is possible that I have drawn big conclusions from small and scattered statements, and as such, have painted a picture that is narrower than the one the Commission intended. If that is the case, then I defend myself by the fact that my purpose has also been to offer frameworks within which to think about the role of science and technology. I have placed *Our Common Future* within a technologically and scientifically optimistic tradition, and address the issue of its conditions for attaining the reorientation of research and research policy it is looking for.

During the 1970s, the faith in technological solutions as neutral solutions came asunder. Technology came to be understood as socially formed. The causes of technological changes should not lie in technology itself, but in economic, social and political power structures. A science and technology that really should be in the service of mankind, rather than that of militarism, patriarchy and capitalism, would have to wait for an upheaval in the power structures and another kind of power distribution in society. However, these perspectives have also been criticised for being static and deterministic. One may stare oneself blind at structures until they appear irrefutable and immutable. Structuralist points of view allow neither changes that have occurred nor possibilities for change to be significant. They tend to become reality-binding rather than motivating action and change.

Both of these conceptual frames have been addressed and attempts have been made to break them up. The focus has been shifted first from internal dynamics to macro-political structures, then from power structures to participants, room for action and micro-politics. Attention is still directed at society's effects on technology but, based on the critiques of structuralism as static and deterministic, the goal is to emphasise room for action. Rather than focusing on how technology is formed and used in power structures, one should look for alternatives that exist or are found in the process. The outcome of technological development is no longer taken for granted, but is negotiated in social relations and contexts. (See Cronberg, 1992; Haraway, 1986, 1989 and 1991; Bijker, Hughes and Pinch, 1987; Bijker and Law, 1992; and Feenberg, 1995.) Both science and technology are social constructs, constituted on and constitutive of concrete political and cultural conditions. Today, there is talk of a seamless web of science, technology and society. No society exists that is not integrated through knowledge and technology. The difference lies in the way that this is done and the relations that are constituted. Room for action opens up as we acknowledge that neither science and technology nor the social, cultural and ecological relations they are bound up in – and bind up – are given once and for all. Both social structures and technologies have proven to be open, susceptible and subject to action and change.

But how do you initiate and mobilise such changes, not to speak of movements for change? How do we bring about the instruments and competence for change that are necessary for such a comprehensive project of change – being realistic regarding the complexity, obstacles and opposition it would involve?

As mentioned earlier, science and technology do not exist isolated from the concrete contexts they work in, and consequently, changes towards sustainability must also include both science and technology and the social, cultural, historical and ecological relations they form a part of. Changes should be implemented in many arenas and ways, and should include as many parties in different localities as possible. Movements for change are faced with the challenge of building bridges and creating alliances between different parties and arenas.

However, I see it as my contribution here to emphasise the necessity of including science and technology as important arenas for work towards change. As they are fundamentally entangled in the development projects that we presently experience as critical – most evidently in natural and poverty crises – science and technology are part of the problem that we have to deal with.

One place to begin is to discuss our conceptions, our understandings, of knowledge and technology. I hasten to add that understanding 'alone' never changes the world. It is integrated in and integrates the world. But this is precisely why it is also a condition for the changes we wish for. Understandings, ideas and conceptions are material conditions, to put it in a way that turns the usual concept of what knowledge is, upside down. To change understanding is hard physical work; changes have to overcome resistance, and be transformed into practices. Understandings are notable for being resistant and material. They reside in our heads and bodies, in our needs and desires, as well as in the physical, economic, social, political, cultural and ecological structures we build up as parts of scientific and technological systems. Here, we encounter a struggle for change that is demanding and difficult, and that includes science and technology as part of the problem.

Both practices and relations in research, as well as the social intercourse with science and technology, rest on assumptions that are a part of our problematic common cultural heritage. Is the only story we have about who we are and what we have become, not to speak of what we *can* become, the tale of Homo Faber and the linearly advancing development based on technology and the utilisation and exploitation of nature as a resource for our anthropocentric projects? What basis do we have, then, for believing that things do not have to be as they are; that the threatening future is a question of will and choice? Here, the importance of discussing understandings of knowledge and technology, and of problematising our conceptual frames, is apparent. If the field of discourses on the role of science and technology in a common future opens up and is admitted to be a field of *different* understandings (a question of values, views on nature, humanity, science and technology), then the focus is shifted from questions of truth and legitimacy to questions of ethics and politics. Science and technology are politics and culture. We must open the arena and show that it is based on various values and politics that we must take responsibility for.[12] Only then can we begin to work with our common understanding, with our symbols and dreams, to form the symbols of new possibilities and alternative futures.

NOTES

1. See conference reports and pronouncements from 'Sustainable Development, Science and Policy', Bergen 8–12 May 1990, 'International Conference on an Agenda of Science for Environment and Development into the 21st Century (ASCEND 21), Vienna, 25–29 November 1991, and *Agenda 21: The United Nations Programme of Action from Rio 1992.* Noteworthy exceptions are represented by *Women's Action Agenda 21* and the report from 'World Women's Congress for a Healthy Planet', Miami, 8–12 November 1991.
2. The Conference on Research Strategies in Environment and Development Studies, Vettre, Asker, Norway, January 1992.
3. *Agenda 21: The United Nations Programme of Action from Rio 1992.*
4. See periodicals like *Science for the People* in the USA, *Science for People* in Europe, *Radical Science Journal*, and Rose and Rose (1976).
5. See Jensen (1972), Goldberg (1975) and Wilson (1975), and with regard to criticism, for example, Rose and Rose (1969 and 1979).
6. See Rose (1992) and Rose in Shiva and Moser (ed.) (1995) for an overview and introduction to feminist critics of science and technology.
7. See Shiva 1989, 1991 and 1995.
8. See Sejersted and Moser (ed.): *Humanistic Perspectives on Technology, Development and Environment. Papers from a Conference* (1992). As a follow-up to this conference, an initiative was taken to establish a new field of activity at the Centre for Technology and Human Values: 'Environment and Development Perspectives on Modern Technology and Science'. The project has been involved in putting environmental crises on the agenda with respect to what they mean for work in the modern research complex. The collective work in this group of formulating challenges and conditions for change, forms the background to the perspectives and arguments in this chapter.
9. The knowledge-generating institutions in modern society can no longer be regarded as enclaves or cocoons for remote and disengaged reflection over a world 'out there'. This should not be a controversial standpoint today. Most researchers would also agree to the social and cultural dependence on modern science and technology: science and technology in society, society in science and technology. Nevertheless, scientists, technologists, politicians and bureaucrats also seem to continue to think of the knowledge-generating institutions as 'on the outside' or in any case, marginal in relation to the 'important' conflicts, sufferings and institutional conditions we live under and with. We certainly do not manage to stop thinking in terms of 'out there' and 'in here', and of the modern research complex as marginal and less important with respect to where problems and changes are generated.
10. An attempt to evaluate biotechnological development within these relations and context is made in Shiva and Moser, 1995. The argument below is based on the contributions in this anthology.
11. Through these relations, biotechnology is also woven into the same order under which modern science and technology arose and developed, several hundred years ago. Shiva (1994) speaks of a new and late modern form of colonisation that takes place through modern biotechnology; the colonisation of nature, seeds and genes. However, it does not replace earlier forms of

colonisation; rather, it is the foundation for, and strengthens relations and power structures that already exist.

12. See Haraway (1986 and 1991) and Levidov and Tait (1995) for development of this argument.

12 Future Challenges of Sustainable Development

William M. Lafferty and Oluf Langhelle

The purpose of the present volume has been to probe the meaning and import of the concept of sustainable development as first put forth by the Brundtland Commission and later pursued through the UNCED process. In concluding our collection of studies, we wish to first present an overall 'meta-perspective' on the concept, and then try to illustrate the implications of our interpretation with reference to climate policy.

12.1 THE DEBATE ON SUSTAINABLE DEVELOPMENT

Let us begin by summarily maintaining that sustainable development is a normative concept which stipulates desirable global conditions with respect to the relationship between humans, the environment and development. The general context for developing and applying the concept is a widely acknowledged need for change on a global basis. Sustainable development was endorsed by the World Commission as an idea designed to mobilise the forces of change for achieving a better balance between humans and nature, and thereby a safer and better world for all.

Few would disagree up to this point. For many, however, the issue appears to be one of simply not trusting the concept to achieve its own declared goals. Wolfgang Sachs (1993), for example, has edited a collection of distinguished articles where several authors have voiced the opinion that sustainable development is the wrong concept at the wrong time. While some of the authors are opposed for diverse ideological reasons, others are negative because they feel that the idea is too diffuse to be used constructively. Another example is provided by Dick Richardson (1994). His assessment of the concept is particularly relevant for its reference to the realm of politics:

So what, then, is the future of sustainable development? The concept as defined by Brundtland is not only a political fudge, it is a sham. It attempts to theoretically obscure the basic contradiction between the finiteness of the Earth, with natural self-regulating systems operating with limits, and the expansionary nature of industrial society. . . . The divide between the anthropocentric and biocentric approaches is unbridgeable, and the attempt by

Brundtland to obfuscate the incongruity by promoting a new terminology was foredoomed to failure (Richardson, 1994:11).

In this view, sustainable development is not only garbled, but deceptive. The position also illustrates a general tendency to anchor criticism in some form of 'deeper' environmental understanding, whether 'ecocentrism', 'deep ecology', 'eco-socialism', or 'eco-feminism'. The persuasion is guided by a conviction as to the 'real' essence of the environment-and-development problem, where it is felt that the official lip-service to sustainable development merely detracts from a more correct understanding. There are, of course, other lines of criticism – lines which focus more on the operationalisation and practicality of the concept without getting into the issue of correctness – but these are less relevant for the distinctions to be made here.

For those who dismiss the debate on sustainable development as either dangerous or uninteresting, there is not much more to say. One must merely register that there are quite a large number of academics and politicians who do not find the concept promising, and who apparently feel that there are other symbols and values which are more capable of mobilising for change. For this, in the end, is what the concept is all about: making an effect on current non-sustainable practices. *Our Common Future* is a document with a mission: a mission to change policies and behaviour so as to achieve a new and more integrated relationship between man and nature, rich and poor, present and future generations.

The changes in question must, moreover, be achieved through rational argumentation and democratic procedures. Though there are those who are increasingly sceptical as to whether the 'ecological crisis' can be resolved democratically, such views are hardly acceptable within the dominant ideology of Western liberalism. It is for this reason that we advocate a more pragmatic (and hopefully more constructive) approach. As we see it, there are a number of very good reasons for taking the politics of sustainable development seriously, regardless of how individual politicians and bureaucrats may use or abuse the idea.

12.1.1   Political Acceptance

Firstly, and in direct opposition to the contention made by Richardson, we maintain that, far from failing, the concept and symbol of sustainable development has succeeded beyond all expectations. In all, more than 150 countries have given their official support to the Rio Declaration and to the action plan *Agenda 21*. No other concept in this area has achieved such acceptance.

Critics may reply, of course, that the concept's extensive popularity is primarily symbolic and secondarily merely a reflection of the power and interests of those who stand to gain from the concept. As we see it, however, consensual understanding of a normative concept is a prerequisite for achieving change, and we assess the potential of sustainable development as positive in this regard. When, previously, has such a clearly prescriptive idea received such diverse and comprehensive voluntary support? Regardless of differences of interpretation, and making no presumptions as to sincerity of commitment, the world-wide acknowledgement of the principle of sustainable development gives credence to the claim of a global ethic. A foundation has been laid which ideological purists may reject, and cynical politicians exploit, but which normative pragmatists should welcome.

12.1.2 Ethical Strength

Our second reason for stressing the practical usefulness of the concept is a philosophical comment on the first. It may be argued that the concept's popularity reflects two central conditions for ethical strength. There are, of course, numerous views as to the nature of ethics. Moral statements aim to convince us of good and bad behaviour, but they do so in different ways, with different arguments as to the legitimacy of their claims. For present purposes, we can be extremely simplistic. With reference to the work of Jon Wetlesen (Chapter 2), we can identify two major modes for achieving ethical legitimacy and compliance: 'realism' and 'consensualism'. The choice of these two orientations is conditioned by two more basic presumptions as to how change will be accomplished: (1) that compliance with norms should be achieved through rational argument directly related to the problematic; and (2) that any sanctions involved must derive from reasonable democratic procedures.

The realist mode argues for compliance on the basis of presumed ontological truth. What is right or wrong is derivable from a correct understanding of the phenomena relevant to the problematic. The oldest and most resilient form of this mode of ethics is the morality of natural law. Once we have understood the innate workings of the 'real world' (as discoverable by science), we will then know how to act with respect to that world. Goodness attaches to the natural, badness to the unnatural. Both positivist and phenomenological approaches to the 'real world' support ethics in this mode.

The consensual mode seeks moral validity through collective agreement. Theories of the 'real world' are too indecisive and contingent to provide adequate ethical foundations. The debate as to correct epistemology leads to the deconstruction of scientific method as a decisive criterion for 'truth'. Morality as a guide for action can only be secured through critical dialogue and consensual acknowledgement. The greater the degree of consensus as to right or wrong, the greater the force of moral prescription, and the greater the chances of moral compliance.

The concept of sustainable development can be shown to derive force from both of these modes of ethical legitimacy. With respect to the aspect of 'physical sustainability', the norm-set is validated by the enormous weight of scientific evidence and argument as to the degenerative effects on the environment from human intervention. It is clearly no accident that several of the more decisive texts and many of the most prominent activists of the early environmental movement came from the natural sciences. Natural-science arguments, supported by natural-science data, have been at the core of demands for global environmental change from the start. They have provided these demands with a legitimacy and force that modern humanism lacked in its attempt to reverse the negative effects of industrialism.

It is an interesting commentary on the foibles of ideological development and change, that modern 'environmentalism' should anchor its moral appeal in positivist science at a point in history when the critical-scientific basis of Marxism was being definitively undermined. Where indeed would the argument for environmentalism-as-progress be if it were not for the natural scientists? This is a point which the Brundtland report makes explicit in its admonition for more direct links between the scientific community and NGOs (WCED, 1987:326–9).

In addition to its 'realist' appeal the demand for sustainable development, in both its physical and equity aspects, derives clear moral support from its widespread endorsement as a consensual norm. Regardless of which school of ethics one adheres to, there can be no doubt that if the goal is mobilisation for change within the realm of democratic procedures and institutions, the stronger the potential for consensus, the better. And whereas philosophers of consensual ethics promote the correctness of their position in terms of an abstract consensus, the concept of sustainable development has been the subject of very real and widespread agreement.

12.1.3   New Politics

During the past twenty years or so, the global arena for environment-and-development politics has emerged as a clearly identifiable 'political system'. There are actors, roles, routines, settings, and an increasingly distinct political culture. Each major political milestone, from the Stockholm Conference in 1972 to the 'Earth Summit +5' conference in 1997, has established new precedents for how future events and procedures should be structured. A pattern of relationships between governments, international administrative organisations, business groups, voluntary organisations and the media has emerged within a common historical framework. (See, for example, Caldwell, 1990; Hempel, 1996; and Princen and Finger, 1994).

The politics of sustainable development are not, however, only the politics of UNCED, UNEP, UNDP, CSD and the EU. They are also the *potential* politics of national and local change under the onus of supranational commitments. Both Gro Harlem Brundtland and her political successors in Norway have surely had cause to regret her reference to the Rio accords as 'promises made by world leaders' (COCF, 1993), but her observation (in the same context) that the promises 'can only be fulfilled in time to secure our future if governments are inspired and pressured by their citizens', stands nonetheless as a rallying cry for political mobilisation and change.

It thus becomes increasingly important to objectify, analyse and make better known the parameters for sustainable-development politics. The emerging global 'game' is of great significance in its own right, but there are also important implications for regional, national and local development. The slogan 'Think globally – act locally' can only be given more widespread and concrete meaning if voters become better schooled in the intricacies of the environment-and-development relationship, and more aware of the moral and practical potential for local–global linkages.

What we are saying, therefore, is that the politics of sustainable development are at once more normatively constrained and more instrumentally specific than any form of global politics thus far developed. Furthermore, it is maintained that there are clear possibilities of 'exploiting' the normative position to exert political pressure on domestic regimes. Governmental leaders become bound up, and to a certain degree carried away by, the momentum of international and regional environment-and-development processes. They either compete in capturing, or belatedly give their active support to, the moral cutting-edge of the persuasion. The role of environmental journalists and NGOs has been crucial in forcing this development, but the functional need for creating 'new politics' at home has also been a factor.

When leaders return from their international summits, they leave behind a wealth of publicly recorded statements, documents, accords, procedures and institutions – records which clearly can be used to press for domestic political compliance. Arne Næss (1991) provides an appropriate description of this point:

> Thanks to the Brundtland Report, the eco-political argumentation has been raised to a higher level. One may declare that a political decision is logically irreconcilable with the accepted Brundtland Report, and that there exists a logical contradiction, an inconsistency. Now, when 'all' politicians pretend to have (moderate) green colours, the debate can be made more efficient. Who will admit to being out of step with oneself? (Næss 1991:37)

12.1.4 Accent on Implementation

One of the characteristics of the 'new politics' deserves to be treated as a separate point – the issue of implementation. Not that there is much to boast about when it comes to actual results: the progress since Rio is less than impressive. But the truth is that the UNCED process has brought with it a deliberate focus on implementation. As a result of the pronounced moralising within the environment-and-development discourse, together with the constant pressure from NGOs for follow-up and results, the procedures for implementation and evaluation have received more and more attention.

Of special interest for the politics of implementation at present is the latest addition to the environment-and-development arena, the United Nations Commission on Sustainable Development (CSD). Established by the General Assembly in December of 1992 under the umbrella of the UN Economic and Social Council (ECOSOC), CSD has a small secretariat and an assembly of representatives from 53 governments. Its specific mandate is to follow up and implement the massive *Agenda 21*.

More than any other document, *Agenda 21* is the successor to *Our Common Future*. Its categories are, to a large degree, those established by the Brundtland Commission. The document addresses (in 479 pages and 40 chapters) topics varying from radioactive waste and toxic chemicals to 'Children and Youth in Sustainable Development'. It was endorsed by virtually all national delegations to Rio as a 'global partnership for sustainable development', with the signatories committing their respective governments to the development and implementation of national 'plans of action'. It is this process that CSD is designed to monitor and promote, and that the UN General Assembly reviewed in June 1997 ('Earth Summit +5').

Figure 12.1 lists 13 general guidelines which the Commission adopted at the outset of its proceedings as temporary guidelines for monitoring and assessment. A quick run-down of the list shows that it is much more concerned with issues of political and economic relevance than with issues related to the natural environment. Part of this has to do with the fact that CSD has limited resources and cannot be expected to monitor environmental phenomena which already are under surveillance by other international bodies. More specifically, however, the profile is attributable to what can be referred to as CSD's 'compensatory role' *vis-à-vis* Rio. It was widely acknowledged in the aftermath of the Earth Summit that two issues of key concern for Southern countries were not adequately covered by the concluding documents: the financing of sustainable development in the South, and the transfer of technologies necessary for more sustainable economic production. CSD was implicitly given responsibility for these tasks, and proceeded forthwith to establish high-profile 'work-groups' on both issues.

These developments mean that CSD has been placed in the 'front line' of sustainable-development implementation. Not only is the Commission to monitor and highlight national efforts with regard to the overall goals of *Agenda 21*, it must also bear the responsibility of carrying forward the crucial North–South issues of financial aid and the transfer of technology.

The CSD must, in other words, keep UNCED 'honest' with respect to both its 'public' and 'hidden' agendas. As with all international agreements and projects, however, the fate of the joint CSD efforts will depend on the follow-up activities of the individual member states. What the activities and results thus far indicate, however, is that *Agenda 21* has received a status as a guideline for change which few would have anticipated in the immediate post-Rio period.

Table 12.1 General guidelines for monitoring implementation of *Agenda 21* (UNCSD)

- Policies and measures at national level to meet *Agenda* 21 objectives, including national sustainable-development strategies and major activities and projects undertaken;
- Institutional mechanisms to address sustainable-development issues, including the participation of NGOs and major groups in these mechanisms;
- Assessments of progress achieved to date, with statistical sheets and tables;
- Measures taken and progress achieved to reach sustainable production and consumption patterns and life-styles, to combat poverty, and limit demographic impact on the planet's life-supporting capacity;
- The impact of the environmental measures undertaken on the national economy, including the social impact of such measures;
- Experiences gained, for example, descriptions of successful policies and projects that can serve as models, and particularly strategies that improve both social conditions and environmental sustainability;
- Specific problems and constraints encountered, including those related to finance and technology and to the adverse impact of economic and trade policies and measures, particularly on developing countries;
- The adverse impact on sustainable development of trade restrictions and distortive policies and measures, and progress in making trade and environment policies mutually supportive in favour of sustainable development;
- Assessments of capacity, or the availability of domestic human, technological, and financial resources;
- Assessments of needs and priorities for external assistance in finance, technology transfer, co-operation, and capacity building, and human-resources development;
- Implementation of *Agenda 21* commitments related to finance (including the 0.7 per cent of GNP aid target) and to technology transfer, co-operations, and capacity building;
- Assessments of the effectiveness of activities and projects of international organisations, including international financial institutions and funding mechanisms;
- Other environment-and-development issues, including those affecting youth, women, and other major groups.

Source: Martin Khor (1994:106–7).

12.1.5   A Global Partnership

Perhaps more than anything else, however, it is the actual content of the concept of sustainable development itself (as understood in the Brundtland Report) which explains the concept's central place in both national documents and the international follow-up process.

To begin with, the Brundtland Report is first and foremost a *political* document. It is not a scientific dissertation, and hence not subjected to the same strict requirements for consistency and precision. As a political document it is based on compromise; a characteristic which is essential for gaining support, and practical for achieving change. When Donald Worster (1993), for example, dismisses compromise as a navigable way for achieving sustainable development, he reveals a poor understanding of political processes. Politics – at least democratic politics – is not possible without compromises: 'Where there are no compromises, there is no democracy' (Cohen, 1971:180).

But even though the Brundtland Report is clearly the result of political compromise, this does not, in our view, equate solely with inconsistency and impreciseness. On the contrary, the report is demonstrably more consistent and precise than is often claimed. Of particular relevance here is the mandate of the World Commission. Here we find the initial questions and problems the Commission was asked to address. The mandate was formulated by the General Assembly as a 'Global Agenda for Change': an 'urgent call' by the United Nations to:

- propose long term environmental strategies for achieving sustainable development by the year 2000 and beyond;
- recommend ways concern for the environment may be translated into greater co-operation . . . and lead to the achievement of common and mutually supportive objectives that take account of the interrelationship between people, resources, environment, and development;
- consider ways and means by which the international community can deal more effectively with environmental concerns;
- help define shared perceptions of long-term environmental issues and the appropriate efforts needed to deal successfully with the problems of protecting and enhancing the environment, a long term agenda for action during the coming decades, and aspirational goals for the world community (WCED, 1987:ix).

It is this 'strategic framework' of *Our Common Future* which structures the further development of the UNCED programme up to the adoption of the 'global partnership for sustainable development' at the Rio Earth Summit. The distributional characteristics of the partnership remain to be spelled out, however. There is no doubt that the challenges confronting the industrialised and developing countries are different. The main challenge for developing countries is to eradicate poverty and develop, through economic growth and internal redistribution. The key tasks for the industrialised countries are three-fold: (1) to assist the eradication of poverty by substantial increases in development aid and changing the rules of the international balance of economic forces; (2) to change consumption and production patterns by reducing energy consumption and CO_2 emissions, in order to allow for necessary compensatory increases in developing countries; and (3) to develop and transfer environmentally sound technology in order to smooth the transition to sustainable development. In addition, both developed and developing countries should triple the total expanse of protected natural areas so as to conserve a representative sample of the earth's ecosystems.

It must be added, however, that the fact that poor nations face different challenges for sustainable development from wealthy nations does not imply that they are free from responsibility for their own production and consumption patterns: 'The simple duplication in the developing world of industrial countries' energy use patterns is neither feasible nor desirable' (WCED, 1987:59). It is the 'changed' (or sustainable) consumption and production patterns – with reduced energy consumption and CO_2 emissions – which must be duplicated. This presupposes, of course, that there actually exists such a consumption and production pattern to duplicate; a prospect which both increased energy consumption and CO_2 emissions in most OECD countries today clearly belie.

The normative essence of the 'global partnership' nonetheless remains: a division of labour between developing and developed countries within a strategic framework for realising sustainable development. It was the function of the Commission to here outline a new and more integrated logic for change: how to translate concern for the environment into greater global co-operation; how to deal more effectively with individual environmental problems; and finally, how to relate aspirations for human development to the natural carrying capacity of the Earth.

In the following, we shall take a closer look at the reasons behind the Brundtland Report's conclusions. We shall do this by focusing on the problem of climate change. We emphasise three conditions which may be used to explain and possibly reconcile the various distributional criteria in the Report: the global perspective; the combination of the normative and the empirical; and the combination of the political and the scientific. It is the combination of these different elements in the Report that partly determines the concept's content, role and function in international political forums; as well as the context for applying sustainable development as a global ethic with national-political implications.

12.2   THE ISSUE OF GLOBAL JUSTICE

The issue of global justice is a central and disputed topic in the debate on sustainable development. What constitutes a just global distribution? Is it sufficient to satisfy only basic human needs on a global basis? Or is it necessary to achieve a more equal distribution of life-chances and goods? One may find support for both viewpoints in *Our Common Future*. While the core definition focuses upon needs, and particularly the basic needs of the world's poor, there are several passages which point in the direction of a more general distributional equity:

> What is required is a new approach in which all nations aim at a type of development that integrates production with resource conservation and enhancement, and that links both to the provision for all of *an adequate livelihood base* and *equitable access to resources* (WCED, 1987:39).

> Sustainable development requires meeting the basic needs of all and extending to all *the opportunity to satisfy their aspirations for a better life* (WCED, 1987:44).

> Living standards that go beyond the basic minimum are sustainable only if consumption standards everywhere have regard for long-term sustainability. Yet many of us live beyond the world's ecological means. . . . Sustainable development requires the promotion of values that encourage consumption standards that are within the bounds of the ecologically possible and to which *all can reasonably aspire* (WCED, 1987:44).[1]

As a political document, the different distributional criteria in the report may, of course, be interpreted as the outcome of a political tug-of-war where various interpretations of equity have been played out against each other. In this respect, the report may be taken to substantiate both the moderate and radical interpretations of John Rawls's (1972b) theory of justice, as described by Jon Wetlesen in this book. While Rawls (1993) may be taken to substantiate the fact that global social justice implies that all can satisfy their basic needs, Thomas Pogge (1989, 1994) may be said to advocate more general egalitarian principles.

There is little doubt that the above quotes from the Brundtland Report point towards a *more* egalitarian distribution of goods than the present. But how much more? As we argued in Chapter 1, it seems unreasonable to interpret *Our Common Future* as advocating an absolutely equal distribution of goods. Still, there exists a conflict between trying to meet the basic needs of all (which can be referred to as *the basic-needs requirement*), and a more egalitarian distribution of goods (which can be referred to as *the equal-distribution requirement*, meaning here a more egalitarian distribution of goods than that implied by *the basic-needs requirement*, but not necessarily an absolutely equal distribution).[2]

As argued by Andreas Føllesdal in Chapter 4, considerations of basic needs cannot justify the claim that all should have an equal level of consumption in both time and space. But does this, as Føllesdal claims, deviate from the

Commission's view? Or are there other considerations which lead the Commission towards the equal-distribution requirement? In other words, what substantiates the equal-distribution requirement, and how is it justified in *Our Common Future*?

In his lecture 'The Law of Peoples' (1993), John Rawls mentions three possible extensions where he thinks the framework of 'justice as fairness' may yield reasonable answers. The concept of sustainable development addresses two of these extensions: to other societies and to future generations.[3] In contrast (and addition) to Rawls's own approach, however, the concept of sustainable development is based on the assumption of *an accelerating ecological interdependence*. This has to some degree been ignored in the different attempts to 'globalise' Rawls's theory of justice, where the extensions have been largely justified from the perspective of *economic* interdependence.

The environmental challenge adds, in other words, a third dimension to the issue of global justice.[4] More forcefully, it can be argued that the accelerating ecological interdependence not only has distributional implications, but that the concept of *sustainability* as such carries its own distributional implications by linking the issue of intra-generational justice to the issue of inter-generational justice. Environmental interdependence is described in *Our Common Future* as follows:

> We are now forced to concern ourselves with the impacts of ecological stress – degradation of soils, water regimes, atmosphere and forests – upon our economic prospects. We have in the more recent past been forced to face up to a sharp increase in economic interdependence among nations. We are now forced to accustom ourselves to an accelerating ecological interdependence among nations. Ecology and economy are becoming ever more interwoven – locally, regionally, nationally, and globally – into a seamless net of causes and effects. (WCED, 1987:5).

The concept of sustainable development is partly developed in response to this ecological interdependence, and the intention is to describe a development path by which peoples of the world can enlarge their spheres of co-operation to ensure both sustainable human progress and human survival. By doing so, we argue that the Commission, through the concept of sustainable development, recommends and envisages distributional criteria which go beyond liberal distributional principles.

12.3 THE DISTRIBUTIONAL CRITERIA OF SUSTAINABLE DEVELOPMENT

In accordance with the classification of goods in Chapter 1, it is possible to distinguish three different distributional criteria in *Our Common Future*. The concept of sustainable development itself contains one direct distributional principle; the notion of need. Sustainable development is development that meets the needs of the present. The report does not distinguish between needs and essential needs, other than giving priority to the essential needs of the world's poor. Essential needs are jobs, food, energy, water and sanitation; and sustainable development prescribes that essential needs should be met for everyone.

The fulfilment of these needs for the present generation must not, however, compromise the ability of future generations to meet their own needs. At a minimum, this implies respecting the minimal requirement of sustainable development: 'physical sustainability'. This leads in turn, however, to two demands which are directed towards living standards which *go beyond* the minimal requirement of fulfilling essential needs; that is, standards of living which are over and above those necessary for satisfying basic needs. These demands have been identified here (in Chapter 1) as consumption standards which are: (1) within the bounds of the ecologically possible (*the principle of physical sustainability*) and (2) formulated so that everyone (in both time and space) can reasonably aspire to achieving them (*the principle of universality*).

As stressed in Chapter 1, these principles are not necessarily egalitarian principles. To aspire is not the same as to attain, and the principles thus seem to open up for an unequal distribution of goods, both within and among countries. But how do these different principles relate to each other, and how are they to be understood? How *much* inequality do they allow for?

We shall illustrate possible connections between the different distributional criteria by looking at the problem of climate change. While patterns of consumption may be unproblematic in a national perspective – with respect to both the requirements for basic needs and for physical sustainability – they may not hold in a global perspective. The crucial question becomes: what will happen if developing countries reach a pattern of production and consumption, and a living standard, equivalent to that of the OECD countries?

12.3.1 Physical Sustainability

According to the Brundtland Report, the ultimate limits for global development are 'perhaps determined by the availability of energy resources and by the biosphere's capacity to absorb the by-products of energy use' (WCED, 1987:58). The energy limits will in all likelihood 'be approached far sooner than the limits imposed by other material resources' (WCED, 1987:58).

A globalisation of Western consumption patterns and standards of living must thus be viewed in the context of the principle of physical sustainability. And there appears to be widespread agreement to the effect that a simple globalisation of Western living standards will result in an ecological catastrophe, and in this respect be incompatible with the principle of physical sustainability. As stated by the Norwegian Minister of the Environment, Thorbjørn Berntsen: 'If India should aspire towards the same level as us, the whole world would collapse.'[5]

But is it not becoming increasingly apparent that India *is* aspiring towards the same standard of living as 'us', and that virtually all the nations of the world are firmly intent on following suit? And why shouldn't they? It is surely morally obnoxious to argue that the OECD countries have an exclusive right to a consumption pattern which cannot be globalised without violating the principle of sustainability, simply because they have attained it first. Let us try to place the problematic in a more systematic context.

As previously stated, the *principle of physical sustainability* constitutes the minimum requirement for sustainable development: 'At a minimum, sustainable development must not endanger the natural systems that support life on Earth: the atmosphere, the waters, the soils, and the living beings' (WCED, 1987:44). As such, the sustainability requirement is linked to environmental problems. Figure 12.1 provides an overview of selected environmental problems along the dimensions of space and time. The figure indicates that there are two problems in particular which are global in scope, and which have effects stretching into the long-term future: the problem of climate change and the depletion of the ozone layer in the atmosphere. Of these, it is the problem of climate change in particular which links the principle of physical sustainability with the distributional issues of sustainable development. The issue of climate change is, therefore, well-suited to an illustration of possible connections between the principle of physical sustainability and the equal-distribution requirement, as well as to whether – and possibly how – the equal-distribution requirement may be substantiated and justified.

12.3.2 The Problem of Climate Change

Climate change is frequently portrayed as the most serious environmental challenge currently facing mankind. Few, however – including the Intergovernmental Panel on Climate Change (IPCC)[6] – seem to be aware of the fact that, more than any other problem, global warming is also what underlies many of the World Commission's recommendations.[7] The problem is taken up several places in the report (WCED, 1987:2, 5, 8, 14, 22, 32, 33, 37, 58, 59, 172, 174, and 176), and the following statement from the Chairman of the World Commission illustrates the point:

The threat of climate change has been known to the world for ten years. And still we have not yet worked out legally binding commitments, procedures, timetables and targets that work. It was while we worked on the WECD that scientists from 29 countries, gathered in Villach, Austria in October 1985, announced the conclusion that climate change was a 'plausible and serious probability'. The World Commission dealt seriously with this problem and, in our report *Our Common Future*, we called for internationally agreed policies and a global convention. (Brundtland, 1996:1. See also WCED, 1987:175 for a similar description.)

Figure 12.1   Environmental problems in time and space

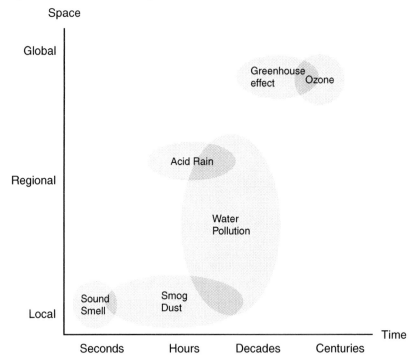

Source: Bergesen, Roland and Sydnes, 1995.

Contrary to the opinion of, for example, Beckerman (1994) (who views the problem of global warming as more or less non-existent and, therefore, of little import for a trade-off between welfare maximisation and sustainable development), the assumption in *Our Common Future* is that the problem of climate change is *real*. Moreover, the problem is seen as a problem of scale, and conceived as an equity issue in the same manner as by the IPCC. The issue involves *distribution*, both between and within generations, and thereby substantiates – better than any other contemporary problem – a claim that the two types of equity are linked.

The IPCC's first Assessment Report of 1990 concluded that continued accumulation of anthropogenic greenhouse gases in the atmosphere would lead to climate change, the rate and magnitude of which would have serious impacts on natural and human systems. IPCC's Second Assessment Report of 1995 states that the conclusions from the first report still hold:

> carbon dioxide remains the most important contributor to anthropogenic forcing of climate change; projections of future global mean temperature change and sea level rise confirm the potential for human activities to alter the Earth's climate to an extent unprecedented in human history; and the long time-scales governing both the accumulation of greenhouse gases in the atmosphere and the response of the climate system to those accumulations, means that many important aspects of climate change are effectively irreversible. Further, that observations suggest 'a discernible human influence on global climate', one of the key findings of this report, adds an important new dimension to the discussion of the climate change issue. (IPCC, 1995a: Foreword)

According to the IPCC, carbon-dioxide emissions, if maintained at the 1994 level, will lead to a nearly constant rate of increase in atmospheric concentrations for at least two centuries, approaching twice the pre-industrial concentration by the end of the twenty-first century. Further, carbon-cycle models indicate that stabilisation of atmospheric CO_2 concentrations at 450, 650 or 1000 ppmv ('parts per million by volume' of carbon-dioxide), could be achieved only if global anthropogenic CO_2 emissions drop to the 1990 levels by, respectively, 40, 140 or 240 years from now, and drop substantially *below* 1990 levels after that. For any of the levels, however, higher emissions in earlier decades require lower emissions later on (IPCC, 1995a:3).

IPCC has also developed a range of scenarios of future greenhouse-gas and aerosol-precursor emissions. These are based on assumptions as to population, economic growth, land-use, technological changes, energy availability and fuel-mix during the period 1990 to 2100. The different scenarios project an increase in global mean-surface temperature of about 1 to 3.5 degrees Celsius by 2100, and an increase in sea level of about 15.95 cm (IPCC, 1995b).

There is still great uncertainty regarding the magnitude of the rise in global temperature, both with respect to the rate of change and the effects there will be at the regional level. There is, however, a risk that climate change may unleash self-reinforcing mechanisms creating dramatic ecological changes that may be difficult or impossible to bring under control again (Bergesen *et al.*, 1995:10), what the IPCC refers to as 'the possibility of surprises' (IPCC, 1995a:45).

In response to IPCC's first Assessment Report of 1990, the UN General Assembly authorised the creation of an International Negotiating Committee (INC) with the task of working out a framework convention on climate change. The UN Framework Convention on Climate Change was agreed in its final form at the fifth meeting of INC, and opened for signature at the UN Conference in

Rio de Janeiro in 1992. As a result of US opposition, the convention omitted any legally binding quantitative emission targets (Harrison, 1997:86).

The Framework Convention did, however, mandate that 'Annex-1 countries' should act 'with the aim of returning individually or jointly to their 1990 levels [of] . . . anthropogenic emissions of carbon dioxide and other greenhouse gases'.[8] Further, the framework convention outlined the organisation, operation, and funding of a Conference of the Parties (COP) to implement and further develop the convention. At COP1 in Berlin 1995, the parties agreed to what is now referred to as 'the Berlin Mandate', a process for negotiating progressively more stringent emission targets for Annex-1 countries than the non-binding convention commitments (Harrison, 1997:87).

The second session of the Conference of the Parties (COP2), was held in Geneva, Switzerland in 1996. For the first time, the developed countries here accepted quantified limits on their net greenhouse-gas emissions. Net emissions are reduced either by cutting emissions from sources, or by increasing sinks. The 'Geneva Ministerial Declaration', however, did not specify any upper limit for atmospheric concentrations of greenhouse gases or for global mean temperatures (Harrison, 1997:91). These questions were left for the third Conference of the Parties (COP3) to decide upon, in Kyoto, Japan in December 1997.

12.4 CLIMATE CHANGE AND SUSTAINABLE DEVELOPMENT

The greenhouse effect is thus a global problem which, in all probability, will worsen and threaten the living conditions of future generations. In this respect, it is an environmental problem which is linked to both the relationship between generations and to the minimum requirement for sustainable development; that natural life-sustaining systems not be endangered. And the declared objective of the Framework Convention on Climate Change is in accordance with this requirement; that is, to stabilise 'greenhouse gas concentrations in the atmosphere at a level that would prevent dangerous anthropogenic interference with the climate system' (O'Riordan and Jäger, 1996, Appendix 1: United Nations Framework Convention on Climate Change).

But what constitutes 'dangerous anthropogenic interference with the climate system'? According to Harrison (1997), Bert Brolin, former Chairman of the IPCC, has consistently argued that this is a *political* – and not a scientific – issue. It seems, however (from the wording of the 'Geneva Ministerial Declaration') that the Ministers have implicitly accepted 'twice the preindustrial levels' (or about 550 ppmv) as a rough measure of what constitutes a 'dangerous level' (Harrison, 1997:89).

And how does this relate back to the question of global justice? In the case of the basic-needs requirement, the relationship is straightforward: if the sustainability requirement is not fulfilled, it is uncertain whether future generations can satisfy their basic needs. In other words, the principle of physical sustainability is a precondition for satisfying the basic-needs requirement *between* generations, and hence a precondition for social equity along this dimension. It is reasonable, therefore, to regard the principle of physical sustainability as both an end in itself (an integral part of the development goal of sustainable development) and a precondition ('proviso') for sustainable development (Malnes, 1990).[9]

This implies, however, that social justice in *Our Common Future* is primarily understood as the fulfilment of basic needs. A world in which large parts of the world's population do not get their basic needs met is clearly an *unjust* world in the view of the World Commission, thus justifying redistribution both within and among countries. Pushing the argument one step further, however, this fact also makes the question of climate change a matter of equity *within our own generation*.

In 1993, the OECD countries accounted for about 51 per cent of global fossil carbon emissions, with half of this from the United States. The former Soviet Union and Eastern European countries accounted for about 17 per cent, with half coming from Russia. Developing countries contributed just under a third of total emissions, with over 40 per cent of this portion coming from China (IPCC, 1995c:95). In addition, past emissions account for the cumulative build-up of gases in the atmosphere, and the industrialised countries account for about two-thirds of cumulative carbon emissions in total (IPCC, 1995c:94).

If we look at the distribution of carbon-dioxide emissions per capita, the average level of emissions in the European Union is 8.72 tons per capita, while the United States accounts for 19.35 tons per capita, and China, Brazil and India respectively 2.2, 1.5 and 0.77 tons per capita (Bergesen et al., 1995:37, 71). The gap between the developing and the industrialised countries is thus formidable.

Since the CO_2 emission level is related to both production and consumption, as well as to standards of living, the problem of climate change is also related to the distribution of benefits within our own generation. With more than 90 per cent of population growth expected in the South, the basic-needs requirement alone dictates that the consumption of energy and fossil fuels will have to be increased in that part of the world. Reflecting this, the Framework Convention on Climate Change recognises that 'economic and social development and poverty eradication are the first and overriding priorities of the developing country parties' (O'Riordan and Jäger, 1996, Appendix 1: United Nations Framework Convention on Climate Change, Article 4.7).

In an extremely important chapter on 'Equity and Social Considerations' (IPCC, Working Group III, 1995c:78–124), the IPCC operates with an almost identical categorisation of the distributive issues arising from climate-change impacts as the different dimensions of social equity put forth in *Our Common Future*. IPCC puts them into four different groups: (1) aggregate welfare impacts over time (intertemporal distribution of expected global utility); (2) welfare impacts between countries (international distribution of expected utility); (3) welfare impacts within countries (interpersonal distribution of expected utility within countries); and (4) the distribution of the cost of risk-bearing associated with each of the above (IPCC, 1995c:100).[10]

The problem of risk is also treated in *Our Common Future* (pp. 49, 60–2 and 323–6), and managing risk is identified as one of the critical objectives for environment and development which follows from the concept of sustainable development (WCED, 1987:49). According to the IPCC, risk is an equity issue for several reasons. Firstly, industrialised countries have, in general, better insurance markets, which makes it possible for individuals to reduce the costs of risks. Secondly, the nature of the impacts from climate change may make the cost of risk-bearing much higher in some developing countries (IPCC, 1995c:101), and, thirdly – as also stated in *Our Common Future* – 'wealthier nations are better placed financially and technologically to cope with the effects of possible climatic change' (WCED, 1987:49).

The major point here, however, is that the IPCC claims that the combination of basic needs and risk-bearing could have far-reaching implications:

> If we accept that individuals have some right to some basic goods – food, shelter, access to environmental resources – and if emitting greenhouse gases threatens the availability of these basic goods, then those responsible for the emissions should be prepared to protect potential victims against losing the right to basic goods (IPCC, 1995c:102).

There is thus an additional relationship between the basic-needs requirement and the climate-change issue from the perspective of risks.

12.5   THE EQUAL-DISTRIBUTION REQUIREMENT

Thus far we have concentrated mainly on the relationship between the basic-needs requirement and climate change. We now turn to the question of how *the equal-distribution requirement* may be substantiated in light of the climate-change issue. As argued by Føllesdal in Chapter 4, considerations of basic needs cannot justify the claim that all should have an equal consumption level in both time and space. This, however, does not, in our opinion, deviate from the view of the World Commission. Another interpretation of the equal-distribution requirement which is both possible and plausible is that it is primarily substantiated by the principle of physical sustainability, and only secondarily supported by the basic-needs requirement.

The problem of climate change has a number of characteristics which can be used to illustrate this connection. First of all, the atmosphere is an international public good, and the atmospheric concentration of anthropogenic greenhouse gases is the result of the combined actions of all countries. The atmosphere has, in this perspective, both of the identifying characteristics of a 'pure public good': 'nonrivalry' and 'nonexcludability'. These are defined by the IPCC as follows:

Nonrivalry means that additional consumers do not have to compete with each other to use the good and therefore drive up its cost: the marginal cost of an additional individual using the good is zero. Nonexcludability means that the marginal cost of exclusion – of stopping an individual from enjoying the good – is prohibitive. Public goods thus permit 'free riding' (IPCC, 1995c:28).

The global climate system can, in other words, be regarded as a 'global commons'. No one has property rights to the atmosphere, and, at this point in time, no institution exists which can enforce or regulate the amount of greenhouse gases that are emitted by the individual countries. In other words, there is nothing at present which can be done if a country chooses to increase its emissions considerably. Lacking an effective global agreement (and as a precondition *for* a global agreement), we are completely dependent upon the individual countries' voluntary participation. The global character of the climate problem, combined with the (lack of) legal structure in the international political system, thus makes a 'solution' dependent on the voluntary co-operation of all parties.

These circumstances, together with the fact that most developing countries in the world seem to aspire to a standard of living equivalent to that of the West, necessitates the principles of physical sustainability and universality. There is simply not enough 'ecological space' for the universalisation of the present living standard of the West. The fact that the industrial world already has used much of the planet's ecological capital is part of the determinative circumstances of environment-and-development problems:

developing countries must operate in a world in which the resources gap between most developing countries and industrial nations is widening, in which the industrial world dominates in the rule-making of some key international bodies, and in which the industrial world has already used much of the planet's ecological capital. This inequality is the planet's main 'environmental' problem, it is also its main 'development' problem. (WCED, 1987:5–6).

While meeting basic needs is, in this light, the first requirement of social justice, keeping within the limited depository capacity of the Earth constitutes the second. Further, as previously mentioned, the OECD countries arguably have no exclusive right to their present standard of living. So, while OECD countries may have no duty towards developing countries beyond helping them to secure basic needs, there is nothing which can prevent developing countries from aspiring to, and eventually attaining, a standard of living equivalent to that of the West.

If the negotiating parties within the Framework Convention on Climate Change were to decide that 'dangerous anthropogenic interference with the climate system' should be understood as 'twice preindustrial levels' (about 550 ppmv), this would define the available depository capacity for greenhouse gases. Even though there is some flexibility within this scale (increasing sinks and so forth), we may in principle regard the depository capacity as a finite dimension which must be shared among the world's countries. Hence, the fundamental question is how this cake is to be divided: who should be allowed to increase their emissions, and who should pay for greenhouse-gas abatement and adaptation?

The question can be reformulated as whether one can, in the long run, imagine a stable solution (that is, one which doesn't violate the principle of physical sustainability), which does not prescribe an equal distribution of the Earth's depository capacity among the world's nations on a *per capita* basis. This for three related reasons: (1) because no one can reasonably be denied his share; (2) because no one needs to be content with less than an equal distribution; and (3) because if one persists in wanting more, one may risk that others also will want more, which may lead in the long run to even worse results for all parties involved.

In our view, the equal-distribution requirement in the Brundtland Report may be interpreted in such a perspective. It is *the principle of physical sustainability* which substantiates the *equal-distribution requirement*. Given the above circumstances, the equal distribution requirement would be the natural outcome of development processes which respect the principle of physical sustainability. In this sense the equal-distribution requirement embodies the 'principle of universality', that is, that consumption standards must be set so that everyone (in time and space) can reasonably aspire to them. As such, the equal-distribution requirement may be regarded as a necessary condition for fulfilling the principle of physical sustainability, and the principle of physical sustainability may in turn be regarded as a condition for social equity between generations (so as to fulfil the basic-needs requirement between generations).

Even if the available depository capacity for greenhouse gases were divided equally among the world nations on a *per capita* basis, and we envision a future where everyone eventually uses their share, this would still not imply an equal distribution of goods. It would be perfectly possible for a country to have a higher standard of living due to differences in the availability of other resources, technology, know-how, and so on. For this reason, it is more precise to say that the principle of physical sustainability – working in tandem with the principle of universality – substantiates limitations in allowable inequality, which includes a more equal – but not necessarily *absolutely* equal – distribution of goods. How equal the global distribution actually turns out to be is dependent on numerous factors: technological development (cleaner forms of energy, and so on); the degree to which OECD countries actually change their production and consumption patterns; the transfer of money and technology from rich to poor countries; and the actual development in developing countries.

The constraint imposed by the share of greenhouse gases would, however, have implications for the production and consumption of a whole range of goods. This relationship is treated here by Stein Hansen (Chapter 10), and more thoroughly documented in the report from the Norwegian project on 'sustainable economics' (Hansen *et al.*, forthcoming). The results from the Norwegian macro-model simulations indicate consequences for a large number of different consumption categories. The projected effects of a gradual rise in the existing Norwegian CO_2 tax are, for example, a change in the overall composition of consumption and a reduction in the level of consumption for goods such as gasoline, the stationary use of oil products, travelling abroad, housing, and so forth (see Chapter 10, Table 10.2).

In this connection, the second category of goods identified in Chapter 1 – goods which do not create serious environmental problems even if everyone should both aspire to and attain them – may, in fact, contain few actual goods. Whether the consumption of specific goods creates serious environmental problems, appears to be a matter of scale and of fossil-fuel dependency. To what degree a lowering of fossil-fuel consumption in the OECD countries actually affects the living standards in these countries, is, therefore, difficult to predict. Ultimately it will depend on technological development and the availability of renewable energy resources, accompanied by a further change in the content of growth towards a dematerialised and energy-intensive pattern.

12.6 THE PRINCIPLE OF UNIVERSALITY: SUSTAINABLE PRODUCTION AND CONSUMPTION

Keeping within the 'ecological space' of the depository capacity for greenhouse gases also raises questions, however. How much fossil fuel to consume, in which manner, and with which implications for the standard of living, are all central problems for sustainable development in both the industrialised and developing countries. The issue was addressed in the Brundtland Report as follows:

Industrialised countries must recognise that their energy consumption is polluting the biosphere and eating into scarce fossil fuel supplies. Recent improvements in energy efficiency and a shift towards less energy-intensive sectors have helped limit consumption. But the process must be accelerated to reduce per capita consumption and encourage a shift to non-polluting sources and technologies. The simple duplication in the developing world of industrial countries' energy use patterns is neither feasible nor desirable (WCED, 1987:59).

It is clear from this statement that the goal is not to duplicate the existing pattern of energy use in the industrial countries, but rather to develop energy-use patterns which are in accord with both the principle of physical sustainability and the principle of universality. This issue lies at the very core of the idea of 'sustainable production and consumption', and is directly linked to the issue of changing the content of growth. The recommended growth rates in *Our Common Future* are viewed as 'environmentally sustainable' only if: (1) industrialised nations can continue the recent shifts in the content of their growth 'towards less material- and energy-intensive activities and the improvement of their efficiency in using materials and energy' (WCED, 1987:51); and (2) there is a change in the content of growth, to make it more equitable in its impact, that is, 'to maintain the stock of capital, to improve the distribution of income, and to reduce the degree of vulnerability to economic crises' (WCED, 1987:51).

These conditions are further elaborated in *Our Common Future*, and they must be seen as essential qualifying conditions on what is otherwise seen as a strong economic-growth bias. They are also issues of key concern for Rio's 'global partnership for sustainable development'. Principle 7 of the Rio Declaration (United Nations, 1993b), states that: 'The developed countries acknowledge the responsibility that they bear in the international pursuit of sustainable development in view of the pressures their societies place on the global environment and of the technologies and financial resources they command.' This is followed up in Principle 8 with an admonition to the states of the world to 'reduce and eliminate unsustainable patterns of production and consumption and promote appropriate demographic policies'.

These principles place a clear burden on Northern countries to examine their production and consumption patterns with respect to standards of sustainable development. The burden is also spelled out in Chapter 4 of *Agenda 21* where the issue of 'changing consumption patterns' is related to other aspects of the action plan (energy, transportation, waste and the transfer of technology), but where the framers of the document also wanted to endow the topic with its own moral weight. We thus read that:

Poverty and environmental degradation are closely interrelated. While poverty results in certain kinds of environmental stress, the major cause of the continued deterioration of the global environment is the unsustainable pattern of consumption and production, particularly in industrialised countries, which is a matter of grave concern, aggravating poverty and imbalances (United Nations, 1993a:34).

Chapter 4 of the *Agenda* goes on to spell out objectives and activities related to the problem, placing, for example, emphasis on the promotion of 'patterns of consumption and production that reduce environmental stress and will meet the basic needs of humanity', and advocating 'domestic policy framework(s) that will encourage a shift to more sustainable patterns of production and consumption'. The chapter also calls for greater scientific analysis of the implications of consumption patterns for sustainable development, and recommends that the achievement of sustainable consumption be given 'high priority'.

Although the burden of creating sustainable patterns of production and consumption is placed on Northern countries, it seems that the accelerating global ecological interdependence also makes this a matter of concern for developing countries. As pointed out by the IPCC:

Whatever the past and current responsibilities and priorities, it is not possible for the rich countries to control climate change through the next century by their own actions alone, however drastic. It is this fact that necessitates global participation in controlling climate change, and hence, the question of how equitably to distribute efforts to address climate change on a global basis (IPCC, 1995c:97).

And this leads us, again, to focus on a relatively small group of very populous countries. If China, India and Brazil are not brought into some form of binding co-operation, any efforts on the part of the industrialised countries will come up short. This fact seriously complicates the responsibilities and burdens to achieve sustainable development, a problem stressed by academics (Bergesen *et al.*, 1995) and clearly visible within the politics and proceedings of the Commission on Sustainable Development. In this latter context, the Norwegian Minister of the Environment, Thorbjørn Berntsen, took an initiative at the first session of the CSD to facilitate further development on sustainable production and consumption within the 'Working Group on Financial Resources'. Without mincing words, Berntsen addressed the session as follows:

Our consumption patterns, and our efforts to multiply them world-wide, will undermine the environmental resource base even if we were to introduce the best available technology world-wide. I am convinced that without real change in our consumption patterns we will not be able to reach the goals in the climate and biodiversity conventions, nor will we effectively fight poverty (as quoted in Khor, 1994:110).

The Norwegian minister also used the occasion to announce a working conference of experts on the topic, held in Oslo in February 1994. The work from this conference led to the tabling of a draft document on sustainable production and consumption at the second 'normal' session of the CSD in New York in May 1994. The document proved, however, to be more controversial than expected, with a major part of the opposition coming from representatives from the rapidly developing South. They were clearly concerned that any slow-down in Northern development would affect their chances for continued growth at home. The conflict threatened, at one point, to torpedo the entire effort on the theme, and – according to Berntsen's own account in the Oslo newspapers – was only resolved by a resolute intervention from the representative from the European Union.

The issue was, however, resolved, and the CSD gave its assent to continue with the work on an action plan for sustainable production and consumption. The next stage in the process was the 'Oslo Ministerial Roundtable' in February 1995. This meeting was designed to be both more pragmatic and more political. With governmental representatives from 26 countries and the European Union (including 14 Ministers/Commissioners of Environment), the conference aimed 'to prepare elements for an international work programme on sustainable production and consumption'.

The final document from the Oslo Roundtable was submitted to the third session of the CSD in April 1995, where it received general support as a basis for further specification and implementation. In addition to outlining several of the basic conceptual issues involved, the Oslo document identifies 'a menu of possible actions' for the 'key actors' involved. These focus generally on three types of activity: (1) improving understanding and analysis, (2) applying tools for modifying behaviour, and (3) monitoring, evaluating and reviewing performance. The structure of the document is relatively specific as to both goals and initiatives for each of these topics.

In his address to the Oslo Roundtable, the then Chairman of the CSD, Klaus Töpfer, added further specifies to what he saw as the future development of the programme:

A systematic analysis of individual country experiences – with 5 to 10 countries reviewed each year – in the design and implementation of policy measures intended to make an impact in the short- and medium-term on their most pressing problems requiring changes in consumption and production patterns; systematic analysis of the impact on developing countries of changes in consumption and production patterns anticipated in the developed countries; reviews (every 3 to 5 years) of the results of quantitative analysis, including the use of global models for long-term projections linking resource use to economic activity in order to assess their policy implications at the national and international levels; and the further development and compilation of indicators of sustainable development (MoE, 1995:43).

The CSD process on sustainable production and consumption has thus focused the burden of environment-and-development responsibility on the

Northern countries in a dramatic way, at the same time that it has revealed a much more complex picture with respect to differing interests in the South and the overall issue of interdependence. The two Oslo conferences contributed, nonetheless, to force the issue of sustainable production and consumption on to the UNCED agenda.

12.7   CONCLUDING REMARKS

In this chapter we have tried to link the concept of sustainable development to some of the major environment-and-development problems facing us today. The purpose has been to provide a better understanding of the various elements of the concept, as well as to describe the context within which the idea was originally developed and is currently designed to function. It is precisely within the tensions of this context – between the normative and the empirical, the political and the scientific, the global and the national – that the Brundtland Report's interpretation of sustainable development retains a constructive potential for change. Not that *Our Common Future* is free of problems and inconsistencies: they clearly exist. But given the fact that the report was the result of an extensive and highly complicated process of compromise, it is our position that the document stands out today as a powerful source of normative inspiration and goal-oriented pragmatics.

As a key aspect of this perspective, we have stressed that the report contains different distributional criteria, and that these criteria are *not* inconsistent within the overall logic of the argument. On the contrary, within the scope of global environment-and-development problems, the various distributional criteria can be shown to be well-substantiated and reasonable, and they clearly go beyond liberal principles of distributive justice. We are convinced, therefore, that sustainable development is a concept which both will and should remain central to further debates on environment and development.

Accepting this, we are nonetheless faced with numerous pressing tasks. First and foremost, there is an overriding need for further elaboration of the internal priorities and operational implications of the concept as an instrument for social steering. We need a better understanding of the processes necessary for converting goals and action-plans into reality, and we need a much stronger awareness of the interdependences between efforts to satisfy 'physical sustainability', on the one hand, and demands for global and generational equity, on the other. Much work is already in progress as a direct result of the impact from the UNCED process on policies, research and social change. But the logic of the implementation problematic – as a distinct global-policy challenge with a demand for new multi-level procedures, responsibilities and policy instruments – is still diffuse.

If we are to achieve more effective management for sustainable development in this context, we must begin by attaining a wider and more profound consensus as to the overriding goals of the process. Just as 'democracy' had to be converted from symbol to practice through critical public debate with respect to evolving procedures and institutions, so too must 'sustainable development' be subjected to a similar process. The present book is a contribution toward this end. It is our hope that by focusing on the concept of sustainable development within a specific context (the Brundtland Report and UNCED), we have contributed to a narrowing of the concept's scope of meaning – and a broadening of its legitimacy and potential for generating change. This does not imply, of course, that we feel the debate has been 'resolved' – nor do we wish it to be so. We wish merely to move the debate in a more operational direction, within what we believe to be a more constructive global-political context. We feel there is reason to expect both a greater degree of agreement on the concept of sustainable development; and a greater degree of effectiveness in its implementation than we have thus far experienced.

Agenda 21 marks an important benchmark in global planning and task specification, and the administrative apparatus connected to the Commission for Sustainable Development (CSD) provides the tools for follow-up and implementation. But these must also be subjected to ongoing scrutiny and improvement. Furthermore, there is a clear need for investing more resources in the procedures for strategic planning (with new forms for participation and co-ordination among the involved parties), and in new indicators and evaluation models for a more consolidated and fruitful public debate. In our view, there are ample idealism and 'alternative ways of thought' in the UNCED documents to focus and guide reform work for many decades to come. The main challenge is to maintain the momentum from the Rio Earth Summit while we continue to work for both a deeper consensus as to the goals of sustainable development, and an improved understanding of the costs and benefits accruing to different steering strategies and policy instruments.

NOTES

1. Our emphasis in all three quotes.
2. How much *more* equal distribution has to be will be taken up later in the discussion.
3. A third extension mentioned by Rawls is to certain cases of health-care which seem to be most relevant for the case of domestic justice (Rawls, 1993:44).
4. Rawls does not think, however, that the problem of what is due to animals and the rest of nature can be answered within this framework (Rawls, 1993:44–5). This is because the liberal conception of justice is a political, and not a meta-

physical, concept. The idea of political justice does not, according to Rawls, cover everything, and should hardly be expected to. The concept of sustainable development, as developed in *Our Common Future* (WCED, 1987), does not give an adequate answer to this problem either. The concept is, however, mainly anthropocentric, even though one can find selected statements which point beyond an anthropocentric bias. These questions are not taken up here.

5. In an interview in Norway's leading non-tabloid newspaper, *Aftenposten*, 19 January 1994.

6. The Intergovernmental Panel on Climate Change (IPCC) was jointly established in 1988 by the World Meteorological Organisation and the United Nations Environment Programme. Its task was to: (1) assess available scientific information on climate change, (2) assess the environmental and socioeconomic impacts of climate change, and (3) formulate response strategies. The IPCC's First Assessment Report was completed in August 1990 and served as the basis for negotiating the UN Framework Convention on Climate Change (IPCC, 1995a: Foreword).

7. Although sustainable development and *Our Common Future* are occasionally referred to in IPCC's Second Assessment Report (1995), the report does not seem to be aware of the direct relevance of *Our Common Future*, and the similarity between the two approaches. After referring to the core definition of sustainable development given by *Our Common Future*, the IPCC report concludes as follows: 'Although the Commission clearly had in mind environmental considerations, its report did not spell out exactly what sustainable development included' (IPCC, 1995c: 40) This is, however, a gross underestimation of, not only the Commission's report, but also the relevance of sustainable development for the climate-change issue.

8. Annex 1 countries include the OECD countries, other developed countries, and most of the European countries of the former Soviet bloc that are considered countries in transition (Harrison, 1997; O'Riordan and Jäger, 1996, Appendix 1: United Nations Framework Convention on Climate Change).

9. Even though the principle of physical sustainability is, in this perspective, a precondition for social equity between generations, social equity is not a necessarily a precondition for the principle of physical sustainability (in the sense of being maintainable). In theory, a dictatorship with extensive poverty and without the most basic civil and political rights, may be 'sustainable'. However, the Brundtland Report maintains that a world 'in which poverty and inequity are endemic will always be prone to ecological and other crises' (WCED, 1987:43). Hence, 'the reduction of poverty itself is a precondition for environmentally sound development' (WCED, 1987:69). This is an empirical condition in the Brundtland Report, indicating that social equity *in practice* is also a precondition for fulfilling the principle of physical sustainability.

10. What is missing from the framework compared with *Our Common Future* is equity across national generations. This, it could be argued, should also be relevant for the IPCC framework.

Bibliography

Ackerman, Bruce (1980). *Social Justice in the Liberal State*. New Haven: Yale University Press.

Adams, W.M. (1990). *Green Development. Environment and Sustainability in the Third World*. London: Routledge.

Alfsen, Knut, Birkelund, H. and Aaserud, M. (1993). 'Secondary Benefits of the EC Carbon/Energy Tax'. Statistics Norway Discussion Papers No. 104. November. Oslo: Statistics Norway.

Alston, Philip and Quinn, G. (1987). 'The Nature and Scope of States Parties' Obligations Under the International Covenant on Economic, Social and Cultural Rights'. *Human Rights Quarterly* 9 (May):156–229.

Alston, Philip (1988). 'Making Space for New Human Rights: The Case of the Right to Development'. *Harvard Human Rights Yearbook* 1 (Spring):3–40.

Alston, Philip (1989). 'On the Purposes of General Comments and Reporting by States Parties: General Comment'. UN doc. E/C.12/1989/CRP.2/Add.1.

Amdur, Robert (1977). 'Rawls' Theory of Justice: Domestic and International Perspectives', *World Politics* 29:438–61.

Amundsen, E.S., Asheim, G.B., Moxnes, E. and Sandvik, B. (1991). 'Hva er bærekraftig utvikling?', *Sosialøkonomen* 45:3.

Andersen, H.W. and Sørensen, K.H. (1992). *Frankensteins Dilemma. En bok om teknologi, miljø og verdier*. Oslo: Ad Notam Gyldendal.

Andresen, S., Skjærseth, J.B. and Wettestad, J. (1993). 'International Efforts to Combat Marine Pollution: Achievements of North Sea Cooperation and Challenges Ahead'. *Green Globe Yearbook*, London and Oslo: Oxford University Press and the Frditjof Nansen Institute, pp. 15–24.

Anker, Peder (1997). 'From Scepticism to Dogmatism and Back'. In Andrew Brennan and Nina Witoszek (eds). *Philosophical Dialogues*. Berkeley: California University Press.

Ariansen, P. (1994). *Beyond Parfit's Paradox. A Guardian for Future Generations. Status Under International Law*. Conference paper. Foundation for International Studies, University of Malta, Valletta, Malta.

Arrow, K. (1951). *Social Choice and Individual Values*. London: Wiley.

Asheim, G.B. (1988). 'Rawlsian Intergenerational Justice as a Markov-perfect Equilibrium in a Resource Technology'. *Review of Economic Studies* 55:469–84.

Asheim, G.B. (1991). 'Unjust Intergenerational Allocations', *Journal of Economic Theory* 54:350–71.

Asheim, G.B. (1994). 'Net National Product as an Indicator of Sustainability'. *Scandinavian Journal of Economics* 96:257–65.

Asheim, G.B. (1996). 'Capital Gains and Net National Product in Open Economies', *Journal of Public Economics* 59 (No. 3):419–34.

Attfield, R. (1983). *The Ethics of Environmental Concern*. Oxford: Basil Blackwell.

Baird, Callicott, J. (1993). 'The Conceptual Foundations of the Land Ethic.' In *Environmental Ethics: Divergence and Convergence*, Susan J. Armstrong & Richard G. Botzler (eds), pp. 386–97.

Barro, R.J. (1974). 'Are Government Bonds Net Wealth?', *Journal of Political Economy* 82:1095–1117.

Barry, Bryan (1973). *The Liberal Theory of Justice*. Oxford: Clarendon Press.

Barry, Bryan (1989). *Theories of Justice*. Berkeley: University of California Press.

Bauman, Z. (1994). 'Morality without Ethics'. *Theory, Culture & Society* 11:1–34.

Beck, U. (1992). *Risk Society. Towards a New Modernity*. London. Sage Publications.

Beckerman, W. (1994). '"Sustainable Development": Is it a Useful Concept?', *Environmental Values* 3:191–209.

Beckerman, W. (1995). 'How Would You Like Your "Sustainability", Sir? Weak or Strong? A Reply to my Critics'. *Environmental Values* 4:169–79.

Beitz, Charles R. (1979). *Political Theory and International Relations*. Princeton: Princeton University Press.

Beitz, Charles R. (1981a). 'Democracy in Developing Societies'. In Peter G. Brown and Henry Shue (eds). *Boundaries: National Autonomy and Its Limits*. Totowa, N.J.: Rowman and Allanhead.

Beitz, Charles R. (1981b). 'Economic Rights and Distributive Justice in Developing Societies'. *World Politics* 33:321–46.

Bergesen, H.O.; Roland, K. and Sydnes, A.K. (1995). *Norge i det globale drivhuset*. Oslo: Universitetsforlaget.

Berntsen, T. (1994). *Miljøvernpolitisk Redegjørelse 1994*, Oslo: Ministry of the Environment.

Bijker, Wiebe E. and Law, J. (eds) (1992). *Shaping Technology/Building Society. Studies in Sociotechnical Change*. Cambridge, Mass: MIT Press.

Bijker, Wiebe E., Hughes, T.P. and Pinch, T. (eds) (1987). *The Social Construction of Technological Systems: New Directions in the Sociology and History of Technology*. Cambridge, Mass: MIT Press.

Bleier, Ruth (ed.) (1986). *Feminist Approaches to Science*. New York: Pergamon Press.

Bowlby, J. (1988). *A Secure Base. Clinical Applications of Attachment Theory*. London: Routledge.

Braidotti, Rosi, Charkiewicz, E., Häusler, S. and Wieringa, S. (1994). *Women, the Environment and Sustainable Development: Towards a Theoretical Synthesis*. London: Zed Books.

Brenna, Brita (ed.) (1995). 'En kyborg til forandring. Nye politikker i moderne vitenskap og teknologi'. Oslo: TMV Publication series.

Brenna, Brita, Moser, I. and Refseth, N. (1994). 'Vitenskap: Kulturen uten kultur? – Vitenskapens tabuer i en postmoderne verden'. *ARR – Idehistorisk Tidsskrift*, 1: 28–41.

Brown Weiss, Edith (1990). 'Our Rights and Obligations to Future Generations for the Environment'. *American Journal of International Law* 84:198–206.

Brown, B.J., Hanson, M.E., Liverman, D.M., and Merideth, R.W. (1988). 'Global Sustainability: Toward Definition'. *Environmental Management* 11: 713–19.

Brown, Lester R. (1981). *Building a Sustainable Society*. New York: Norton.

Brown, Lester R. (ed.) (1993). *State of the World*. Washington, DC: Worldwatch Institute.

Brundtland, G.H. (1994). 'Vekst, verdiskapning og miljøutfordringen', *Aftenposten*, 5 March 1994.

Brundtland, G.H. (1996). 'Burden-sharing Under the Climate Convention', Speech held at *Global Change Forum*, Oslo, SAS Hotel, 13 June 1996.

Bryk, Dale S. (1991). 'The Montreal Protocol and Recent Developments to Protect the Ozone Layer'. *Harvard Environmental Law Review* 15:275–98.

Bull, Hedley (1977). *The Anarchical Society*. New York: Columbia University Press.

Bye, Torstein and Glomsrød, S. (1994). 'Hva er kostnaden ved miljøforbedringer?' Talk at the User-Group Conference under the programme committee of the SAMMEN programme, Research Council of Norway, 17 October 1994.

Caldwell, L.K. (1990). *International Environmental Policy: Emergence and Dimensions*. Durham and London: Duke University Press.

Calvo, G. (1978). 'Some Notes on Time Inconsistency and Rawlsian Maximin Criterion'. *Review of Economic Studies* 45:97–102.

Carson, Rachel (1962). *Silent Spring*. Greenwich, Connecticut: Fawcett Publications.

Chichilnisky, G. (1993). 'What is Sustainable Development?', mimeo, Stanford University and Columbia University.

—— (1996). 'An Axiomatic Approach to Sustainable Development'. *Social Choice and Welfare*, 13:231–57.

Clark, C.W. (1976). *Mathematical Bioeconomics*. New York: John Wiley.

Clark, C.W. (1985). *Bioeconomic Modelling and Fisheries Management*. New York: John Wiley.

COCF (Centre for Our Common Future) (1993). *Agenda for Change: A Plain Language Version of Agenda 21 and the other Rio Agreements* (Compiled by Michael Keating), Geneva: Centre for Our Common Future.

Cohen, C. (1971). *Democracy*. New York: The Free Press.

Commoner, B. (1972). *The Closing Circle: Nature, Man and Technology*. New York: Bantam.

Connolly, W.E. (1983). *The Terms of Political Discourse*. Princeton: Princeton University Press.

Cornia, G.A., Jolly, R. and Stewart, F. (eds) (1987). *Adjustment with a Human Face: Protecting the Vulnerable and Promoting Growth*, 2 vols. A study by UNICEF. Oxford: Oxford University Press, Clarendon Press.

Cronberg, Tarja (1992). *Technology in Social Sciences: The Seamless Theory*. Lyngby: DTH.

Daly, H.E. (1977). *Steady-State Economics. The Economics of Biophysical Equilibrium and Moral Growth*. San Francisco: W.H. Freeman and Company.

Daly, H.E. (1992a). *Steady-state Economics*. London: Earthscan Publications.

Daly, H.E. (1992b). 'Allocation, Distribution, and Scale: Towards an Economics that is Efficient, Just and Sustainable'. *Ecological Economics* 6:185–93.

Daly, H.E. (1993). 'The Economist's Response to Ecological Issues'. In *Sustainable Growth: A Contradiction in Terms?*, Report of the Visser'tHooft Memorial Consultation, The Ecumenical Institute, Chaeuteau de Bossey, 39–52.

Daly, H.E. and Cobb, J.B. (1989). *For the Common Good: Redirecting the Economy toward Community, the Environment, and a Sustainable Future*. Boston: Beacon Press.

Danielson, Peter (1973). 'Theories, Intuitions, and the Problem of World-Wide Distributive Justice', *Philosophy and the Social Sciences* 3–4:331–40.

Dasgupta, P. and Heal, G. (1979). *Economic Theory and Exhaustible Resources*. Cambridge University Press.

Den norske MAB-komiteen (1994). 'Mennesket i naturen: Biosfæreområder som verktøy for bærekraftig forvaltning av naturens ressurser', Research Report from the Norwegian Man-and-the-Biosphere Committee, Oslo, Research Council of Norway, Division for Environment and Development.

Devall, B. and Sessions, G. (1985). *Deep Ecology: Living as if Nature Mattered*. Layton, Utah: Gibbs M. Smith

Diamond, J.M. (1975). 'The Island Dilemma'. *Biological Conservation* 7:129–45.

Diamond, J.M. (1984). 'Historic Extinctions: Rosetta Stone for Understanding Prehistoric Extinctions'. In P.S. Martin and R.F. Klien (eds), *Quarternary Extinctions: A Prehistoric Revolution*. Tucson: University of Arizona Press.

DiLorenzo, T. (1993). 'The Mirage of Sustainable Development'. *The Futurist* (September/October):14–19.

Dixit, A., Hammond, P. and Hoel, M. (1980). 'On Hartwick's Rule for Regular Maximin Paths of Capital Accumulation and Resource Depletion'. *Review of Economic Studies* 47:551–6.

Dixon, J.A. and Fallon, L.A. (1989). *The Concept of Sustainability: Origins, Extensions, and Usefulness for Policy*. Washington, DC: The World Bank. Environment Department, Division Working Paper No. 1989–1.

DN Notes (1993). 'Naturens tålegrenser. Referat fra seminar i 1991 og 1992'. Trondheim, Direktoratet for naturforvaltning (Directorate for Natural Resource Management).

Dobson, A. (1996). 'Environment Sustainabilities: An Analysis and a Typology'. *Environmental Politics* 3:401–28.

Donnelly, Jack (1985). 'In Search of the Unicorn: The Jurisprudence and Politics of the Right to Development'. *California Western International Law Journal* 15:473–98.

Donnelly, Jack (1989). *Universal Human Rights in Theory & Practice*. Ithaca, NY: Cornell University Press.

Doyal, L. and Gough, I. (1991). *A Theory of Human Need*. London, Macmillan.

Dryzek, J. (1987). *Rational Ecology: Environment and Political Economy*. Oxford: Blackwell.

Dunning, John H. (1993). *Multinational Enterprises and the Global Economy*. Wokingham: Addison-Wesley.

Dworkin, Ronald (1993). *Life's Dominion: an Argument about Abortion, Euthanasia, and Individual Freedom*. New York: HarperCollins.

Eckersley, R. (1992). *Environmentalism and Political Theory. Toward an Ecocentric Approach*. London: UCL Press.

Eckersley, R. (1993). 'Free Market Environmentalism: Friend or Foe?', *Environmental Politics* 2 (No. 1):1–19.

Eckersley, R. (1996). 'Markets, the State and the Environment: an Overview'. In R. Eckersley (ed.), *Markets, the State and the Environment. Towards Integration*. London: Macmillan.

Ehrlich, Paul (1972). *The Population Bomb*. New York: Ballantine.

Elster, J. (1977a). *Om utbytting*. Oslo: Pax Forlag.

Elster, J. (1977b). *Rasjonalitet og rasjonalisme*. Oslo: Gyldendal.

Elster, Jon (1984). 'Skeptiske tanker om samfunnsplanlegging'. *Forskning og Framtid* 1:27–36.

Eriksen, T.H. (1992). 'Vi og de andre – kultur, makt og miljø'. In N.C. Stenseth and K. Hertzberg (eds). *Ikke Bare Si Det, Men Gjøre Det! Om Bærekraftig Utvikling*, Oslo: Universitetsforlaget, pp. 137–45.

Erikson, Robert (1993). 'Descriptions of Inequality: The Swedish Approach to Welfare Research'. In Martha Nussbaum and Amartya K. Sen (eds). *The Quality of Life*. Oxford: Clarendon Press, pp. 67–83.

Esty, C. Daniel (1994). 'Greening the GATT: Trade, Environment and the Future'. Washington, DC: Institute for International Economics, July 1994.

Feenberg, Andrew (1995). *Alternative Modernity: The Technical Turn in Philosophy and Social Theory*. Berkeley: University of California Press.

Fromm, E. (1957). *The Art of Loving*. London: George Allen & Unwin.

Føllesdal, Andreas (1991). *The Significance of State Borders for International Distributive Justice*. Doctoral dissertation, Harvard University, Cambridge, Massachusetts, University Microfilms No. 9211679.

Føllesdal, Andreas (1995). 'Justifying Human Rights: The Challenge of Cross-Cultural Toleration'. *European Journal of Law, Philosophy and Computer Science* 4:38–49.

Føllesdal, Andreas (1996). 'Minority Rights: A Liberal Contractualist Case'. In Juha Raikka (ed.) 1996, *Do We Need Minority Rights? Conceptual Issues*. The Hague, London, Boston: Kluwer Academic Publishers.

Førsund, F. and S. Strøm (1980). *Miljø og Ressursøkonomi*. Oslo: Universitetsforlaget.

GAO (United States General Accounting Office) (1992). *International Agreements Are Not Well Monitored*. Report, January 1992, Washington, DC: US General Accounting Office.

Gallie, W.B. (1962). 'Essentially Contested Concepts'. In Max Black (ed.), *The Importance of Language*. Englewood Cliffs, NJ: Prentice Hall.

Gaston, K.J., Williams, P.H., Eggleton, P. and Humphries, C.J. (1995). 'Large Scale Patterns of Biodiversity: Spatial Variation in Family Richness'. *Proceedings of the Royal Society*, Biological Sciences B, 260:149–54.

General Assembly, United Nations (1986). Declaration on the Right to Development. New York, United Nations, Resolution 41/128.

Giddens, A. (1994). *Beyond Left and Right. The Future of Radical Politics*. London: Polity Press.

Gilpin, Robert (1987). *The Political Economy of International Relations*. Princeton: Princeton University Press.

Goldberg, Steven (1975). *On Male Dominance: The Inevitability of Patriarchy*. New York: William Morrow and Co.

Goodin, Robert E. (1979). 'The Development–Rights Tradeoff: Some Unwarranted Economic and Political Assumptions'. *Universal Human Rights* 1:31–42.

—— (1992). *Green Political Theory*. Cambridge: Polity/Blackwell.

Gray, J. (1989). *Liberalism: Essays in Political Philosophy*, London: Routledge.

Gray, J. (1993). *Beyond the New Right. Markets, Government and the Common Environment*. London: Routledge.

Grey, W. (1993). 'Anthropocentrism and Deep Ecology, *Australian Journal of Philosophy* 71:463–75.

Guha, Ramachandra (1989). 'Radical American Environmentalism and Wilderness Preservation: A Third World Perspective'. *Environmental Ethics* 11: 71–83.

Gulbrandsen, Elisabeth (1994). 'Refleksivitet og autoritet'. In *Kjønn og Kunnskapsproduksjon*, Publication series, Centre for Womens' Research, University of Trondheim, Trondheim, Norway.

Hammond, P. (1994). 'Is there Anything New in the Concept of Sustainable Development?'. In L. Camriglio, L. Pineschi, D. Siniscalo and T. Treves (eds), *The Environment after Rio: International Law and Economics*. London: Graham and Trotman.

Hansen, Stein (1992). 'Er økonomisk vekst forenlig med bærekraftig utvikling?'. In N.C. Stenseth og K. Hertzberg (eds). *Ikke Bare Si Det, Men Gjøre Det! Om Bærekraftig Utvikling*. Oslo: Universitetsforlaget, pp 183–91.

Hansen, Stein (1992). *Er vi rede til nullvekst? U-landssolidaritet med miljøprofil*. Oslo: J.W. Cappelens Forlag.

Hansen, Stein (1993). 'The Evolution of Environmental Concerns in Economy-wide Policies and Adjustment Lending: Experience from the Energy Sector'. EED Report 1993/11, Oslo, Fridtjof Nansen Institute.

Hansen, Stein, Jespersen, P.F. and Rasmussen, I. (1995). *Bærekraftig økonomi*. Oslo: Ad Notam Gyldendal.

Hansen, Stein, Jespersen, P.F. and Rasmussen, I. (forthcoming). *Prospects for a Sustainable Economy: A Study of Norwegian Policy Options*. London: Macmillan.

Haraway, Donna (1986). 'Primatology is Politics by Other Means'. In Ruth Bleier (ed.), *Feminist Approaches to Science*. New York: Pergamon Press.

Haraway, Donna (1989). *Primate Visions: Gender, Race, and Nature in the World of Modern Science*. Routledge, New York.

Haraway, Donna (1991). *Simians, Cyborgs, and Women. The Reinvention of Nature*. London: Free Association Books.

Hardin, G. (1974). 'Lifeboat Ethics: The Case Against Helping the Poor'. *Psychology Today* 8:38–43, 123–6.

Hardin, G. (1968). 'The Tragedy of the Commons'. *Science* 162:1243–48.

Hardin, G. (1985). *Filters Against Folly*. New York: Penguin Books.

Hardin, G. (1993). *Living within Limits: Ecology, Economics, and Population Taboos*. Oxford: Oxford University Press.

Hardin, G. (1994). 'Who Cares for Posterity?'. In L.P. Pojman (ed.), *Environmental Ethics, Readings in Theory and Application*. Boston: Jones and Bartlett, pp. 219–24.

Harding, Sandra (1986). *The Science Question in Feminism*, Ithaca: Cornell University Press.

Hare, Richard M. (1976). 'Rawls' Theory of Justice – I & II'. In N. Daniels (ed.), *Reading Rawls*. New York: Basic Books, 1976, pp. 81–107.

Hareide, D. (1991). *Det gode Norge: På vei mot et medmenneskelig samfunn*. Oslo: Gyldendal.

Harrison, N.E. (1997). 'Unexpected Events in Geneva: Progress Toward a Protocol on Climate Change'. *Journal of Environment & Development* 6:85–92.

Harsanyi, J.C. (1953). 'Cardinal Utility in Welfare Economics and in the Theory of Risk-Taking', *Journal of Political Economy* 61:434–5.

Hartwick, J. (1977). 'Intergenerational Equity and the Investing of Rents from Exhaustible Resources'. *American Economic Review* 66:972–4.

Haugland, T. Olsen, Ø. and Roland, K. (1990). 'Stabilising CO_2 Emissions by Carbon Taxes – A Viable Option?'. EED Report 1990/11. Oslo: Fridtjof Nansen Institute.

Hayek, F.A. (1960). *The Constitution of Liberty*, Chicago: The University of Chicago Press.

Hayek, F.A. (1973). *Law, Legislation and Liberty. Volume 1: Rules and Order*, Chicago: The University of Chicago Press.

Hayek, F.A. (1976). *Law, Legislation and Liberty. Volume 2: The Mirage of Social Justice*. Chicago: The University of Chicago Press.

Hayek, F.A. (1979). *Law, Legislation and Liberty. Volume 3: The Political Order of a Free People*. Chicago: The University of Chicago Press.

Hayek, F.A. (1989). *The Fatal Conceit. The Errors of Socialism*. In W.W. Bartley III (ed.), *The Collected Works of F.A. Hayek*, Vol. 1, Chicago: University of Chicago Press.

Heffernan, James D. (1993). 'The Land Ethic: A Critical Appraisal'. In Susan J. Armstrong and Richard G. Botzler (eds), *Environmental Ethics: Divergence and Convergence*, New York: McGraw Hill, pp. 398–404.

Hempel, Lamont C. (1996). *Environmental Governance: The Global Challenge*. Washington, DC: Island Press.

Hovi, J. (1992). 'Å være dumsnill fungerer ikke: Bærekraftig forvaltning av felles-ressurser'. In N.C. Stenseth and K. Hertzberg (eds), *Ikke bare si det, men gjøre det! Om bærekraftig utvikling*. Oslo: Universitetsforlaget, pp. 339–47.

Hovi, J. and Rasch, B.E. (1993). *Strategisk handling*. Oslo: Universitetsforlaget.

Hubbard, Ruth (1990). *The Politics of Women's Biology*, New Brunswick, NJ: Rutgers University Press.

Hulten, C.R. (1992). 'Accounting for the Wealth of Nations: The Net Versus Gross Output Controversy and its Ramifications'. *Scandinavian Journal of Economics* 94 (Supplement):9–24.

Hurrell A. and Kingsbury, B. (eds) (1992). *The International Politics of the Environment: Actors, Interests and Institutions*. New York: Oxford University Press.

Hägerhäll, Bertil (1993). 'The Evolving Role of NGOs'. In G. Sjöstedit (ed.), *International Environmental Negotiations: Process, Issues and Context*. Stockholm, Utenrikspolitiska Institutet, pp. 50–77.

Håkonsen, Lars and Mathiesen, L. (1994). 'Towards a more Comprehensive Cost Measure for CO_2 Reductions'. Unpublished mimeo, Norges Handelshøyskole, 11 November 1994. Working notes for the 'Sustainable Economics' project.

Håland, W. (1986). *Psykoterapi. Relasjon, utviklingsprosess og effekt*. Oslo: Universitetsforlaget.

Haavelmo, T. (1971). 'Forurensningsproblemet fra samfunnsvitenskapelig syns-punkt' *Sosialøkonomen* 4:5–8.

Haavelmo, T. and Hansen, S. (1992). 'Strategier for bekjempelse av fattigdom i u-landene'. In R. Goodland, H. Daly, S.E. Serafy and B. Droste, *Økonomisk Politikk for en Bærekraftig Utvikling: Oppfølging av Brundtlandkommisjonen*. Oslo: J.W. Cappelens Forlag/UNESCO.

IPCC (1995a). *Climate Change 1995. The Science of Climate Change. Contributions of Working Group I to the Second Assessment Report of the Intergovernmental Panel on Climate Change*, New York: Cambridge University Press.

IPCC (1995b). *Climate Change 1995. Impacts, Adaptions and Mitigation of Climate Change: Scientific-Technical Analyses. Contributions of Working Group II to the Second Assessment Report of the Intergovernmental Panel on Climate Change*. New York: Cambridge University Press.

IPCC (1995c). *Climate Change 1995. Economic and Social Dimensions of Climate Change. Contributions of Working Group III to the Second Assessment Report of the Intergovernmental Panel on Climate Change*. New York: Cambridge University Press.

IUCN/UNEP/WWF (1980). *World Conservation Strategy. Living Resource Conservation for Sustainable Development*. Gland, Switzerland: IUCN/UNEP/WWF.

IUCN/UNEP/WWF (1991). *Caring for the Earth. A Strategy for Sustainable Living.* Gland, Switzerland: IUCN/UNEP/WWF.

Jacob, M.L. (1996). *Sustainable Development. A Reconstructive Critique of the United Nations Debate*. University of Gothenburg, Department of Theory of Science and Research.

Jacobs, M. (1991). *The Green Economy: Environment, Sustainable Development and the Politics of the Future*. London: Pluto Press.

Jacobs, M. (1995). 'Sustainable Development, Capital Substitution and Economic Humility: A Response to Beckerman'. *Environmental Values* 4:57–68.

Jensen, Arthur (1972). *Genetics and Education*. London: Methuen.

Jenssen, A.T. (1989). *Hva vil vi med samfunnsutviklingen? Sentrale verdier og verdiendringer i Norge*. Oslo: Prosjekt Alternativ Framtid.

Johnson, Lawrence E. (1991). *A Morally Deep World: An Essay on Moral Significance and Environmental Ethics*. New York: Cambridge University Press.

Johnston, R.J. (1989). *Environmental Problems: Nature, Economy and State*. London: Belhaven Press.

Kaland, P.E. and Brekke, N.G. (1994). 'Lyngheisenteret på Lygra i Nordhordaland', In *Fylkestinget i Bergen, Hefte II*, case 57, pp. 11–47.

Kaplan, A. (1964). *The Conduct of Inquiry: Methodology for Behavioral Science*. San Francisco: Chandler Publishing Company.

Katz, Erik and Oechsli, L. (1993). 'Moving Beyond Anthropocentrism: Environmental Ethics, Development, and the Amazon'. *Environmental Ethics* 15 (Spring):49–59.

Kavka, G.S. (1982). 'The Paradox of Future Individuals'. *Philosophy and Public Affairs* 11:93–112.

Keller, Evelyn Fox (1985). *Reflections on Gender and Science*. New Haven: Yale University Press.

Keller, Evelyn Fox (1992). *Secrets of Life, Secrets of Death. Essays on Language, Gender and Science*. New York and London: Routledge.

Kirkby, J., O'Keefe, P. and Timberlake, L. (eds) (1995). *The Earthscan Reader in Sustainable Development*. London: Earthscan.

Khor, M. (1994). 'The Commission on Sustainable Development: Paper Tiger or Agency to Save the Earth?'. In *Green Globe Yearbook 1994*. Oslo and Oxford: Scandinavian University Press and Oxford University Press, pp. 103–13.

Kloppenburg, J.R. (1988). *First the Seed*. Cambridge: Cambridge University Press.

Koopmans, T.C. (1967). 'Intertemporal Distribution and Optimal Aggregate Economic Growth'. In *Ten Economic Studies in the Tradition of Irving Fisher*, London: Wiley.

Kukathas, Chandran (1989). *Hayek and Modern Liberalism*. Oxford: Clarendon Press.

La Court, T.D. (1990). *Beyond Brundtland: Green Development in the 1990s*. London: Zed Books.

Lafferty, W.M. (1996). 'The Politics of Sustainable Development: Global Norms for National Implementation'. *Environmental Politics* 5:185–208.

—— and Meadowcroft (eds) 1990. *Democracy and the Environment: Problems and Prospects*. Cheltenham: Edward Elgar.

Langhelle, O. (1996). 'Norway: Progress Toward Sustainability?'. In D.C. Pirages (ed.), *Building Sustainable Societies. A Blueprint for a Post-Industrial World*. New York: M.E. Sharpe.

Lem, S. (1994). *Den tause krigen mot de fattige og mot miljøet – og hva som må gjøres*. Oslo: Forlaget Forum.

Levidov, Les and Tait, J. (1995). 'The Greening of Biotechnology: GMOs as Environment-Friendly Products'. In V. Shiva and I. Moser (eds), *Biopolitics: A Feminist and Ecological Reader on Biotechnology*. London: Zed Books.

Liftin, Karen (1991). 'Ozone Politics: Power and Knowledge in the Montreal Protocol'. Paper presented for delivery at the 1991 Annual Meeting of the International Studies Assosiation, Vancouver, BC, 20–24 March 1991.

Lorenz, K. (1966). *On Aggression*. New York: Harcourt, Brace & World.

Luke, T. (1988). 'The Dreams of Deep Ecology'. *Telos. A Quarterly Journal of Critical Thought* 76:65–92.

Lunde, L. (1991). 'Science or Politics in the Global Greenhouse? The Development Towards Scientific Consensus on Climate Change'. Oslo: The Fridtjof Nansen Institute, Report Series, 1991:8.

Lundström, M. (1992). *Is Anti-Rationalism Rational? The Case of F.A. Hayek*. Paper presented at The European Consortium for Political Research, Joint Sessions of Workshops, 'The New Institutionalism', Limerick, Ireland, 30 March–4 April, 1992.

Mace, G.M. and Lande, R. (1991). 'Assessing Extinction Threats: Towards a Reevaluation of IUCN Threatened Species Categories'. *Conservation Biology* 5:148–57.

Magnus, A. *et al.* (1979). *Penga eller livet? Studiebok om økologi og samfunn*. Oslo: Sosialistisk opplysningsforbund.

Malnes R. (1990). *The Environment and Duties to Future Generations*. Oslo: Fridtjof Nansen Instituttet.

Manne, A.S. and Richels, R.G. (1994). 'The Costs of Stabilising Global CO_2 Emissions: A Probabilistic Analysis Based on Expert Judgements'. *The Energy Journal* 15 (No. 1):31–56.

Marglin, S.A. (1963). 'The Social Rate of Discount and the Optimal Rate of Investment'. *Quarterly Journal of Economics* 77:95–111.

Marietta, Don E., Jr. (1993). 'Environmental Holism and Individuals'. In Susan J. Armstrong and R.G. Botzler (eds), *Environmental Ethics: Divergence and Convergence*, New York: McGraw Hill, pp. 405–10.

Maslow, A.H. (1962). *Toward a Psychology of Being*. New York: Van Nostrand.

McManus, P. (1996). 'Contested Terrains: Politics, Stories and Discourses of Sustainability'. *Environmental Politics* 5:48–73.

Meadowcroft, J. (1996). *Planning, Democracy and the Demands of Sustainable Development*. Paper presented at IPSA Roundtable on The Politics of Sustainable Development, Oslo, Norway, April 26.

Meadowcroft, J. (1997). *Democratic Planning and the Challenges of Sustainable Development*. Report prepared for ProSus (Project for Research and Documentation for a Sustainable Society), Research Council of Norway, Oslo.

Merchant, Carolyn (1980). *The Death of Nature: Women, Ecology and the Scientific Revolution*. New York: Harper and Row.

Mishan, E. (1977). 'Economic Criteria for Intergenerational Comparisons'. *Futures* 9:383–403.

MoE (Ministry of Environment, Norway) (1995). 'Oslo Ministerial Roundtable: Conference on Sustainable Production and Consumption', Report. Oslo.

Moxnes, E. (1989). *Sustainable Development*. Bergen: Chr. Michelsen Institute. Report 30701–1.

Myers, N. (ed.) (1984). *Gaia: an Atlas of Planet Management*. Garden City, NY: Anchor Press/Doubleday.

Mysen, H.T. (1993). 'Climate Cost Function'. Report to the SAMMEN research programme's research seminar, 16 November, 1993, Research Council of Norway, Oslo.

Mäler, K.G. (1989). 'Sustainable Development'. Economic Development Institute, The World Bank.

Mäler, K.G. (1990). 'Sustainable Development', in *Sustainable Development, Science and Policy*. The Conference Report. Bergen 8–12 May 1990. NAVF.

Mäler, K.G. (1991). 'National Accounts and Environmental Resources'. *Environmental and Resource Economics* 1:1–15.

Nash, Roderick Frazier (1989). *The Rights of Nature*. Madison: University of Wisconsin Press.

Naturvårdsverket (Swedish Environmental Protection Agency') (1992). 'Åtgärder mot klimatförendringar'. Rapport 4120, Stockholm.

NAVF (1990). *Sustainable Development, Science and Policy*. Conference Report, Bergen 8–12 May, Oslo, NAVF (Norwegian Research Council for Science and the Humanities).

New Scientist (1988). 'Now it Makes Business Sense to Save the Ozone Layer'. London, 29 October 1988.

Nilsen, F.S. (1989). *Samfunnsordninger og samfunnsmoral. En komparativ sosialantropologisk analyse*. Oslo: Prosjekt Alternative Framtid.

Norderhaug, M. (1994). *For mange? Befolkningsveksten i det 21. århundre*. Oslo: Cappelen.

Norton, B.G. (1986). 'Conservation and Preservation: A Conceptual Rehabilitation', *Environmental Ethics* 8:195–220.

Norton, B.G. (1982). 'Environmental Ethics and The Rights of Future Generations'. *Environmental Ethics* 4:319–37.

Norton, B.B. (1989). 'Intergenerational Equity and Environmental Decisions: a Model Based on Rawls' Veil of Ignorance'. *Ecological Economics* 1:137–59.

Nozick, R. (1974). *Anarchy, State and Utopia*. Oxford: Basil Blackwell.

Nybom, Thorsten (1993). 'Forskning och politik: Om det kvalificerade kunskapssökandets konstitutionella förutsättningar och framtid', Forum for universitetshistorie, Oslo, University of Oslo.

Næss A. (1991). 'Den dypøkologiske bevegelse: aktivisme ut fra et helhetssyn'. In S. Gjerdåker, L. Gule, B. Hagtvet (eds), *Den uoverstigelige grense. Tanke og handling i miljøkampen*, Bergen and Oslo: Chr. Michelsens Institutt/J.W. Cappelens Forlag, pp. 21–43.

Næss, A. (1973). 'The Shallow and the Deep, Long-Range Ecology Movement: A Summary'.*Inquiry* 16:95–100.

Næss, A. (1984). 'A Defense of the Deep Ecology Movement'. *Environmental Ethics* 6:265–70.

Næss, Arne (1989). *Ecology, Community and Lifestyle*. (Translated and edited by David Rothenberg). Cambridge: Cambridge University Press.

Ofstad, H. (1971). *Vår forakt for Svakhet. En Analyse av Nazismens normer og vurderinger.* Oslo: Pax Verlag.

O'Riordan, T. (1981). *Environmentalism.* London: Pion Limited.

O'Riordan, T. (1993). 'The Politics of Sustainability'. In K.R. Turner (ed.), *Sustainable Environmental Economics and Management: Principles and Practice.* London: Belhaven Press, pp. 37–69.

O'Riordan, T. and Jäger, J. (eds) (1996). *Politics of Climate Change. A European Perspective.* London: Routledge.

Oelschlaeger, Max (1991). *The Idea of Wilderness.* New Haven: Yale University Press.

Olson, Mancur (1993). 'Dictatorship, Democracy, and Development'. *American Political Science Review* 87:567–76.

Ophuls, W. and Boyan, S.A. (1992). *Ecology and the Politics of Scarcity Revisited: the Unraveling of the American Dream.* New York: W.H. Freeman and Company.

Oslo and Paris Commissions (1993). 'North Sea Quality Status Report', London.

Østerud, Ø. (1994). 'Nasson og stat som teoterisk ut fordring', in S. Goerdåker, T. Skolnes and Y. Tvedt, *Nassonalstaten under press?* Oslo: Cappelen.

Paehlke, R.E. (1989). *Environmentalism and the Future of Progressive Politics.* New Haven: Yale University Press.

Page, T. (1977). *Conservation and Economic Efficiency.* Johns Hopkins University Press.

Parfit, D. (1984). *Reasons and Persons.* Oxford: Clarendon Press.

Passmore, J. (1980). *Man's Responsibility for Nature, Ecological Problems and Western Tradition.* (2nd edn). London: Duckworth.

Pearce, D. and Atkinson, G. (1993). 'Capital Theory and the Measurement of Sustainable Development: an Indicator of "Weak" Sustainability'. *Ecological Economics* 8:103–8.

Pearce, D., Markandya, A. and Barbier, E.B. (1989). *Blueprint for a Green Economy.* London: Earthscan.

Pearce, D., Barbier, E. and Markandya, A. (1990). *Sustainable Development: Economics and Environment in the Third World.* London: Earthscan Publications.

Pearce, D.W. and Warford, J.J. (1993). *World without End: Economics, Environment, and Sustainable Development.* Oxford: Oxford University Press.

Pezzey, J. (1989). 'Economic Analysis of Sustainable Growth and Sustainable Development'. Environment Department Working paper No. 15, The World Bank.

Pezzey, J. (1992a). 'Sustainable Development Concepts: An Economic Analysis', World Bank Environment Paper Number 2, Washington, DC, The World Bank.

Pezzey, J. (1992b). 'Sustainability: An Interdisciplinary Guide'. *Environmental Values* 1:321–62.

Pogge, Thomas W. (1989). *Realizing Rawls.* Ithaca: Cornell University Press.

Pogge, Thomas W. (1994). 'An Egalitarian Law of Peoples', *Philosophy & Public Affairs* 23:195–224.

Princen, T. and Finger, M. (1994). *Environmental NGOs in World Politics.* London and New York: Routledge.

Rahbek, C. (1995). 'The Elevational Gradient of Species Richness: A Uniform Pattern?'. *Ecography* 18:200–5.

Ramsey, F. (1928). 'A Mathematical Theory of Saving'. *Economic Journal* 38:543–9.

Randers, J. (1994). 'The Quest for a Sustainable Society – a Global Perspective'. In G. Skirbekk (ed.), *The Notion of Sustainability and its Normative Implications*, Oslo, Scandinavian University Press.

Rawls, J. (1971). *A Theory of Justice*. Cambridge, Mass.: Harvard University Press.

Rawls, J. (1972). *A Theory of Justice*. London: Oxford University Press.

Rawls, John (1993a). *Political Liberalism*. New York: Columbia University Press.

Rawls, J. (1993b). 'The Law of Peoples'. In S. Shute and S. Hurley (eds), *On Human Rights: The Oxford Amnesty Lectures 1993*. New York: Basic Books, pp. 41–82.

Redclift, M. (1987). *Sustainable Development. Exploring the Contradictions*. London: Routledge.

Redclift, M. (1993). 'Sustainable Development: Needs, Values, Rights'. *Environmental Values* 2:3–20.

Regan, T. (1979). 'Examination and Defence of One Argument Concerning Animal Rights'. *Inquiry* 22:189–219.

Reid, D. (1995). *Sustainable Development. An Introductory Guide*, London: Earthscan Publications.

Repetto, R. (1986). *World Enough and Time*. New Haven: Yale University Press.

Richardson, D. (1994). *The Politics of Sustainable Development*. Paper presented to the International Conference on the Politics of Sustainable Development within the European Union, University of Crete, 21–3 October 1994.

Ring, K. (1988). 'Near-Death Experiences: Implications for Human Evolution and Planetary Transformation'. In S. Grof and M.L. Valier, *Human Survival and Consciousness Evolution*. Binghamton, NY: State University of New York Press.

Rodman, J. (1993). 'Ecological Sensibility'. In Susan J. Armstrong and Richard G. Botzler (eds), *Environmental Ethics: Divergence and Convergence*, New York: McGraw Hill, pp. 382–5.

Rose, Hilary (1992). 'Victorian Values in the Test-Tube: the Politics of Reproductive Science and Technology'. In Francis Sejersted and I. Moser (eds) (1992), *Humanistic Perspectives on Technology, Development and Environment*, University of Oslo, TMV Publication series No. 3/92.

Rose, Hilary (1995). 'Feminist/Gender Studies of Science: An Overview of the Field'. In V. Shiva and I. Moser (eds), *Biopolitics: A Feminist and Ecological Reader on Biotechnology*. London: Zed Books.

Rose, Hilary and Rose, Steven (1969). *Science and Society*. Harmondsworth: Allen Lane & Penguin.

Rose, Hilary and Rose, Steven (1976). *The Radicalisation of Science*. London: Pantheon Books.

Rose, Hilary and Rose, Steven (1979). *Ideology of/in the Sciences*. Boston: Schenkman.

Rose, Steven; Lewontin, R.C. and Kamin, L.J. (1984). *Not in our Genes: Biology, Ideology and Human Nature*. London: Pantheon Books.

Rosendal, G.K. (1995). 'The Conservation of Biological Diversity: A Viable Instrument for Conservation and Sustainable Use'. In H.O. Bergersen and G. Parman (eds), *Green Global Yearbook 1995*. Oxford: Oxford University Press, pp. 69–81.

Sachs, W. (ed.) (1993). *Global Ecology. A New Arena of Political Conflict*. London: Zed Books.

Samdahl, D.M. and Robertson, R. (1989). 'Social Determinants of Environmental Concern: Specification and Test of the Model'. *Environment and Behaviour* 21:57–81.

Sartori, Giovanni (1987). *The Theory of Democracy Revisited*. (2 vols) Chatham, NJ: Chatham House Publishers.

Scanlon, T.M. (1982). 'Contractualism and Utilitarianism'. In Amartya Sen and Bernard Williams (eds), *Utilitarianism and Beyond*, Cambridge: Cambridge University Press, pp. 103–28.

Scanlon, T.M. (1993). 'Partisan for Life'. *The New York Review of Books*, 15 July 45–50.

Schachter, Oscar (1982). 'International Human Rights'. *Recueil des Cours* 178(5):327–51.

—— (1985). *International Law in Theory and Practice: General Course in Public International Law* (Dordrecht: Martinus Nijhoff).

Schramm, Gunter and Warford, J.J. (1989). *Environmental Management and Economic Development*. Washington, DC: The World Bank and Johns Hopkins University Press.

Schulz, C.E. (1992). 'Hva er bærekraftig utvikling?'. In Nils Chr. Stenseth og Karine Hertzberg (eds), *Ikke Bare Si Det, Men Gjøre Det! Om Bærekraftig Utvikling*, Oslo: Universitetsforlaget.

Schulz, C.E. (1995). *De rikes etterspørsel etter de fattiges natur*. Report No. 1995:1 from the Project for an Alternative Future, Oslo: Prosjekt Alternativ Framtid.

Seippel, Ø. and Langhelle, O. (1993). 'Norsk Miljøfilosofi – Arne Næss'. *Tidsskriftet Alternativ Framtid*, No. 3:51–66.

Seippel, Ø. (1995). *Fra Natur til Handling: En empirisk analyse av forholdet mellom natursyn, forbruk og politisk atferd*, Report No. 1995:3 from the Project for an Alternative Future, Oslo: Prosjekt Alternativ Framtid.

Seippel, Ø. and Lafferty, W.M. (1996). 'Religion, menneske eller økologi'. *Norsk Statsvitenskaplig Tidsskrift* 12 (2):113–39.

Sejersted, F. (1988). 'Norsk Idyll? Forhandlingssamfunnet som forutsetning for demokratiet'. *Nytt Norsk Tidsskrift* 1:10–23.

Sejersted, F. (1989). *Er det mulig å styre samfunnsutviklingen?* Working Paper, Oslo, TMV Center, No. 11.

Sejersted, F. (ed.) (1991). *Teknologi og kultur – et humanistisk bidrag til en analyse av vårt moderne tekniske samfunn*, Report. Oslo, TMV Center.

Sejersted, Francis and Moser, I. (eds) (1992). *Humanistic Perspectives on Technology, Development and Environment*. Oslo, TMV Center, Publication series No. 1992:3.

Semb-Jansson, A. (1989). 'Challenges in the North'. 30th Annual Meeting of the Canadian Commission for UNESCO. Yellowknife, NWT, pp. 143–7.

Sen, Amartya K. (1988). 'Property and Hunger'. *Economics and Philosophy* 4:57–68.

Sessions, G. (1995). 'Ecocentrism, Wilderness and the Global Ecosystem Protection', in George Sessions (ed.) *Deep Ecology for the Twenty-first Century*. (Boston: Shambhala).

SFT (Norwegian Pollution Control Authority) (1994). 'Foruresning i Norge'. Oslo: SFT.

Shanmugaratnam, N. (1992). 'Den bærekraftige utviklingen i møtepunktet mellom debattene om utvikling og miljø'. *Vardøger* 21:85–105.

Shapin, Steven and Schaffer, Simon (1985). *Leviathan and the Air-Pump: Hobbes, Boyle, and the Experimental Life*, Princeton, NJ: Princeton University Press.

Shiva, Vandana (1989). *Til livets opphold. Kvinner, Økologi og Utvikling.* Oslo: Forlaget Oktober.

Shiva, Vandana (1991). *The Violence of the Green Revolution. Third World Agriculture, Ecology and Politics.* London: Zed Books.

Shiva, Vandana (1994). 'The Seed and the Earth: Biotechnology and the Colonisation of Regeneration'. In Vandana Shiva (ed.), *Close to Home: Women Reconnect Ecology, Health and Development Worldwide.* Gabriola Island, BC: New Society Publishers.

Shiva, Vandana (1995). '*Biotechnology Development and Conservation of Biodiversity*'. In V. Shiva and I. Moser (eds), *Biopolitics: a Feminist and Ecological Reader on Biotechnology.* London: Zed Books.

Shiva, Vandana and Ingunn Moser (1995). *Biopolitics: a Feminist and Ecological Reader on Biotechnology.* London: Zed Books.

Skirbekk, G. (ed.) (1994). *The Notion of Sustainability and its Normative Implications.* Oslo: Scandinavian University Press.

Skjærseth, Jon Birger (1992). 'The "Successful" Ozone-Layer Negotiations – Are there Any Lessons to be Learned?'. *Global Environmental Change*, December 1992:292–300.

Skjærseth, Jon Birger (1993). 'EF-lobbying i drivhuset – institusjonell endring og nye strategier'. *Internasjonal Politikk* 51(2):211–17.

Skjærseth, Jon Birger (1994). 'Selvbestemmelsesrett under press fra transnasjonale miljøproblemer'. In S. Gjerdåker, T. Skålnes and T. Tvedt, *Nasjonalstaten Under Press?* Oslo and Bergen: CMI/Cappelen.

Skonhoft, A. (1995). 'Tap av biologisk mangfold og utrydding av arter: Hvilken innsikt gir økonomiske studier?'. *Norsk økonomisk tidsskrift* 109:231–54.

Skåre, Mari (1994). 'Whaling: a Sustainable Use of Natural Resources or a Violation of Animal Rights?'. *Environment* 36 (No. 7).

Smith, F.L. and Jeffreys, K. (1993). 'A Free-Market Environmental Vision'. In D. Boaz and E.H. Crane (eds), *Market Liberalism. A Paradigm for the 21st Century*, Washington DC: Cato Institute.

Sohn, Louis B. (1982). 'The New International Law: Protection of the Rights of Individuals Rather than States.' *American University Law Review* 32:1–64.

Solow, R.M. (1974). 'Intergenerational Equity and Exhaustible Resources'. *Review of Economic Studies* (Symposium, 1974), pp. 29–45.

Solow, R.M. (1993). 'Special Lecture: an Almost Practical Step Towards Sustainability'. *Resources Policy* 19:162–72.

Soussan, J.G. (1992). 'Sustainable Development'. In S.R. Bowlby and A.M. Mannion (eds), *Environmental Issues in the 1990's.* London: John Wiley & Sons.

Spitz, R.A. (1946). 'Hospitalism: an Inquiry into the Genesis of Psychiatric Conditions in Early Childhood'. In O. Fenichel *et al.* (eds), *The Psychoanalytic Study of the Child.* New York: International Universities Press.

Steidlmeier, P. (1993). 'The Morality of Pollution Permits', *Environmental Ethics*, 15:133–50.

Stenseth, N.C. (1991). 'Forvaltning av biologiske fellesressurser i et lokalt og globalt perspektiv'. In N. Chr. Stenseth, N. Trandem and G. Kristiansen (eds), *Forvaltning av våre fellesressurser.* Oslo: Ad Notam, pp. 11–70.

Stenseth, N.C. (1992a). 'Bærekraftig utvikling – bak flosklene'. In N.C. Stenseth and K. Hertzberg (eds), *Ikke bare si det, men gjøre det! Om bærekraftig utvikling.* Oslo: Universitetsforlaget, pp. 19–36.

Stenseth, N.C. (1992b). 'Skal vi lage omelett, må vi knuse egg'. In N.C. Stenseth and K. Hertzberg (eds), *Ikke bare si det, men gjøre det! Om bærekraftig utvikling*. Oslo: Universitetsforlaget, pp. 329–38.

Stenseth, N.C. and Semb-Johansson, A. (1986). 'Katastrofe i u-hjelpens fotspor'. *Aftenposten*, 5 February 1986.

Stenseth, N.C. and Hertzberg, K. (eds) (1992). *Ikke bare si det, men gjøre det! Om bærekraftig utvikling*. Oslo: Universitetsforlaget.

Stenseth, N.C., Hovi, J. and Hoel, A.H. (1993). 'Bærekraftig forvaltning av biologiske fellesressurser'. In N.C. Stenseth *et al.* (eds), *Vågehvalen – valgets kval*. Oslo: Ad Notam Gyldendal, pp. 249–75.

Stenseth, N.C., Paulsen, K. and Karlsen, R. (1995). *Afrika – natur, samfunn og bistand*. Oslo: Ad Notam Gyldendal.

Stokke, O. (ed.) (1991). *Sustainable Development*. London: Frank Cass.

Stone, C.D. (1994). *Reflections on the Moral and Institutional Challenges of 'Sustainable Development'*. The Hart Lecture, University of London, School of Oriental and African Studies, London.

Strand, Jon (1994). 'Er miljøpolitikk sysselsettingsfremmende? En analyse av mulighetene for "doble gevinster" gjennom skjerpet miljøbeskatning'. Report No. 6, Oslo, Project for a Sustainable Economy (Prosjekt Alternativ Framtid).

Strumse, E. (1991). *Miljøbevissthet og økologisk bærekraftige beslutninger. Litteraturoversikt og implikasjoner for forskning og miljørettede tiltak*. Hovedoppgave psykologi (Graduate thesis in Psychology), University of Bergen.

Svarstad, H. (1991). 'Den bærekraftige utviklingen: Retorikk og samfunnsanalyse'. *Sosiologi i dag* 2:36–57.

Sylvan, Richard (1985). 'A Critique of Deep Ecology'. *Radical Philosophy* 40:2–12 and 41:10–12.

Tietenberg, T.H. (1984). *Environmental and Natural Resource Economics*. Glenview, Ill.: Scott, Foresman & Co.

Torrissen, G. (1994). 'Bærekraftig utvikling og bruk av fossil brensler'. Hovedoppgave (Graduate thesis in Economics), Department of Economics, University of Oslo, Oslo, Norway.

Trevarthen, C. (1975). 'Early Attempts at Speech'. In R. Lowin (ed.), *Child Alive*. London: Temple Smith.

Turner, K.R. (ed.) (1993). *Sustainable Environmental Economics and Management: Principles and Practice*. London: Belhaven Press.

UNDP (1994). *Human Development Report 1994*. Danish Edition, distributed by Mellemfolkeligt Samvirke og FN-forbundet for De Forenede Nationers Udviklingsprogram: *Mennesket i Centrum*, Copenhagen.

UNICEF (1994). *The Progress of Nations*. Paris: UNICEF.

United Nations (1993a). *Report of the United Nations Conference on Environment and Development, Rio de Janeiro, 3–14 June 1992, Volume I: Resolutions Adopted by the Conference*. New York: United Nations.

United Nations (1993b). *Report of the United Nations Conference on Environment and Development, Rio de Janeiro, 3–14 June 1992, Volume II: Proceedings of the Conference*. New York: United Nations.

United Nations (1993c). *Report of the United Nations Conference on Environment and Development, Rio de Janeiro, 3–14 June 1992, Volume III: Statements made by Heads of State or Government at the Summit Segment of the Conference*. New York: United Nations.

United States General Accounting Office (GAO) (1992). 'International Agreements Are Not Well Monitored'. Washington, DC: GAO.

Utenriksdepartementet (Norwegian Ministry of Foreign Affairs) (1993). 'Om resultatet av Uruguay-runden (1986–1993) og om samtykke til ratifikasjon av Avtale om opprettelse av Verdens Handelsorhanisasjon (WTO) m.m.', St.prp.nr. 65 (1993–94) (Parliamentary White Paper).

van Boven, Theo (1979). 'United Nations Policies and Strategies: Global Perspectives'. In B.G. Ramcharam (ed.), *Human Rights: Thirty Years After the Universal Declaration*, pp. 83–92.

Van De Veer, Donald (1979). 'Of Beasts, Persons, and the Original Position'. *The Monist* 62:368–77.

Victor, P.A. (1991). 'Indicators of Sustainable Development: Some Lessons from Capital Theory'. *Ecological Economics* 4:191–214.

Viederman, S. (1994). 'Five Capitals and Three Pillars of Sustainability'. Working Paper from the Jessie Smith Noyes Foundation, mimeo.

Walzer, Michael (1981). 'Philosophy and Democracy'. *Political Theory* 9:379–99.

WCED (The World Commission on Environment and Development) (1987). *Our Common Future*. Oxford and New York: Oxford University Press.

Wells, D. (1993). 'Green Politics and Environmental Ethics: A Defense of Human Welfare Ecology'. *Australian Journal of Political Science* 28:515–27.

Westbrook, David A. (1991). 'Environmental Policy in the European Economic Community: Observations on the European Environment Agency'. *Harvard Environmental Law Review* 15:257–98.

Wetlesen, J. (1991). *What is the Relevance of a Rights-Based Ethics in an Ecological Context?* Oslo: Department of Linguistics and Philosophy, University of Oslo.

Wetlesen, J. (1993). 'Who has a Moral Status in the Environment?'. In Nina Witoszek and Elizabeth Gulbrandsen (eds), *Culture and Environment: Interdisciplinary Approaches*. Nature and Humanities Series, Vol. I, pp. 98–129.

Wilson, E.O. (1975). *Sociobiology: the New Synthesis* (Cambridge: Harvard University Press).

——. (1988). *Biodiversity*. Washington, DC: National Academy Press.

Wilson, E.O. (1992). *The Diversity of Life*. London: Penguin Books.

WMO/UNEP (1992). *Intergovernmental Panel on Climate Change, IPCC Supplement*, February 1992.

World Bank (1994). *Making Development Sustainable*. Washington DC: The World Bank.

World Conservation Monitoring Centre (1992). *Global Biodiversity. Status of the Earth's Living Resources*. London: Chapman & Hall.

Worster, D. (1993). 'The Shaky Grounds of Sustainability'. In W. Sachs (ed.), *Global Ecology. A New Arena of Political Conflict*. London: Zed Books, pp. 132–45.

Wyller, T.C. (1991). 'Miljøkrisen og demokratiet'. In S. Gjerdåker, L. Gule and B. Hagtvet (eds), *Den uoverstigelige grense. Tanke og handling i miljøkampen*. Bergen and Oslo: Chr. Michelsens Institute and J.W. Cappelens Forlag.

Yearley, S. (1992). 'Green Ambivalence about Science: Legal-Rational Authority and the Scientific Legitimation of a Social Movement'. *British Journal of Sociology* 43(4):511–32.

Index